Netherlands Insolvency Law

The Netherlands Bankruptcy Act and the Most Important Legal Concepts

NETHERLANDS INSOLVENCY LAW

The Netherlands Bankruptcy Act and the Most Important Legal Concepts

Peter J.M. Declercq

T · M · C · ASSER PRESS
The Hague

Published by T.M.C. ASSER PRESS,
P.O.Box 16163, 2500 BD The Hague, The Netherlands

Sold and distributed in the U.S.A. and Canada
by Kluwer Law International,
101 Philip Drive, Norwell, MA 02061, U.S.A.

In all other countries, sold and distributed
by Kluwer Law International,
P.O.Box 85889, 2508 CN The Hague, The Netherlands.

ISBN 90-6704-144-0

PREFACE

The great novelty of *Netherlands Insolvency Law* is that it is the first book in the English language covering the Netherlands insolvency law as a whole. It is a practical book for use by internal and external legal counsel, Dutch and non-Dutch companies, students, academics and practitioners alike, presenting not only the principal concepts but also the current state of affairs of the Netherlands insolvency law. The reader is offered not only the black letter law, but also impartial discussions presenting differing views on particular aspects of the insolvency law. Furthermore, *Netherlands Insolvency Law* briefly addresses recent developments such as the EU Insolvency Regulation and the progress made on the ongoing total revision of the Netherlands Bankruptcy Act in the "*Marktwerking, Deregulering en Wetgevingskwaliteit* (MDW)"-project.

Declercq has successfully managed to strike such a balance that, on the one hand, the book offers the reader more than an average introduction, while on the other hand, it is not weighed down in a quagmire of technical detail. Declercq's experience and international exposure as an insolvency lawyer in one of the most reputable law firms in the Netherlands has probably contributed in this respect.

Netherlands Insolvency Law promises to become a standard textbook to a wide-ranging audience.

ANTONIUS I.M. VAN MIERLO
Professor of Law
Erasmus University Rotterdam

January 2002

TABLE OF CONTENTS

ABBREVIATIONS

AB

Algemene Bepalingen
(*General Provisions*)

BBA

Buitengewoon Besluit Arbeidsverhoudingen 1945
(*Extraordinary Resolution Employment-Relations 1945*)

Bill 27 244

Wetsvoorstel 27 244 inzake wijziging van de Faillissementswet in verband met het bevorderen van de effectiviteit van surséance van betaling en faillissement
(*Bill 27 244 concerning the amendment of the Netherlands Bankruptcy Act in respect of enhancement of the effectiveness of suspension of payment and bankruptcy*)

BV

Besloten vennootschap met beperkte aansprakelijkheid
(*a private or closed company with limited liability*)

BW

Burgerlijk Wetboek
(*Netherlands Civil Code*)

DEM

German marks (local currency of Germany prior to the introduction of the Euro)

EU Insolvency Regulation

The Council Regulation (EC) No. 1346/2000 on insolvency proceedings adopted on 29 May 2000

Finality Directive

Directive number 98/26/EU, dated May 19, 1998, Pb EG Number l 166/45

Fw

Faillissementswet
(*Netherlands Bankruptcy Act*)

HR

Hoge Raad der Nederlanden
(*Netherlands supreme court*)

Hw

Huurwet
(*Rent Act*)

Inv	Invorderingswet 1990 (*Tax Recovery Act 1990*)
JOR	Jurisprudentie Onderneming & Recht
MDW-Project	Marktwerking, Deregulering en Wetgevingskwaliteit-project (*Competition, Deregulation and Legislative Quality-project*)
MvA	Memorie van Antwoord (*Memorandum of reply*)
MvT	Memorie van Toelichting (*Explanatory memorandum*)
NbBW	Nieuwsbrief Burgerlijk Wetboek
NJ	Nederlandse Jurisprudentie
NJB	Nederlands Juristenblad
NLG	Netherlands guilders (local currency of the Netherlands prior to the introduction of the Euro)
NV	Naamloze vennootschap (*public company with limited liability*)
Ow	Overgangswet (*Transitional Act*)
Pw	Pachtwet (*Lease Act*)
q.q.	*qualitate qua*
RvdW	Rechtspraak van de Week
Rv	Wetboek van burgerlijke rechtsvordering (*Netherlands Code of Civil Procedure*)
Sv	Wetboek van strafvordering (*Netherlands Code of Criminal Procedure*)

TvI

Tijdschrift voor Insolventierecht

TVVS

Tijdschrift voor Vennootschappen, Verenigingen en Stichtingen

TWHOZ

Tijdelijke wet huurkoop onroerend goed
(*Temporary Act on the hire-purchase of immoveable goods*)

US

American dollars (local currency of the United States of   America)

WBA

Wet Bestuurdersaansprakelijkheid
(*Act on the Liability of Directors*)

WBF

Wet Bestuurdersaansprakelijkheid in geval van faillissement
(*Act on Liability of Directors in case of Bankruptcy*)

WFR

Weekblad voor Fiscaal Recht

WMCO

Wet melding collectief ontslag
(*Act on the notification of collective dismissal*)

WOR

Wet op de ondernemingsraden
(*Act on the Works Councils*)

WPNR

Weekblad voor Privaatrecht, Notariaat en Registratie

Wtk

Wet toezicht kredietwezen 1992
(*1992 Act on the supervision of the credit system*)

WW

Werkeloosheidswet
(*Unemployment Act*)

INTRODUCTION

Bankruptcy is considered to be a litmus-test of legal devices. Therefore, in legal counseling the question of whether or not a legal device will survive bankruptcy is of an utmost importance. Bearing that in mind, it is striking to note that general interest among a broader group of people as to what insolvency really is and how to deal with cases of insolvency has only developed in the last decade and a half in the Netherlands. Some larger bankruptcies in the Netherlands like OGEM, BCCI, DAF, FOKKER, TULIP and AIR HOLLAND (for the second time) have added to this "revival" of insolvency law in the Netherlands because they received a substantial amount of media-attention. At the same time, a fair number of lawyers seem to have (re)discovered the (legal) challenges the field of insolvency law presents. Insolvency law has also been positively (re)valued in the academic world, with some universities deciding to commence their own departments of insolvency law[1].

Along with the increased attention and interest in insolvency law, there has also been a shift in how bankruptcy is viewed: while in the past, bankruptcy was considered to be something which one was struck with involuntarily, it now seems that people often consider an insolvency proceeding as a tool one could (and should), in certain circumstances, choose voluntarily. To companies faced with the need to reorganize their business, the threshold for seriously considering (the existence of) the option of a bankruptcy (possibly also followed by a subsequent restart[2]) or another insolvency proceeding, has been lowered considerably

---

1   Further evidence of this revival of insolvency law in the Netherlands are (i) the more frequent publications of articles on insolvency law related topics by law professors and legal practitioners alike, (ii) the foundation in 1995 of the legal magazine TvI focusing entirely on insolvency law and insolvency law related topics, and (iii) the decision made by Netherlands attorneys specialized in insolvency law in 1991 to found an association called "INSOLAD". In close co-operation with the "Grotius Academy", INSOLAD designed its own specialization courses in insolvency law. The successful completion of these specialization courses is one of the mandatory requirements for a full membership of INSOLAD.

2   For the purposes of this book, a restart is described as a continuation of (a part of) the business activity of the debtor by another legal entity - which could, but does not necessarily have to, be related to the debtor - whereby:
    (1) the debtor ceases to exist after a bankruptcy;
    (2) a part of the debts of the debtor remain unpaid; and/or
    (3) a part of the employees of the debtor, after their employment agreements have been terminated by the trustee in bankruptcy, remain unemployed and thus are not taken over by the other legal entity.
    The term "restart" will appear a number of times throughout this book, but will not be discussed further in this book. For a selection of books dealing with "restart", see the Further Reading section in the back.

in recent years. However, in considering the option it is evident that both proper knowledge and legal counseling on the subject are essential.

The revival of insolvency law in the Netherlands has further resulted in a flow of information on the subject, from which it is hard to sift out information that is pertinent to one's needs. My aim is to provide the reader with an understanding of the Netherlands Bankruptcy Act ("Fw"), which is the main source of insolvency law in the Netherlands, by laying out the primary law in an order and manner which is logical and comprehensible. Where necessary, I have looked for guidance primarily in the parliamentary notes to the rules and the interpretation of the rules in landmark cases. Where grey areas and/or where differing views exist, I have indicated them. I have tried to avoid displaying my own opinion about insolvency issues as much as possible.

Structure of the book

As of 1 December 1998, three insolvency proceedings exist under Netherlands law, namely:
(1) suspension of payment or moratorium;
(2) bankruptcy; and
(3) debt reorganization of natural persons.
The focus will be on bankruptcy in the Netherlands and the most important legal concepts pertaining to bankruptcy. In comparison, the discussion of suspension of payment will be relatively brief. The topic of debt reorganization of natural persons has been left out entirely.

CHAPTER 1 is a discussion of the Fw together with its most important underlying principles. At the end of Chapter 1 the most important recent development, the EU Insolvency Regulation, is discussed. The EU Insolvency Regulation will become effective in the Netherlands from 31 May 2002 and some of its consequences for the Netherlands insolvency practice are briefly touched upon. An English version of the EU Insolvency Regulation is included as an Annex.

Unlike the order in which the different insolvency proceedings are dealt with in the Fw, I have elected to first address the procedure of suspension of payment in Chapter 2 and subsequently move to a (more detailed) discussion of the procedure of bankruptcy under Netherlands law in Chapter 3. The reason for this is that, in reality, suspension of payment comes before bankruptcy; it is not possible to have it the other way around[3].

---

3   This odd order in the Fw whereby the procedure of bankruptcy is dealt with prior to the procedure of suspension of payment can be explained by the fact that, originally, the procedure of suspension of payment was regulated in the Netherlands Code of Commerce ("*Wetboek van Koophandel*") and was transferred to the Fw only at a later stage.

CHAPTERS 2 AND 3 will touch upon the steps that need to be taken to file for the insolvency proceeding concerned. These chapters will further identify who the main players are in each insolvency proceeding and which rights and duties they have. There are two stages in a suspension of payment:
(1) the provisional suspension of payment; and
(2) the final suspension of payment.
In a bankruptcy three different stages will be distinguished:
(1) the preservation stage;
(2) the executorial stage; and
(3) the verification or closing stage.
For each stage there will be a discussion of what can generally be expected. At the end of each chapter the Competition, Deregulation and Legislative Quality-project ("MDW-Project") will be discussed as the most relevant recent development. The MDW-Working Group investigates if, how and when the current Netherlands insolvency laws need to be amended. For both suspension of payment and bankruptcy the most important consequences that may result from the MDW-Project will be looked into.

The most important (legal) concepts under Netherlands law that present themselves (especially) in a bankruptcy, will be addressed in CHAPTER 4. These are:
(1) the *actio pauliana*;
(2) set-off;
(3) the corporate liability concepts of:
     (i)   liability of directors;
     (ii)   liability of supervisory directors; and
     (iii) liability of shareholders; and
(4) the concept of wrongful act.
A number of landmark cases will be briefly discussed in order to make (the consequences and application of) these concepts in practice more accessible to the reader.

In CHAPTER 5, the last chapter of the book, the two most important security rights in the Netherlands are discussed:
(1) pledges; and
(2) mortgages.
Here the general aspects of pledges and mortgages will be described, together with the legal requirements to create them and exercise rights of foreclosure. Different types of pledges will be addressed and some situations of concurrence – both involving pledges and mortgages – will be touched upon.

Throughout the book SUMMARIES are included after certain sections or subsections to highlight the key points. A FURTHER READING section with a selection of recommended reading materials for further research can be found in the back of the book. This selection is a personal one and is by no means aiming at being exhaustive. As well as an INDEX, a table of cases and a bibliography, the book also has a section TRANSLATED TERMS in the back in which English terms are translated into the original Netherlands terms and *vice versa*. The idea behind the two lists is to avoid littering the body of the book with Netherlands terms and to provide the reader with the possibility to verify which translations have been used.

Acknowledgements

Finally, I would like to take this opportunity to thank the following people for their indispensable support in completing the manuscript of this book and getting it published: my colleague Jan Willem de Boer for his essential help in developing the idea for this book; Michael Veder and my colleagues Symen de Ranitz and Jako van Hees for their constructive comments; my firm De Brauw Blackstone Westbroek for their general support; Professor Van Mierlo for his expertise, practical tips, trust and enthusiasm; my publishers Philip van Tongeren and Marjolijn Bastiaans of T.M.C. Asser Press for their professionalism in publishing this book; and, last but not least, my wife Sun-Hee for her angelic patience and her uncompromising editing of earlier drafts.

London, December 2001   PETER J.M. DECLERCQ

Chapter 1
THE NETHERLANDS BANKRUPTCY ACT

The main source of Netherlands insolvency law is the Fw, which dates back from 1893 and, although revised in bits, has remained virtually unchanged until to-day[1]. The Fw regulates the following two insolvency regimes, which apply to both private persons and legal entities:

(1) suspension of payment or moratorium; and

(2) bankruptcy.

The biggest change to the Fw to date was made on 1 December 1998 when the following third insolvency regime, applicable to private persons only, was included in the Fw:

(3) debt reorganization of natural persons.

The Emergency Arrangement

In addition to the three insolvency proceedings mentioned above under (1)-(3), it should be noted that a special insolvency regime exists for credit institutions falling within the scope of the 1992 Act on the supervision of the credit system ("Wtk"). For purposes of the Wtk, a credit institution is defined as:

> "an enterprise or institution which business is (i) to receive funds repayable on demand or subject to notice being given and (ii) to grant credits or investments on its own account[2]".

Branch offices situated in the Netherlands of credit institutions situated outside of the Netherlands may also be subject to the Wtk[3].

The special insolvency regime for these credit institutions is called the "Emergency Arrangement" and is set forth in Chapter X of the Wtk[4]. The Emergency Arrangement can been seen as a substitute for suspension of payment, which does not apply to credit institutions falling within the scope of the Wtk[5]. This is

---

1   There are, however, authors who consider substantial changes to the Fw necessary. See, for example, *"Wetgever: de hoogste tijd voor een insolventiewet"*, by Prof. mr R.D. Vriesendorp, *TvI*, 3, pp. 63-68 and the January/February 2000 issue of TvI which features articles on future insolvency law.

2   See article 1 paragraph 1 sub (a) Wtk.

3   See article 5 Wtk.

4   See articles 71 to 80 Wtk.

5   See article 70 paragraph 2 Wtk and article 250(a) Fw.

not the case for bankruptcy and the bankruptcy rules set forth in the Fw apply to credit institutions falling within the scope of the Wtk.

A discussion of the special rules and procedures following an Emergency Arrangement, as well as the involvement of the Central Bank of the Netherlands, falls outside the scope of this book. The Emergency Arrangement and credit institutions falling within the scope of the Wtk will be briefly discussed only in the context of the exception to the principle of fixation pursuant to the Finality Directive (§ 1.2.1.2.2).

1.1   The three insolvency regimes

The three insolvency proceedings mentioned above appear in the following articles in the Fw:
(1)   Articles 1- 212f Fw provide for the rules applicable to bankruptcy;
(2)   Articles 213-283 Fw provide for the rules applicable to suspension of payment; and
(3)   Articles 284-362 Fw provide for the rules applicable to debt reorganization of natural persons.

Suspension of payment and bankruptcy

Each of suspension of payment and bankruptcy, in theory, serve its own specific purpose. In a suspension of payment the key concept is continuation, while in a bankruptcy the key concept is liquidation. A suspension of payment can already be requested if a debtor foresees it will not be able to pay all its creditors when claims become due and payable[6]. The purpose of a suspension of payment is to give the debtor an opportunity to reorganize, search for (new) means of financing (its debts) and continue its business. A bankruptcy, on the other hand, is declared where a debtor has ceased to pay its debts[7]. The purpose of a bankruptcy is to (ultimately) liquidate all assets of the debtor for the benefit of its creditors. If the debtor is a company, the bankruptcy, in principle, results in the dissolution of the company[8]. Liquidation in a bankruptcy should, however, not be understood to preclude continuation of the business of the debtor altogether. A composition in bankruptcy (§ 3.4.3.3) could, for example, also result in a continuation of the debtor's business, as could a restart in bankruptcy[9].

---

6   See article 213 Fw.
7   See article 1 Fw.
8   See article 173 paragraph 1 Fw read in conjunction with article 2:19 paragraph 1 sub c BW.
9   See footnote 2 of the Introduction.

Debt reorganization of natural persons

Similar to bankruptcy, debt reorganization of natural persons is aimed at the liquidation of the debtor's assets. However, debt reorganization of natural persons differs substantially from both bankruptcy and suspension of payment in that, after the debtor has met all its obligations under the debt reorganization, the remaining debts of the debtor are no longer enforceable by the creditors of the debtor. The key concept of debt reorganization of natural persons is therefore liquidation resulting in a clean slate for the debtor. In addition to the release of the debtor from a "life-long imprisonment" by his debts, the other purposes of debt reorganization of natural persons are to reduce the number of bankruptcies of natural persons and to increase the willingness of creditors of natural persons to conclude settlements with them[10].

In this book, the focus will be on insolvencies of companies, not those of natural persons. Therefore, a further discussion of the debt reorganization of natural persons is left out. One should, however, be aware of the fact that when dealing in a professional context with a counter party who is not conducting business through a company, a risk exists that such a counter party could request for a debt reorganization at a certain point in time, with consequences outlined above.

Summary
THREE INSOLVENCY REGIMES

Suspension of payment
law	:	articles 213-283 Fw
key concept	:	continuation
purpose	:	to reorganize and search for (new) means of financing
test	:	debtor foresees that it will not be able to pay its creditors when debts become due and payable

Bankruptcy
law	:	articles 1-212f Fw
key concept	:	liquidation
purpose	:	to liquidate assets for the benefit of creditors
test	:	debtor has ceased to pay its debts

---

10   See generally the introductory remarks by Prof. mr B. Wessels in respect of Title III Fw in *"Tekst & Commentaar Faillissementswet"*, Prof. mr B. Wessels/Mr Ph. van Sint Truiden (editors), Kluwer 2nd edition 1999, Deventer, pp. 271-281. For a selection of books dealing with "debt reorganization of natural persons", see the Further Reading section at the back.

Debt reorganization of natural persons
> law   :   articles 284-362 Fw
> key concept :   liquidation resulting in a clean slate
> purpose   :   to liquidate assets for the benefit of creditors
>   resulting in a clean slate for the debtor
> test   :   debtor reasonably foresees that he will not be able to
>   continue to pay his debts or debtor has ceased to pay
>   his debts

1.2   The leading principles underlying the Netherlands Bankruptcy Act

The following leading principles underlying the Fw will be further explored below in respect of both suspension of payment and bankruptcy:
(1) the principle of fixation (§1.2.1);
(2) the principle of *paritas creditorum* (§1.2.2);
(3) the principle of universality (§1.2.3); and
(4) the principle of territoriality (§1.2.4).

1.2.1   THE PRINCIPLE OF FIXATION

The principle of fixation is used to indicate that, as of the day the insolvency proceeding is adjudicated, the legal position of those involved in the insolvency proceeding becomes unchangeable[11]. This principle follows from article 23 Fw in respect of bankruptcy and from article 228 Fw in respect of suspension of payment[12]. In Chapter 2 (§ 2.1) it will be explained that, in comparison to a bankruptcy (§ 3.1), the scope of a suspension of payment is limited and therefore the
effect of the principle of fixation is also limited. In both suspension of payment
and bankruptcy, the principle of fixation takes effect retroactively as of 00.00
hours of the day the insolvency proceeding is adjudicated (see § 1.2.1.2 for exceptions).

The right to administer and dispose

The consequences of suspension of payment differ from those of bankruptcy with
regards to the right of the debtor to administer and dispose of its assets. In a suspension of payment the debtor loses its right to administer and dispose of its assets *on its own*. The debtor remains, however, entitled to act in conjunction with,
and with the consent of, a court appointed administrator in the suspension of pay-

---

11   This principle has been recognized by the Netherlands supreme court in a number of cases, one
      of which is the Mr Mulder q.q/CLBN-case (HR 17 February 1995, *NJ* 1996, 471). For further
      details in respect of this case, see § 4.2.1.1.5.
12   See also the OAR/ABN-case (HR 18 December 1987, *NJ* 1988, 340)

ment[13]. As of 00.00 hours of the day the suspension of payment is declared the debtor and the administrator become Siamese twins in this respect. In a bankruptcy the debtor loses its right to administer and dispose of its assets completely[14]. Where the debtor is a company, in both insolvency regimes the same applies to the directors of the debtor. Corporate bodies, such as the board of directors of such debtor, do not cease to exist as a consequence of a suspension of payment or a bankruptcy. In suspension of payment, the board of the debtor and the administrator act as Siamese twins (§ 2.3.1). In bankruptcy, the board of the debtor maintains its corporate law rights to the extent the exercise thereof does not interfere with the task entrusted to the trustee in bankruptcy to administer and liquidate the bankrupt estate (§ 3.3.1). For example, if the debtor is also a director of one of its subsidiaries, it will in general be the board of the debtor, and not the trustee in bankruptcy, that will act in this capacity. It should further be noted that in both insolvency regimes the debtor remains, despite being deprived of its right to administer and to dispose of its assets (on its own), capable of acting.

Consequences

As from the adjudication of the insolvency regime, a debtor is no longer entitled to act (on its own). If the debtor, nevertheless, does act (on its own), the estate is only liable for obligations entered into by the debtor to the extent such obligations arise from transactions which benefit the estate (*i.e.* the proceeds of those transactions come "in the hands" of the court appointed administrator in a suspension of payment or trustee in bankruptcy)[15].

As a result of the loss by the debtor of its right to administer and dispose of its assets (on its own), the following matters no longer have effect[16] :
(1) assignments made in advance;
(2) pledges made in advance (on future receivables or other future assets of the debtor); and
(3) proxies or mandates provided for by the debtor prior to the existence of the insolvency regime.

As of 00.00 hours of the day an insolvency regime is adjudicated there is, by virtue of law, an automatic general arrest of all assets of the debtor that fall within

---

13 See article 228 paragraph 1 Fw.
14 See article 23 Fw read in conjunction with article 68 Fw.
15 In relation to bankruptcy this follows from article 24 Fw and in relation to suspension of payment from article 228 paragraph 2 Fw.
16 In respect of advanced assignments and pledges see article 35 paragraph 2 Fw and § 5.2.1.1. In respect of proxies see article 3:72 sub (a) and (b) BW and in respect of mandates see article 7:422 paragraph 1 BW.

the scope of the insolvency regime[17]. Any arrests made by parties to whom the insolvency regime applies on assets of the debtor prior to an insolvency regime being declared will, as from the adjudication of the insolvency regime onwards, cease to exist[18]. Depending on the way an insolvency regime ends and what happens during the course of the insolvency procedure, such arrests can return into existence after the insolvency regime is terminated[19].

The assets belonging to the estate include[20]:
(1) all assets of the debtor as of the time the insolvency regime is adjudicated; and
(2) all assets acquired during the course of the insolvency regime, regardless of whether or not these assets are held by third parties.

The application of the principle of fixation can have far reaching consequences in practice. These become especially apparent when issues are dealt with concerning, for example:
– the assessment of the status of a claim (does a claim qualify as a claim against the estate?) (§ 3.6.2);
– the possibility of setting-off claims which arose at different points in time (§ 4.2); or
– the finalization of acts, commenced prior to the adjudication of an insolvency regime, after the insolvency regime has been adjudicated (§ 1.2.1.1).

The application of the principle of fixation in article 35 Fw shall be addressed below (§ 1.2.1.1). The two exceptions to the principle of fixation (§ 1.2.1.2) will also be examined more closely.

1.2.1.1   Application of the principle of fixation in article 35 Netherlands Bankruptcy Act

Article 35 Fw
As mentioned in § 1.2.1 above, the principle of fixation in respect of a bank-

---

17 See article 20 Fw. As suspension of payment is limited in scope and basically only affects non-preferential or ordinary creditors (§ 2.1), consequently the "general" arrest is also limited to those assets of the debtor that fall within the scope of the suspension of payment.
18 In relation to bankruptcy this follows from article 33 Fw and in relation to suspension of payment from article 230 Fw.
19 See article 195 Fw.
20 See article 20 Fw. For assets that fall outside a bankruptcy, see articles 21 and 21a Fw.
21 From the Mr Veenendaal q.q./Hoefslag-case (HR 15 March 1991, *NJ* 1992, 605) it follows that the rule set forth in article 35 Fw also applies to suspension of payment.

ruptcy follows from article 23 Fw. This principle is applied in article 35 Fw, the first paragraph of which provides[21] :

> "If on (*or after; PJMD*) the day of the adjudication of a bankruptcy all acts necessary for a transfer by the debtor have not yet been performed, such transfer can no longer validly take place."

The second paragraph of article 35 Fw makes it clear that the transfers of future goods which are only obtained by the debtor after its bankruptcy is adjudicated cannot be invoked against the bankrupt estate. This equally applies to the creation of non-possessory pledges[22] over future goods prior to the adjudication of a debtor's bankruptcy.

An exception is made in the second paragraph of article 35 Fw in respect of fruits and plants not yet harvested but to which a debtor, prior to the adjudication of its bankruptcy, was already entitled pursuant to a property (or proprietary) right, a rental agreement or a lease agreement.

As a consequence of the principle of fixation, the debtor becomes, retroactively as of 00.00 hours of the day its bankruptcy is adjudicated, unauthorized to administer and dispose of its assets. Examples of asset disposals that are no longer possible include:
(1) a disposal by way of sale and transfer of assets; or
(2) a disposal by way of encumbrance of assets with a security right (such as a pledge or mortgage).

Rule of third party protection

In respect of transfers of moveable non-registered goods and bearer or order rights, there is a rule of third party protection under Netherlands law[23] :

> "Notwithstanding a lack of authority of the debtor to administer and dispose of the good or the right concerned, a transfer thereof by the debtor is considered valid when (i) the transferee acts in good faith and (ii) the transfer is for consideration."

A similar rule of third party protection exists in respect of the granting of a pledge over a moveable non-registered good[24] by an unauthorized debtor[25] .

In the context of article 35 Fw, a transferee is considered to act in good faith – and can successfully claim protection under the above-mentioned rule of the third

---

22 For further details on non-possessory pledges, see § 5.2.1.1.
23 See article 3:86 BW.
24 For further details in respect of pledges on moveable non-registered goods, see § 5.2.1.1.
25 See article 3:238 BW.

party protection – if the transfer took place prior to the announcement of the bankruptcy. Article 14 paragraph 3 Fw provides that, immediately after the bankruptcy of a debtor has been declared, the announcement of the bankruptcy must be placed in the National Gazette of the Netherlands and in one or more newspapers indicated by the supervisory judge in bankruptcy.

An announcement of the bankruptcy in the register of bankruptcies, within the meaning of article 19 Fw, does not automatically terminate an invocation of third party protection by the transferee[26]. However, in respect of the acquisition of registered goods (for example, immoveable goods), the announcement of a bankruptcy in the register of bankruptcies, within the meaning of article 19 Fw, does prevent a transferee from invoking the rules of third party protection in the context of article 35 Fw[27]. Since the register of bankruptcies, as meant in article 19 Fw, is kept by the courts internally, it should be noted that tracking down the exact time of announcement of a bankruptcy in that register may not – in practice – always be easy[28].

1.2.1.2   Exceptions to the principle of fixation

The following two exceptions to the principle of fixation will be addressed in this section:
(1) The first exception to the principle of fixation concerns undue payments (§ 1.2.1.2.1), which illustrates the consequences of the principle of fixation in respect of the assessment of the status of a claim in a bankruptcy. This follows from the judgment of the Netherlands supreme court in the *Ontvanger/Mr Hamm q.q.*-case[29].
(2) The second exception to the principle of fixation concerns the settlement of finality in payment and securities and settlement systems (§ 1.2.1.2.2). This is an implementation of the Finality Directive of the European Parliament and the Council of the European Union[30].

---

26 See comment 4 to article 35 Fw by Prof. mr R.H. van Erp in *"Tekst & Commentaar Faillissementswet"*, Prof. mr B. Wessels/Mr Ph. van Sint Truiden (editors), Kluwer 2nd edition 1999, Deventer, pp. 46-47.
27 See article 3:24 paragraph 2 sub(c) BW.
28 See in this context especially *"Levering van registergoederen en aandelen tijdens faillissement: curator en notaris in een lastig parket"*, by Mr J.J. van Hees, in *"De curator, een octopus"*, Prof. mr S.C.J.J. Kortmann c.s. (editors), W.E.J. Tjeenk Willink 1996, Deventer, pp. 123-138.
29 HR 5 September 1997, *NJ* 1998, 437.
30 Directive number 98/26/EU, dated May 19, 1998, Pb EG Number l 166/45.

1.2.1.2.1   Exception pursuant to the Ontvanger/Mr Hamm q.q.-case

The ONTVANGER/MR HAMM Q.Q.-case

In the *Ontvanger/Mr Hamm q.q.*-case a third party made a payment to a debtor by accident. Unfortunately, at the time of payment the debtor had already been declared bankrupt. The leading question in this case was what could be expected from the trustee in bankruptcy, when faced with the following two options:
(1)   The trustee in bankruptcy immediately repays, contrary to the normal rules for distribution of monies to (estate) creditors in a bankruptcy, the undue amount received by accident.
(2)   The (unfortunate) third party does not have a claim for immediate repayment, but instead has only an ordinary claim of a (non-preferential or ordinary) estate creditor who will have to wait for repayment – together with any other estate creditors that may exist – until the trustee in bankruptcy is able to assess whether or not any payment can be made to estate creditors.

In the latter case, a risk exists that other claims will be paid with the monies that were accidentally paid by the third party to the bankrupt estate, leaving the third party with its claim (partly) unpaid.

Judgment of the Netherlands supreme court

In the *Ontvanger/Mr Hamm q.q.*-case, the Netherlands supreme court held:

> If a trustee in bankruptcy is confronted with a payment by a third party that results from a manifest error, for example, concerning the person to whom the payment should be made, then, a trustee in bankruptcy should cooperate in undoing the error (and thus immediately repay the third party with the amount received by accident from the third party).

From this decision it follows that in cases of manifest errors, the Netherlands supreme court uses the principle of reasonableness and fairness to allow for an exception to the principle of fixation.

1.2.1.2.2   Exception pursuant to the Finality Directive

The Finality Directive

The Finality Directive of both the European Parliament and the Council of the European Union deals with "systems" which – in short – can be described as "formal arrangements between three or more participants with common rules and standardized arrangements for the execution of transfer orders between the participants." One of the goals of the Finality Directive is to have the EU member

states amend their (insolvency) laws so as to minimize the disruption to a system
caused by insolvency proceedings declared against a participant in that system.

In the Netherlands, the Finality Directive is implemented in both the Wtk and the
Fw. The amendments to both Acts were aimed at avoiding the retroactive effect
(as of 00.00 hours) pursuant to the principle of fixation in the case of:
(1) the application of the Emergency Arrangement (for credit institutions falling
     within the scope of the Wtk);
(2) the adjudication of bankruptcy; or
(3) the granting of suspension of payment.

As of 1 January 1999, the following articles were added to the Fw and came into
effect:
–   articles 212a-212f for bankruptcy; and
–   articles 281g and 281h for suspension of payment.
A detailed explanation of these new articles falls outside the scope this book.
Therefore the discussion will be limited to a summary of some key issues[31] .

The exception to the principle of fixation pursuant to article 212b Fw

Article 212a Fw contains definitions of terms such as "system", "institution",
"participant", "transfer order" and "central counter party". The essence of the exception is in article 212b paragraph 1 Fw:

> "The declaration of bankruptcy of an institution will not have, contrary to the articles
> 23 and 35 (*Fw; PJMD*), retroactive effect as of the beginning of the day (*00.00 hours;
> PJMD*) on which the bankruptcy was adjudicated in respect of a transfer order, an or-
> der for set-off or any payment, transfer, set-off or other act resulting from such transfer
> order, which is necessary to complete the execution of the order in the system, which
> was made by an institution prior to the time of its declaration of bankruptcy."

This provision aims to assure that transfer orders made by an institution between
00.00 hours and the time of the declaration of the bankruptcy of the institution,
can no longer be revoked by a trustee in bankruptcy.

Paragraph 2 of article 212b Fw addresses the situation where:
(1) a transfer order (as mentioned in paragraph 1 of article 212b Fw) is
     introduced into a system subsequent to the time of the declaration of
     bankruptcy of the institution; and
(2) the transfer order is executed on the day the bankruptcy is adjudicated.

---

31 See generally *"Over art. 212A-212F Faillissementswet (nieuw)"*, by Prof. mr B. Wessels in
    NbBW, 4, 1999, pp. 38-42.

In such a situation, articles 23, 24, 35, 53 paragraph 1 and 54 paragraph 2 Fw and article 3:72 sub a BW cannot be invoked against third parties if:
(i)   the order is executed in the system on the day bankruptcy is declared; and
(ii) either the central counter party, or the settlement agent or the clearing house can prove that they did not and could not have any knowledge about the declaration of bankruptcy.
The condition mentioned under (ii) above is referred to as "the additional requirement of good faith".

The rules set forth in paragraphs 1 and 2 of article 212b Fw are also applicable – pursuant to article 212b paragraph 3 Fw – to the creation of a security right by the institution in connection to the participation in the system for the benefit of another participant or the Central Bank of the Netherlands.

Suspension of payment

The exception to the principle of fixation set out above for bankruptcy applies also to a suspension of payment pursuant to the articles 281g and 281h Fw.

1.2.2   THE PRINCIPLE OF *PARITAS CREDITORUM*

Another leading principle in the Fw is equality of treatment of creditors, better known as the principle of *paritas creditorum*[32]. The implication of this principle is *not* that all creditors are treated the same, but taking into account their respective preferences, priorities and ranks, they are treated equally.

Article 3:277 BW

The basis for the principle of *paritas creditorum* is in article 3:277 paragraph 1 BW:

> " Creditors have, amongst themselves, an equal right, after payment of the costs of execution, to be paid from the net proceeds of the assets of the debtor in proportion to their respective claims, except for grounds of preference recognized by law."

Similar to the principle of fixation (§ 1.2.1), the principle of *paritas creditorum* is a rule of public order from which deviation is, in principle, not allowed. A legal concept which is motivated by the principle of *paritas creditorum* and which, in

---

32   This principle follows from article 3:277 BW and has been recognized by the Netherlands supreme court in a number of cases, amongst which are the Mr Loeffen q.q./Bank Mees & Hoop I-case (HR 8 July 1987, *NJ* 1988, 104) and the Mr Loeffen q.q./Bank Mees & Hoop II-case (HR 22 March 1991, *NJ* 1992, 214).

essence, aims to restore the *paritas creditorum* is the legal concept of *actio pauliana*. A detailed discussion of the *actio pauliana* is in § 4.1.

Statutory exceptions to the principle of paritas creditorum

From article 3:277 paragraph 1 BW it follows that preferential rights recognized by law do not violate the principle of *paritas creditorum*. Two of the most important contractual preferential rights recognized by law in the Netherlands are:
(1) pledges; and
(2) mortgages.
Both security rights are addressed in more detail in Chapter 5.

Paragraph 2 of article 3:277 BW allows a creditor to agree with its debtor to subordinate its claim against the debtor in respect of all or a number of creditors of the debtor (§ 3.6.3.3). This subordination of claims is also not considered to be in violation of the principle of *paritas creditorum*.

Case law exceptions to the principle of paritas creditorum

The exception to the principle of fixation pursuant to the *Ontvanger/Mr Hamm q.q.*-case (§ 1.2.1.2.1) is – strictly speaking – also an exception to the principle of *paritas creditorum*.

Another important exception to the principle of *paritas creditorum* is based on two cases of the Netherlands supreme court concerning the claims of utility companies, such as energy providers, in respect of goods or services delivered by them to the debtor. In the *Veluwse Nutsbedrijven*-case[33] and more recently in the *Mr Van der Hel q.q./Edon*-case[34], the Netherlands supreme court ruled in favor of factual preference of energy providers by holding:

(1) Without a guaranty of full payment of unpaid claims which arose prior to the adjudication of the bankruptcy of the debtor, the energy provider is entitled to validly suspend its (future) supply of goods or services to the debtor.
(2) The trustee in bankruptcy is then forced to evaluate the importance of continuation of the business of the debtor against the importance of the principle of *paritas creditorum*, which evaluation in fact may prejudice the equal treatment of creditors.

The rulings of the Netherlands supreme court in this context are inspired by the so-called *"exceptio non adimpleti contractus"*-defense of creditors. This defense is set forth in article 6:262 paragraph 1 BW, which reads:

---

33   HR 20 March 1981, *NJ* 1981, 640.
34   HR 16 October 1998, *NJ* 1998, 896.

"In the event one of the parties does not perform its obligation, the counter party is entitled to suspend the performance of its opposite obligations."

However, a suspension of (future) supply of goods or services is not considered acceptable in all circumstances[35] and such suspension may very well be in violation of the principle of reasonableness and fairness towards the bankrupt estate and/or the other creditors of the debtor. In the same two cases, the Netherlands supreme court held:

(3) An energy provider is not entitled to suspend future supply of goods or services to the debtor for unsettled claims arisen prior to the bankruptcy of the debtor where:
    (i) they are supplied in a domestic context (as opposed to a professional context); and
    (ii) they could be considered as first necessities of life of the debtor.
(4) This exception does not apply where:
    (i) the suspension is in respect of an office building only; or
    (ii) the suspension only concerns a possible continuation of the business of the debtor by the trustee in bankruptcy.

1.2.3 THE PRINCIPLE OF UNIVERSALITY

Both the principle of universality and the opposite principle of territoriality (which will be discussed in the next section of this Chapter) are adhered to in the Fw and come into play when insolvencies have international aspects.

Scope

Pursuant to the principle of universality[36] all assets of the debtor – wherever situated – fall (in principle) within the bankrupt estate in the Netherlands[37]. Obviously, in practice, this principle is limited by the sovereignty of other States and their jurisdictions. The effective powers of an administrator or a trustee in bankruptcy in a Netherlands suspension of payment and a Netherlands bankruptcy, respectively, will be determined by the law of the foreign State involved. It should also be noted that the operation of this principle will be affected by the EU Insolvency Regulation that will come into force in the Netherlands on 31 May 2002. For a more detailed discussion of the EU Insolvency Regulation, see § 1.3.1.

---

35 See generally *"Monopolist, afkoelingsperiode en faillissement"*, by Mr N.E.D. Faber in *NbBW*, 11, 1998, pp. 124-128.
36 The principle of universality follows (indirectly) from article 203 Fw.
37 This principle has been recognized by the Netherlands supreme court in a number of cases, including the Comfin-case (HR 15 April 1955, *NJ* 1955, 542).

Obligation to compensate

In the Netherlands foreign creditors of the debtor can also have their claim verified in a Netherlands insolvency proceeding[38]. Those creditors (as well as Netherlands creditors) should, however, be aware that if they – after the debtor has
been declared bankrupt in the Netherlands – take recourse against assets of the
debtor situated outside the Netherlands that are not encumbered with a valid security right in their favor or in respect of which they cannot benefit from another
ground of preference, they will be obliged to compensate the bankrupt estate for
the amount recovered by them[39]. This obligation to compensate applies also in
suspension of payment, but not in debt reorganization of natural persons[40].

Monitoring the compliance by creditors of their duty to compensate the estate
will not always be an easy task for a trustee in bankruptcy or an administrator. In
practice, the following "solutions" are used for taking into consideration monies
already recovered by creditors outside the Netherlands for which the estate has
not (yet) been compensated by those creditors[41]:

(1) A trustee in bankruptcy or an administrator could refuse to verify the
     (remainder of the) claim of the creditor until the estate is compensated with
     the recovered amount;
(2) A trustee in bankruptcy or an administrator could accept to verify the claim
     of the creditor taking the position that every creditor is entitled to have its
     claim verified for the full amount until that creditor is fully satisfied[42];
(3) A trustee in bankruptcy or an administrator could deduct the amount
     recovered by the creditor from the claim submitted by the creditor for
     verification; and
(4) A trustee in bankruptcy or an administrator could treat the recovered amount
     as an advanced distribution and deduct the recovered amount by the creditor
     from a distribution in the insolvency procedure if one is made.

---

38 See article 9 AB and see also article 127 paragraph 3 Fw, from which it follows that foreign
    creditors, situated outside the Kingdom of the Netherlands in Europe, are subject to less restric-
    tive rules on late submission of claims for verification in bankruptcy provided they can show
    delay was caused by their living abroad (§ 3.4.3.2).
39 See article 203 Fw.
40 See article 251 Fw.
41 See also:*"Grensoverschrijdende aspecten van insolventieprocedures buiten verdrag"* , by Mr
    R.J. van Galen and Mr J.C. van Apeldoorn, in *"Mededelingen van de Nederlandse Vereniging
    voor Internationaal Recht*, number 117", Kluwer 1998, Deventer, pp. 68-69.
42 Inspired by the provision concerning joint and several liability as set forth in article 136 Fw.

Option (4) is generally considered to be the most common and accepted approach[43].

In situations where a trustee in bankruptcy or administrator knows of the existence of a debtor's assets situated outside the Netherlands and there are fears of recourse by creditors of the debtor against these assets, the following action could be taken to make recourse by creditors unattractive: the trustee in bankruptcy or the administrator could attempt – provided such is allowed under the applicable laws of the jurisdiction where the assets are situated – to dilute the individual claims of such creditors by making an arrest (possibly precautionary in nature) on the assets concerned (or the proceeds thereof) for an amount of the total deficit in the bankruptcy of the debtor or the relevant deficit in the suspension of payment of the debtor.

1.2.4   THE PRINCIPLE OF TERRITORIALITY

Scope

Pursuant to the principle of territoriality a foreign insolvency proceeding has no effect in the Netherlands. As a consequence, the assets of a (foreign) debtor situated in the Netherlands are not considered to be part of the foreign estate[44]. However, the Netherlands have concluded treaties with some States dealing with a (limited) recognition of a foreign bankruptcy[45]. With regards treaties concluded with EU member states, they will soon be replaced by the EU Insolvency Regulation. For more details on the consequences of the EU Insolvency Regulation for the principle of territoriality, see § 1.3.1.3.

For the remainder of this section it is assumed that neither any treaty nor the EU Insolvency Regulation applies.

Complications

It does not take a lot of imagination to understand that matters are substantially complicated where there are concurrent insolvency proceedings of the same debtor in different States, as each insolvency proceeding will have its own spe-

---

43   Options (2) and (3) are arguably in violation of the principle of *paritas creditorum* (§ 1.2.2). See also Van Galen/Van Apeldoorn, *supra* footnote 41, at page 69.

44   See in this respect the Vleeschmeesters-case (HR 31 May 1996, *NJ* 1998, 108).

45   See, for example, the Netherlands-Belgian Execution Treaty of March 28, 1925, especially articles 20-25 on bankruptcy. For recognition within the Kingdom of the Netherlands of court orders granting suspension of payment or declaring bankruptcy in the Netherlands, see article 40 of the Statute of the Kingdom (*Statuut van het Koninkrijk*).

cific (national) rules and its own (court or otherwise) appointed trustee in bankruptcy or administrator.

Experience tells us[46] that in such situations cooperation between all interested
parties (especially larger creditors such as lenders) is essential. Only then can
practical solutions be reached for issues like the following:
–   How should creditors submit their claims in the different insolvency
    regimes?
–   How should such claims be ranked and how should their priority be
    established in and between the different insolvency regimes?
–   How, when and to whom should and can (interim) distribution be made and
    by whom?
–   Until which date can accrued interest be included in a claim?
–   Who has the decisive vote in respect of a course of action and what are the
    remedies (if any) of interested parties?

This is just an indication of some of the issues that interested parties in cross-border insolvencies involving Netherlands aspects may run into as a consequence of,
in part, the principle of territoriality adhered to in the Fw. A more detailed discussion falls outside the scope of this book.

Summary
OF LEADING PRINCIPLES

The Fw adheres to the following four main principles:

Principle of fixation
(1) The principle of fixation results in an automatic general arrest of all
    assets of the debtor (retroactive as of 00.00 hours of the day on which
    the insolvency proceeding was adjudicated).
(2) As a consequence of the principle of fixation, the debtor loses its right
    to administer and dispose of its assets.
    (i) In a bankruptcy, the right is lost completely.
    (ii) In a suspension of payment, the debtor needs prior authorization of
         the administrator to exercise the right.
(3) Further consequences of the principle of fixation are that incomplete
    assignments in advance, pledges in advance, proxies and mandates no
    longer have effect.

---

46   See generally Van Galen/Van Apeldoorn, *supra* footnote 41, at § IV.2 and § V.

(4) When the debtor acts in violation of the principle of fixation, the bankrupt estate is only bound by transactions which benefit the bankrupt estate.

(5) The estate also includes assets acquired during the course of the insolvency.

(6) Exceptions to the principle of fixation are:
  (i) undue payments (pursuant to the *Ontvanger/Mr Hamm q.q.*-case); and
  (ii) transfer orders that are covered by the Finality Directive (artt. 212a-212f Fw and artt. 281g and 281h Fw).

Principle of paritas creditorum

(1) The principle of *paritas creditorum* means equal treatment of creditors, taking into consideration their respective preferences, priorities and ranks.

(2) Valid preferential rights recognized by law do not violate the principle of *paritas creditorum* and the same applies to valid subordinations.

(3) Case law exceptions exist, such as the factual preference based on the *exceptio non adimpleti contractus*-defense for energy providers following from the *Veluwse Nutsbedrijven*-case and the *Mr Van der Hel q.q./Edon*-case.

Principle of universality

(1) Pursuant to the principle of universality, assets of the debtor situated outside the Netherlands fall within a Netherlands insolvency proceeding. The effective powers in respect to those goods are, however, ultimately determined by the foreign law of the foreign State on which territory the assets are situated.

(2) Creditors taking recourse on assets of the debtor situated outside the Netherlands that are not encumbered with a valid security right in their favor, or in respect of which they cannot benefit from another ground of preference, are legally obliged to compensate the bankrupt estate for the amount recovered by them. Monitoring compliance of this duty is difficult, but practice has found ways of dealing with it.

Principle of territoriality

(1) Pursuant to the principle of territoriality a foreign insolvency is not recognized in the Netherlands, unless otherwise agreed in treaties or the EU Insolvency Regulation applies.

(2) If different insolvency regimes in different States are applicable to the same debtor, cooperation between the interested parties is essential.

1.3   Recent developments

The most important recent development that will have an impact on Netherlands insolvency law is the adoption on 29 May 2000 of the Council regulation (EC) No 1346/2000 on insolvency proceedings (the "EU Insolvency Regulation"). An English version of the EU Insolvency Regulation is included as an *Annex.*

The EU Insolvency Regulation shall enter into force on 31 May 2002 [47]. From that date, the EU Insolvency Regulation shall be binding in its entirety and shall be directly applicable in the Netherlands and the other EU member states (save for Denmark)[48]. The EU Insolvency Regulation will not, however, be applicable to insolvency proceedings where the centre of the debtor's main interests is situated outside the jurisdictions of the EU member states (*i.e.* the Community)[49]. This means that the EU Insolvency Regulation shall not govern:

(1) the consequences of the opening of an insolvency proceeding in an EU member state concerning a debtor, the centre of whose main interests is situated outside the Community; and
(2) the consequences of the opening of an insolvency proceeding in third party states (*i.e.* non-EU member states).

In § 1.3.1 below the scope of the EU Insolvency Regulation (§ 1.3.1.1) and the most important features of the EU Insolvency Regulation (§ 1.3.1.2) will be briefly addressed. In addition, the most likely consequences of the EU Insolvency Regulation for the Netherlands insolvency practice will be highlighted (§ 1.3.1.3).

1.3.1   THE EU INSOLVENCY REGULATION

The structure of the EU Insolvency Regulation is as follows:

Chapter I   – "general provisions".
Chapter II   – "recognition of insolvency proceedings".
Chapter III – "secondary insolvency proceedings".
Chapter IV   – "provision of information for creditors and lodgement of their claims".

---

47   See article 47 of the EU Insolvency Regulation.
48   These other EU member states are Austria, Belgium, France, Finland, Germany, Greece, Ireland, Italy, Luxembourg, Portugal, Spain, Sweden, and the United Kingdom. The EU Insolvency Regulation is not applicable in Denmark.
49   This follows from recital 14 of the EU Insolvency Regulation. See also *"De Europese Insolventieverordening"* by Prof. mr S.C.J.J. Kortmann and Mr P.M. Veder in *WPNR* 6421, 2000, pp. 764-774, at p. 765 under 2.2.2.

Chapter V – "transitional and final provisions".

The relevant insolvency proceedings that are covered by the EU Insolvency Regulation are listed, for each member state, in Annex A to the EU Insolvency Regulation. For the Netherlands the relevant insolvency proceedings are:
(1) suspension of payment;
(2) bankruptcy; and
(3) debt reorganization of natural persons.
The relevant "liquidators" are listed in Annex C to the EU Insolvency Regulation and for the Netherlands they are (i) the administrator in a suspension of payment, (ii) the trustee in bankruptcy, and (iii) the administrator in a debt reorganization of natural persons.

1.3.1.1 The scope of the EU Insolvency Regulation

The EU Insolvency Regulation explicitly acknowledges the fact that as a result of widely differing substantive laws it is not practical to introduce insolvency proceedings with universal scope throughout the Community[50]. This is taken into account in the following two ways:

(1) The EU Insolvency Regulation provides for special rules on applicable law in the case of particularly significant rights and legal relationships (such as *e.g.* rights *in rem* and employment agreements).
(2) Alongside the main insolvency proceedings with universal (*i.e.* European) scope, the EU Insolvency Regulation also provides for national insolvency proceedings covering only assets situated in the State where those proceedings were opened (*i.e.* the secondary insolvency proceedings).

The EU Insolvency Regulation further aims to provide for immediate recognition in all other EU member states of judgments concerning the opening, conduct and closure of insolvency proceedings which come within its scope, and of judgments handed down in direct connection with such insolvency proceedings[51]. Recognition of judgments delivered by a court of an EU member state is to be based on the principle of mutual trust.

In addition, the EU Insolvency Regulation aims to set out uniform rules on the conflict of laws which replace, within their scope of application, national rules of private international law. Unless otherwise stated, the general rule pursuant to the EU Insolvency Regulation is that the law of the EU member state of the opening of an insolvency proceeding should be the applicable law (*i.e.* the *lex concur-*

---

50 See recital 11 of the EU Insolvency Regulation.
51 See recital 22 of the EU Insolvency Regulation.

sus)[52]. This rule on conflict of laws should be valid both for the main insolvency proceedings and for the local (or secondary) insolvency proceedings. The *lex concursus*:

(1) determines all the effects of the insolvency proceedings, both procedural and substantive, on the persons and the legal relationships concerned; and
(2) governs all the conditions for the opening, conduct and closure of the insolvency proceedings.

Material scope of the EU Insolvency Regulation

Article 1 of the EU Insolvency Regulation provides the following:

(1) The EU Insolvency Regulation shall apply to collective insolvency proceedings (*i.e.* the "insolvency proceedings" listed in Annex A to the EU Insolvency Regulation) which entail the partial or total divestment of a debtor[53] and the appointment of a liquidator (*i.e.* the "liquidators" listed in Annex C to the EU Insolvency Regulation).
(2) The EU Insolvency Regulation shall not apply to insolvency proceedings concerning insurance undertakings, credit institutions, investment undertakings which provide services involving the holding of funds or services for third parties, or to collective investment undertakings.

Formal scope of the EU Insolvency Regulation

The EU Insolvency Regulation applies only to proceedings where the centre of the debtor's main interests is situated in the Community[54]. In that respect the "centre of main interests" should correspond to the place where the debtor conducts the administration of his interests on a regular basis and is therefore ascertainable as such by third parties[55]. In the case of a company or a legal person, the place of the registered office shall be presumed to be the centre of its main interests in the absence of proof to the contrary[56].

---

52   See recital 23 of the EU Insolvency Regulation.
53   In the Netherlands version of the EU Insolvency Regulation "the partial or total divestment of the debtor" is translated as: "*het geheel of gedeeltelijk verliezen door de schuldenaar van het beheer en de beschikking over zijn vermogen*".
54   See recital 14 of the EU Insolvency Regulation.
55   See recital 13 of the EU Insolvency Regulation.
56   See article 3 paragraph 1 of the EU Insolvency Regulation.

Scope in time of the EU Insolvency Regulation

Article 43 of the EU Insolvency Regulation indicates that the provisions of the EU Insolvency Regulation shall only apply to insolvency proceedings opened after its entry into force. Acts undertaken by a debtor prior to 31 May 2002 shall continue to be governed by the law which was applicable to them at the time they were undertaken.

1.3.1.2   The most important features of the EU Insolvency Regulation

In order to achieve the aim of improving the efficiency and effectiveness of insolvency proceedings having cross-border effects, the EU Insolvency Regulation indicates that it is necessary and appropriate that provisions on the following topics in the area of cross-border insolvencies should be contained in a Community law measure which is binding and directly applicable in the EU member states[57]:

(1) Jurisdiction;
(2) Recognition; and
(3) Applicable law.

Ad. (1) Jurisdiction

The basis for international jurisdiction can be found in article 3 of the EU Insolvency Regulation. There are two types of insolvency proceedings:
(i)   main insolvency proceedings; and
(ii) national or secondary proceedings.

Main insolvency proceedings
The courts of the EU member state where the centre of a debtor's main interests is situated shall have jurisdiction to open the main insolvency proceeding.

National or secondary insolvency proceedings
Where the centre of the debtor's main interests is situated within the territory of an EU member state, the courts of another EU member state shall have jurisdiction to open national or secondary insolvency proceedings against the debtor, provided that the debtor possesses an establishment within the territory of that other EU member state. For the purposes of the EU Insolvency Regulation "establishment" means any place of operations where the debtor carries out a non-transitory economic activity with human means and goods[58].

---

57   See recital 8 of the EU Insolvency Regulation.
58   See article 2 sub (h) of the EU Insolvency Regulation.

It should be noted that the consequences of such national or secondary insolvency proceedings shall be restricted to the assets of the debtor situated in the territory of that other EU member state. For the purposes of the EU Insolvency
Regulation "the member state in which assets are situated" means, in the case
of[59] :

–   *tangible property* – the EU member state where the property is situated;
–   *property and rights, the ownership of or the entitlement to which must be
    entered in a public register* – the EU member state under the authority of
    which the register is kept; and
–   *claims* – the EU member state within the territory of which the third party
    required to meet them has the centre of his main interests.

Ad. (2) Recognition

The principle of recognition of insolvency proceedings is embodied in article 16
of the EU Insolvency Regulation. Any judgment opening insolvency proceedings
handed down by a court of an EU member state having jurisdiction pursuant to
the EU Insolvency Regulation, shall be recognized in all the other EU member
states from the time it becomes effective in the State where the proceedings were
opened. The effects of recognition are as follows[60] :

(i)   The judgment opening the main insolvency proceedings shall, with no
       further formalities, produce the same effects in any other EU member state
       as the State where the proceedings were opened, unless:
       (a)   the EU Insolvency Regulation provides otherwise (see *e.g.* the public
             policy exception below and article 10 of the EU Insolvency Regulation
             for employment agreements); and
       (b)   national or secondary proceedings are opened in that other EU member
             state;
(ii)   The effects of the national or secondary insolvency proceedings may not be
       challenged in other EU member states; and
(iii) As far as national or secondary insolvency proceedings are concerned, only
       with creditor's consent shall any restriction of creditor's rights – in
       particular, a stay or discharge – produce effects vis-à-vis assets situated
       within the territory of another EU member state.

In addition to the recognition of a judgment concerning the opening of insolvency proceedings, the EU Insolvency Regulation also provides for the recognition of other judgments[61] . Also judgments which concern the course and closure

---

59   See article 2 sub (g) of the EU Insolvency Regulation.
60   See article 17 of the EU Insolvency Regulation.
61   See article 25 of the EU Insolvency Regulation.

of insolvency proceedings and approved compositions are recognized with no further formalities, provided that:

(i)   those judgments are handed down by a court whose judgment concerning the opening of the insolvency proceedings is recognized pursuant to the EU Insolvency Regulation; and

(ii) those judgments do not result in a limitation of personal freedom or postal secrecy in the EU member states that are required to recognize those judgments[62].

The same applies to judgments derived directly from insolvency proceedings and which are closely linked with them, even if they were handed down by another court.

The public policy exception

Pursuant to article 26 of the EU Insolvency Regulation any EU member state may refuse to recognize insolvency proceedings opened in another EU member state, or to enforce a judgment handed down in the context of such proceedings, where the effects of such recognition or enforcement would be manifestly contrary to that State's public policy, in particular its fundamental principles or the constitutional rights and liberties of an individual.

Third parties' rights in rem

The EU Insolvency Regulation provides for the protection of third parties' rights in rem[63]. The opening of insolvency proceedings does not affect the rights in rem of third parties in respect of tangible or intangible, moveable or immoveable assets belonging to the debtor, which are situated within the territory of another EU member state at the time of the opening of the insolvency proceedings.

Honoring of an obligation to a debtor

In addition, the EU Insolvency Regulation provides that a third party is deemed to have discharged an obligation if[64]:

(i)   the person honored an obligation in an EU member state for the benefit of a debtor, who is subject to insolvency proceedings opened in another EU member state, pursuant to which insolvency proceedings the obligation should have been honored for the benefit of liquidator of such proceedings; and

(ii) the person was unaware of the opening of the insolvency proceedings mentioned above under (i).

---

62   See paragraph 3 of article 25 of the EU Insolvency Regulation.
63   See article 5 of the EU Insolvency Regulation.
64   See article 24 paragraph 1 of the EU Insolvency Regulation.

Ad. (3) Applicable law

The general rule concerning applicable law is contained in article 4 of the EU Insolvency Regulation. Paragraph 1 of this article states:

> "Save as otherwise provided in this (*EU Insolvency; PJMD*) Regulation, the law appli-
> cable to insolvency proceedings and their effects shall be that of the member state
> within the territory of which such proceedings are opened."

This *lex concursus* determines (i) the conditions for the opening of insolvency
proceedings, (ii) their conduct and (iii) their closure.

The second paragraph of article 4 of the EU Insolvency Regulation provides a
non-exhaustive list of issues (listed from (a) to (m)) that are determined by the *lex
concursus*. In addition, the EU Insolvency Regulation explicitly mentions the applicable law in respect of, *inter alia*, the following issues:

–   *Set-off* – the law applicable to the insolvent debtor's claim (article 6);
–   *Reservation of title* – the law of the EU member state within the territory of
    which the asset is situated (article 7);
–   *Agreements relating to immoveable property* – the law of the EU member
    state within the territory of which the immoveable property is situated
    (article 8);
–   *Payment systems and financial markets* – the law of the EU member state
    applicable to the payment or settlement system or to the financial market
    (article 9);
–   *Employment agreements* – the law of the EU member state applicable to the
    agreement of employment (article 10);
–   *Rights subject to registration* – the law of the EU member state under the
    authority of which the register is kept (article 11); and
–   *Pending lawsuits* – the law of the EU member state in which the lawsuit is
    pending (article 15).

Other features of the EU Insolvency Regulation
Aside from the main rules on jurisdiction, recognition and applicable law, the EU
Insolvency Regulation also provides for:
(i)   rules on publication of insolvency proceedings outside of the EU member
      state in which they were opened[65];
(ii) rules on the duty of cooperation and communication of information[66];

---

65   See articles 21, 22, 23, 40 and 42 of the EU Insolvency Regulation.
66   See article 31 of the EU Insolvency Regulation.

(iii) rules on the position of secondary insolvency proceedings vis-à-vis main insolvency proceedings[67]; and
(iv) rules on creditor rights[68].

1.3.1.3 The consequences of the EU Insolvency Regulation for the Netherlands insolvency practice

What will be the consequences of the EU Insolvency Regulation for the Netherlands insolvency practice? Before attempting to answer this question, it is important to once again emphasize the scope of the EU Insolvency Regulation.

(1) As mentioned above in § 1.3.1.1, the EU Insolvency Regulation does not aim to replace the substantive laws on insolvency proceedings of the EU member states. Therefore the substantive laws on Netherlands insolvency law will, in principle, not be changed as a result of the EU Insolvency Regulation.
(2) In addition, it should be noted that the EU Insolvency Regulation will not be applicable to insolvency proceedings where the centre of the debtor's main interests is situated outside the jurisdictions of the EU member states.

Without aiming to be exhaustive, the EU Insolvency Regulation is likely to have an impact on the following areas of the Netherlands insolvency practice[69]:

(i)   The principle of territoriality applicable to recourse to assets situated in the Netherlands.
(ii)   Agreements with mutual performances; employment agreements; rental agreements with respect to immoveable property.
(iii) The concept of set-off.
(iv)   The *actio pauliana.*
(v)   Secondary insolvency proceeding in the Netherlands as a means to maintain national rights of preference and priority.
(vi)   Security rights *in rem* over assets situated in the Netherlands.

Ad. (i)   The principle of territoriality applicable to recourse to assets situated in the Netherlands

In situations where the EU Insolvency Regulation will apply, the operation of the principle of territoriality, as discussed in § 1.2.4, will be substantially compromised.

---

67 See articles 27-30 and 33-38 of the EU Insolvency Regulation.
68 See articles 32, 39 and 41 of the EU Insolvency Regulation.
69 See also Kortmann/Veder, *supra* footnote 49, at pp. 768-773 under 3.

Pursuant to the EU Insolvency Regulation, individual recourse to assets situated in the Netherlands will no longer be possible, provided that[70]:

(a) main insolvency proceedings have been opened in another EU member state; and

(b) pursuant to the law of that EU member state, creditors are not entitled to take individual measures of recourse.

If creditors obtain total or partial satisfaction of their claims on assets belonging to the debtor situated in the Netherlands in violation of the above rule, those creditors will be under the obligation to return what they have obtained to the liquidator of the main insolvency proceedings in the other EU member state[71].

The same applies to the legal consequences of the termination of main insolvency proceedings in another EU member state. Pursuant to current Netherlands private international law, the legal consequences of foreign (EU and non-EU) insolvency proceedings cannot be invoked in the Netherlands to the extent that creditors, whose claims have not been completely satisfied, would not be able to have recourse to assets of the debtor situated in the Netherlands after the foreign insolvency proceedings have been terminated[72]. This will be different for situations where the EU Insolvency Regulation shall be applicable. After termination of foreign (EU) insolvency proceedings, individual recourse by creditors, whose claims have not been completely satisfied, to assets situated in the Netherlands will no longer be possible, if it is prohibited by the law governing the foreign (EU) main insolvency proceeding that has been terminated[73].

Ad. (ii) Agreements with mutual performances; employment agreements; rental agreements with respect to immoveable property

Agreements with mutual performances
In § 3.5.2.2, rules applicable to agreements with mutual performances will be addressed in the context of a Netherlands bankruptcy. Pursuant to the EU Insolvency Regulation, the consequences of opening insolvency proceedings for such ongoing agreements will be governed by the *lex concursus*[74]. This means that in insolvency proceedings opened in the Netherlands, the Netherlands bankruptcy rules on agreements with mutual performances may apply, irrespective of the choice of law made in the agreements as to the governing law. However, this also

---

70 This follows from article 4 paragraph 2 sub (b) and (f) of the EU Insolvency Regulation read in conjunction with article 17 paragraph 1 of the EU Insolvency Regulation.

71 See article 20 paragraph 1 of the EU Insolvency Regulation.

72 This follows from the De Vleeschmeesters-case of the Netherlands supreme court dated 31 May 1996 (*NJ* 1998, 108).

73 This follows from article 4 paragraph 2 sub (k) of the EU Insolvency Regulation read in conjunction with article 25 paragraph 1 of the EU Insolvency Regulation.

74 See article 4 paragraph 2 sub (e) of the EU Insolvency Regulation.

means that a choice of Netherlands law may be set aside by foreign bankruptcy rules in the case where the opening of foreign insolvency proceedings are covered by the EU Insolvency Regulation.

Employment agreements
In contrast to agreements with mutual performances, pursuant to the EU Insolvency Regulation, the consequences of opening insolvency proceedings on employment agreements will be exclusively governed by the law of the EU member state applicable to the employment agreement[75]. The governing law will have to provide the answers to questions such as whether or not a trustee in bankruptcy is entitled to terminate an employment agreement, and if so which notice period he should observe in doing so. In § 3.5.2.5, the rules applicable to employment agreements will be addressed in relation to a Netherlands bankruptcy of an employer[76].

Rental agreements with respect to immoveable property
In § 3.5.2.4, the rules applicable to rental agreements will be addressed in the context of a Netherlands bankruptcy of a tenant. Pursuant to the EU Insolvency Regulation, the consequences of opening insolvency proceedings on rental agreements with respect to immoveable property will be exclusively governed by the law of the EU member state where such immoveable property is situated. This means that a trustee in bankruptcy in the Netherlands will have to consult French law for the answer to the question of if and how he could terminate a rental agreement entered into by the debtor in respect of immoveable property situated in France.

Ad. (iii) The concept of set-off

The Netherlands legal concept of set-off in bankruptcy is addressed In § 4.2. The general rule pursuant to the EU Insolvency Regulation is that the conditions under which set-offs may be invoked is governed by the *lex concursus*[77]. However, in article 6 of the EU Insolvency Regulation it is specified that the opening of insolvency proceedings shall not affect the right of creditors to demand the set-off of their claims against the claims of the debtor, provided that such a set-off is permitted by the law applicable to the insolvent debtor. This leads to the conclusion that pursuant to the EU Insolvency Regulation the right of set-off must be derived from the law that governs the claim of the debtor against which the credi-

---

75 See article 10 of the EU Insolvency Regulation.
76 For further reading on the position of the employee with an international employment agreement in cases of bankruptcy, see, *inter alia*, "*De curator, de werknemer, zijn internationale dienstbetrekking en haar beëindiging*", by Prof. mr M.V. Polak, in "*De curator, een octopus*", Prof mr. S.C.J.J Kortmann c.s. (editors), W.E.J. Tjeenk Willink 1996, Deventer, pp. 313-328.
77 This follows from article 4 paragraph 2 sub (d) of the EU Insolvency Regulation.

tor wishes to set-off his counter-claim. Whether or not this reference in the EU Insolvency Regulation to the law governing the claim of the debtor includes a reference to the rules concerning set-off in bankruptcy of that law is uncertain[78].

Ad. (iv) The actio pauliana

The *actio pauliana* in the Netherlands is discussed in § 4.1. Pursuant to the EU Insolvency Regulation the rules relating to the voidness, voidability or unenforceability of legal acts detrimental to all creditors in an insolvency proceeding must be governed by the *lex concursus*[79]. As it is a tool to invalidate legal acts conducted by the debtor that are detrimental to the creditors of the debtor, under the EU Insolvency Regulation the *actio pauliana* will therefore, in principle, also be governed by the *lex concursus*.

However, from article 13 of the EU Insolvency Regulation, it follows that the general rule referring to the *lex concursus* is not applicable in case where the person who benefited from an act detrimental to all the creditors provides proof that:

(a)   said act is subject to the law of an EU member state other than that of the State of the opening of the insolvency proceedings; and

(b)   the law mentioned above under (a) does not allow any means of challenging the detrimental act in the relevant case.

This means that article 13 of the EU Insolvency Regulation provides effectively for a "veto" by the *lex causae* (*i.e.* the applicable law as referred to in article 13 of the EU Insolvency Regulation).

Ad. (v)   Secondary insolvency proceedings in the Netherlands as a means to maintain national rights of preference and priority

Pursuant to the EU Insolvency Regulation, any creditor who has his habitual residence, domicile or registered office in an EU member state other than the State of the opening of proceedings, has the right to lodge claims in the insolvency proceedings in writing[80]. Creditors can include tax authorities and social security authorities of the EU member states. Consequently, Netherlands creditors can lodge their claims in a foreign insolvency proceeding.

---

78   See Kortmann/Veder, *supra* footnote 49, at pp. 772-773 under 3.8, where they argue against a reference to the rules concerning set-off in bankruptcy of the law governing the claim of the debtor.

79   This follows from article 4 paragraph 2 sub (m) of the EU Insolvency Regulation.

80   See articles 32 and 39 of the EU Insolvency Regulation.

Whether or not those claims will be verified, admitted and what their rank will be, is governed by the *lex concursus* applicable to the foreign insolvency proceeding. If a Netherlands creditor is uncertain whether or not its Netherlands right of preference will be recognized in the foreign insolvency proceedings, it may be advisable to have the debtor also declared bankrupt in the Netherlands by way of a secondary insolvency proceeding[81]. When main insolvency proceedings have already been opened in another EU member state, the debtor's insolvency does not have to be examined again in the Netherlands for the opening of secondary insolvency proceedings in the Netherlands[82]. The secondary insolvency proceeding in the Netherlands will be governed by Netherlands law[83]. Therefore, Netherlands law on the ranking of claims will be applicable as far as the distribution of the proceeds of the assets of the debtor situated in the Netherlands is concerned.

The different types of creditors in a bankruptcy are addressed in § 3.6. For a brief discussion of the fiscal privileged ground right of the Netherlands tax authorities, see § 5.2.3.1.

Ad. (vi) Security rights in rem over assets situated in the Netherlands

Pledges and mortgages
The two most important security rights *in rem* in the Netherlands are discussed in Chapter 5.

Pursuant to article 5 of the EU Insolvency Regulation, the opening of insolvency proceedings in an EU member state shall not affect the rights *in rem* of creditors or third parties in respect of tangible or intangible, moveable or immoveable assets belonging to the debtor which are situated within the territory of another EU member state at the time of the opening of the insolvency proceedings. For creditors having pledges or mortgages over assets situated in the Netherlands, this means that they can exercise their rights in accordance with Netherlands law. They do not have to accept any limitations that secured creditors are subjected to by virtue of the *lex concursus*.

Uncertainty exists, however, as to the exact scope of the "unaffectedness" that is meant by the EU Insolvency Regulation. It is unclear, for example, whether or not in this context Netherlands holders of a right of pledge or a right of mortgage

---

81   See article 16 paragraph 2 of the EU Insolvency Regulation.
82   See article 27 paragraph 1 of the EU Insolvency Regulation.
83   See article 28 of the EU Insolvency Regulation.

can be subjected to an insolvency stay[84] ordered by the liquidator in a foreign insolvency proceeding[85].

Reservation of title or ownership
The right to reserve title or ownership is addressed in § 3.4.2.1 where recollection of goods by third parties in a bankruptcy is discussed.

Similar to what is contemplated in article 5 of the EU Insolvency Regulation for security rights *in rem*, article 7 of the EU Insolvency Regulation provides for reservation of title or ownership. In that article it is contemplated that opening of insolvency proceedings in an EU member state against the purchaser of an asset shall not affect the seller's rights based on a reservation of title or ownership where, at the time of the opening of the insolvency proceedings, the asset is situated within the territory of an EU member state other than the State of the opening of the insolvency proceedings.

In addition, paragraph 2 of article 7 of the EU Insolvency Regulation makes it clear that opening of insolvency proceedings against the seller of an asset, after delivery of this asset, shall not:
(a)   constitute grounds for rescinding or terminating the sale; and
(b)   prevent the purchaser from acquiring title or ownership where, at the time of opening of the insolvency proceedings, the asset sold is situated within the territory of an EU member state other than the State of the opening of the insolvency proceedings.

Summary
EU INSOLVENCY REGULATION

Annex
An English version of the EU Insolvency Regulation is included as an Annex to this book.

---

84   For more details on insolvency stay in a suspension of payment see § 2.2.3 and in a bankruptcy see § 3.4.1.1.
85   See Kortmann/Veder, *supra* footnote 49 at pp. 769-770 under 3.3, where they expect "unaffectedness" to be interpreted in an extensive manner. Despite that, Kortmann and Veder argue in favor of not giving too broad an interpretation of "unaffectedness". According to them it is sufficient if the EU Insolvency Regulation could assure that rights *in rem* are no more affected as a result of the opening of a foreign insolvency proceeding as when a national insolvency proceeding is opened.

Scope
(1) From 31 May 2002 the EU Insolvency Regulation shall be binding in its entirety and directly applicable in the Netherlands and the other EU member states (save for Denmark).
(2) The EU Insolvency Regulation applies only to proceedings where the centre of the debtor's main interests is situated in the Community.

Jurisdiction
(1) Main insolvency proceedings are opened in the EU member state in which the centre of a debtor's main interests is situated.
(2) National or secondary insolvency proceedings can be opened in the EU member state within the territory of which the debtor possesses an establishment, provided that the centre of the debtor's main interests is situated within the territory of an EU member state.

Recognition
(1) Any judgment opening insolvency proceedings handed down by a court of an EU member state having jurisdiction pursuant to the EU Insolvency Regulation shall be recognized in all the other EU member states from the time it becomes effective in the State of the opening of the proceedings.
(2) Judgments which concern the course and closure of insolvency proceedings and approved compositions are also recognized, provided certain conditions are met.
(3) In respect of recognition, a public policy exception exists for EU member states.

Applicable law
(1) The general rule concerning applicable law pursuant to the EU Insolvency Regulation is that the law of the EU member state within the territory of which insolvency proceedings are opened (*i.e.* the *lex concursus*), is the applicable law.
(2) For a number of issues, the EU Insolvency Regulation mentions different applicable laws.

Consequences for the Netherlands insolvency practice
The EU Insolvency Regulation is likely to have on impact on the following areas of the Netherlands insolvency practice:
(1) The principle of territoriality applicable to recourse to assets situated in the Netherlands.
(2) Agreements with mutual performances; employment agreements; rental agreements with respect to immoveable property.
(3) The concept of set-off.

(4) The *actio pauliana.*

(5) Secondary insolvency proceeding in the Netherlands as a means to maintain national rights of preference and priority.

(6) Security rights *in rem* over assets situated in the Netherlands.

The most likely consequences of the EU Insolvency Regulation in the above areas are briefly discussed in § 1.3.1.3.

Chapter 2
SUSPENSION OF PAYMENT

This Chapter aims to provide the reader with a general outline of the main features of the insolvency regime of suspension of payment as set forth in the Fw. One of the reasons for having only a general discussion of suspension of payment is the rather low frequency – in comparison to bankruptcies – of suspensions of payment in the Netherlands.

At present, suspension of payment is being (re-)evaluated in light of the Ministry of Economic Affairs' MDW-Project concerning the modernization of the Netherlands insolvency laws. The working group established to work on the MDW-project (the "MDW-Working Group") has expressed a feeling that suspension of payment fails to work efficiently in the Netherlands. The MDW-Working Group consists of representatives of the relevant Ministries (*i.e.* the Ministries of Economic Affairs, Justice, Finance and Social Affairs) with an external chairman in the person of Mr M.J.G.C. Raaijmakers, professor of law at the Catholic University of Brabant. While the regime was especially designed to help companies in financial distress to restructure (the viable parts of) their business, the great majority of suspensions of payment quickly result in a bankruptcy in the Netherlands. At the end of this Chapter, the MDW-Project will be discussed in more detail (§ 2.6).

However, before examining the possible direction suspension of payment will take in the future, the purpose, nature, scope and consequences of suspension of payment will be addressed in § 2.1. In doing so, some of the reasons for the reluctance in the Netherlands to properly (*i.e.* timely) use the instrument of suspension of payment will be indicated[1]. In § 2.2 the steps for requesting suspension of payment will be looked into and in § 2.3 the focus will be on the following two court appointed key players in the suspension of payment (1) the administrator and (2) the supervisory judge in the suspension of payment.

In § 2.4 two different stages in a suspension of payment will be discussed: (1) provisional suspension of payment and (2) final suspension of payment. The different ways of ending a suspension of payment will be addressed in § 2.5.

---

1 See generally *"Surséance van betaling"* by Mr A.L. Leuftink, Kluwer 1995, Deventer, Chapter 1, pp. 1-11.

2.1   Purpose, nature, scope and consequences

Purpose and nature

The procedure of suspension of payment is set out in articles 213-283 Fw. It aims to give the debtor in financial distress an opportunity to reorganize its business and search for (new) means of financing its debts. While bankruptcy was originally designed to liquidate the business of a debtor, the purpose of the regime of suspension of payment was to facilitate the continuation of the business of the debtor. In practice, however, suspension of payment rarely serves this purpose. Oftentimes it only operates as an introduction to a subsequent bankruptcy of the debtor, hence its characterization as a "mitigated bankruptcy".

The vicious circle

As is the case for bankruptcy, suspension of payment is also burdened with negative connotations in the Netherlands. When a debtor decides to request for a suspension of payment, this negative perception results in a dramatic loss of confidence in the debtor by third parties[2]. Consequently, debtors have felt obliged to postpone a request for suspension of payment for longer than is prudent. When a request is finally made, it is usually too late and the suspension of payment inevitably results in a bankruptcy of the debtor. This vicious circle is hard to break.

By including a composition proposal to a request for suspension of payment[3], the "loss of confidence"-effect may be reduced.

Risk of liability

In the Netherlands, a formal obligation for a debtor to request suspension of payment when certain criteria are met does not exist. However, when a debtor is evidently too late in requesting a suspension of payment, the debtor does run the risk of incurring liability in that respect. For more details on corporate liabilities and liabilities based on wrongful act, see § 4.3 and § 4.4.

Scope

One of the goals of suspension of payment is to give a debtor, confronted with short-term liquidity problems, some financial breathing space. The achievement of this goal is seriously obstructed by the limited scope of suspension of payment. Basically, a suspension of payment only affects non-preferential or ordi-

---

2   See Leuftink, *supra* footnote 1, at pp. 9-10.
3   For more details on composition in a suspension of payment, see § 2.5.2.

nary creditors, creditors who have no claim secured by either mortgage or pledge, or any other privileged right[4].

As a consequence of this limited scope, creditors such as the Netherlands tax authorities fall outside the scope of suspension of payment. However, secured and/or preferential creditors are covered by a suspension of payment in the following cases:

(1) To the extent secured and/or preferential creditors cannot take recourse on the goods over which they have security or privilege[5];

(2) When secured and/or preferential creditors submit their claims with an administrator, as this may result in the privilege or priority attached to their claims being lost and thereby transforming their claims into non-preferential or ordinary claims[6].

In respect of the situation mentioned above under (2), it should be noted that the administrator has an active duty to warn creditors about the severe consequence of voluntarily submitting their claims[7].

Consequences

As of the day provisional suspension of payment is granted, the following consequences flow:

(1) Creditors covered by the suspension of payment may no longer take further recourse against the debtor[8]. Instead they must submit their claims (duly evidenced, preferably, by documents) to an administrator for verification in case of a composition[9].

(2) All measures of recourse already taken by creditors are suspended by virtue of law as of the day the provisional suspension of payment takes effect[10]. As soon as final suspension of payment is granted or a ratification by the court of a composition has become final (*i.e.* not subject to further appeal), any

---

4   See article 232 Fw.
5   See article 232 sub (a) Fw.
6   See article 257 paragraph 2 Fw.
7   See the Van der Pluijm/Schreurs-case (HR 16 February 1996, *NJ* 1997, 607)
8   See article 230 paragraph 1 Fw. From paragraph 3 of article 230 Fw it follows that the rule of paragraph 1 does not apply to recourse taken in connection with claims secured by a priority right insofar as it concerns goods that are subject to the priority right.
9   See article 257 Fw. For more details on a composition in a suspension of payment, see § 2.5.2.
10 See article 230 paragraph 2 Fw. From paragraph 3 of article 230 Fw it follows that the rule of paragraph 2 does not apply to arrests made in connection with claims secured by a priority right insofar as it concerns goods that are subject to the priority right.

arrests made prior thereto, cease to exist[11]. Such consequence may already take effect at an earlier time if – upon request of the administrator(s) – a competent court has so ordered.

(3)   For debts subject to suspension of payment, there is a special rule in respect of limitation periods and/or terms of forfeiture similar to that applicable in the case of a bankruptcy (§ 3.1)[12]. Limitation periods and terms of forfeiture which would otherwise lapse during the suspension of payment or within six months after the termination thereof, continue to run – by virtue of law – for a period of six months after the termination of the suspension of payment[13].

(4)   The suspension of payment does not suspend or affect pending court proceedings, nor does it prevent the commencement of new ones[14].

(5)   As far as payment of debts during the course of the suspension of payment is concerned, the principal rule is that during the entire course of the suspension of payment, payments of all debts (i) not falling within the scope of article 232 Fw (which – in short – provides that claims with a priority right, claims for costs of living, care or upbringing and installments due under hire-purchase agreements and hire-purchase agreements relating to vessels, do not fall within the scope of suspension of payment) and (ii) existing prior to the suspension of payment, may only be made to all joint creditors in proportion to their respective claims[15]. When the debtor – with the consent of the administrator – deviates from this principal rule, the prejudiced creditors could attempt to hold the administrator liable for any damages they sustain as a consequence thereof.

(6)   As in a bankruptcy, a suspension of payment does not take effect in favor of guarantors pursuant to a surety or several and jointly liable co-debtors of the debtor (§ 3.1)[16]. This means that guarantors pursuant to a surety and co-debtors may be called on their surety or liability, respectively.

(7)   In contrast to a trustee in bankruptcy, an administrator in a suspension of payment is not granted its own right to invalidate acts by the debtor based on the concept of *actio pauliana*. As a consequence, the creditors in a suspension of payment keep their right to invalidate acts by the debtor based

---

11   See comment 3 to article 230 Fw by Mr A.A.J. Wissink in *"Tekst & Commentaar Faillisse-mentswet"*, Prof. mr B. Wessels/Mr Ph. van Sint Truiden, Kluwer 2nd edition 1999, Deventer, p. 217.
12   See article 230 paragraph 4 Fw.
13   See article 36 Fw and also comment 2 to article 36 Fw by Mr R.H. van Erp in *"Tekst & Commentaar Faillissementswet"*, Prof. mr B. Wessels/Mr Ph. van Sint Truiden, Kluwer 2nd edition 1999, Deventer, p. 46.
14   See article 231 paragraph 1 Fw. From article 231 paragraph 3 Fw it follows that without the cooperation of the administrator(s), the debtor may not act in court, either as applicant or as defendant in legal proceedings relating to rights and obligations of the estate.
15   See article 233 Fw.
16   See article 241 Fw.

on *actio pauliana* as set forth in article 3:45 BW during the suspension of payment[17].

Summary
PURPOSE, NATURE, SCOPE AND CONSEQUENCES OF SUSPENSION OF PAYMENT

Purpose and nature
To provide the debtor with financial breathing space to reorganize and continue its business.

Scope
Generally, suspension of payment only affects non-preferential or ordinary creditors.

Consequences
(1) Suspension of payment has a severe "loss of confidence"-effect.
(2) Creditors covered by a suspension of payment may no longer take further recourse on their own against the debtor.
(3) Limitation periods and terms of forfeiture are extended.
(4) All measures of recourse already taken by creditors which are affected by the suspension of payment are suspended by virtue of law.
(5) Pending court proceedings are not affected and the commencement of new ones is not prevented.
(6) A suspension of payment does not take effect in favor of guarantors pursuant to a surety or several and jointly liable co-debtors of the debtor.

2.2   Steps for requesting suspension of payment

The petitioner

A suspension of payment can only be requested by the debtor itself, not by its creditors or other third parties[18]. In order to file a petition with the district court in its place of residence, the debtor needs to procure the services of an attorney of record from that district. This attorney of record, together with the debtor, must sign the petition requesting the granting of a suspension of payment[19]. Where the

---

17   For a further discussion of the concept of *actio pauliana*, see § 4.1.
18   See article 213 paragraph 1 Fw.
19   See article 214 paragraph 1 Fw.

debtor is a private person, the debtor must have an individual profession or business in order for a suspension of payment to be granted[20].

The petition

Where the debtor is a company, the petition for suspension of payment should include, as a minimum, the following[21] :

(1) a recent official registration with the relevant Chamber of Commerce and Industries;
(2) a copy of the articles of association of the debtor; and
(3) a list of assets and liabilities, indicating the creditors (preferably accompanied with their addresses) to whom the suspension of payment shall apply.

In contrast to a petition for bankruptcy by the debtor (§ 3.2.1), a shareholders' resolution ordering the directors of the debtor to file for suspension of payment is not required. As a consequence, the board of directors of a debtor may (ab)use suspension of payment as a backdoor to lead the company into bankruptcy, without having to deal with the shareholders of the company[22].

In respect of larger companies having a supervisory board and to which the so-called "*Structuurregeling*"[23] is applicable, the decision of the board of directors to request for suspension of payment must further be approved by the board of supervisory directors of the debtor[24]. If the debtor has a Works Council, it should be noted that in the *IJsselwerf*-case[25], the Netherlands supreme court held that there is *no* duty to have prior consultation with the Works Council in respect of the anticipated request for suspension of payment because:

(1) the purport of a decision to request suspension of payment is not to make an important change in the organization of the debtor or in the distribution of labor; and
(2) if granted, a suspension of payment does not affect the organization of the debtor.

According to the WOR, an entrepreneur maintaining an enterprise in which, as a rule, at least 50 persons are employed, is obliged to establish a Works Council for the purposes of consultation with and representation of the employees of the en-

---

20 See article 213 paragraph 2 Fw.
21 See Chapter 12 on suspension of payment from the *"Directives in bankruptcies and suspensions of payment"*, in *"Vademecum Advocatuur: Wet & Regelgeving"*, 2001, pp. 485-511.
22 See Leuftink, *supra* footnote 1, at pp. 8-9.
23 See articles 2:152-164 BW and articles 2:262-274 BW; see also § 4.3.2.
24 See article 2:164 paragraph 1 sub i BW and article 2:274 paragraph 1 sub i BW.
25 HR 6 June 2001, *NJ* 2001, 477.

terprise[26]. The obligation to establish a Works Council may also result from a provision to this effect in a collective bargaining agreement[27]. The WOR defines "enterprise" as every organization operating in society as an independent entity where work is being performed on the basis of an employment agreement[28]. This definition implies that the enterprise does not necessarily have to be a corporate entity. "Entrepreneur" is defined as any natural person who, or legal entity which, maintains an enterprise[29]. A Works Council has in certain circumstances, *inter alia*, a right to render advice[30], a right of approval [31] and a right to be informed[32].

Concurrence of requests

Where there is a concurrent request for suspension of payment and a prior third party request for bankruptcy, the request for suspension of payment will be heard first[33]. Therefore, in practice, the request for suspension of payment may also be (ab)used as a defense against a third party request for bankruptcy.

2.2.1 THE APPLICABLE TEST(S)

Test

A debtor can request suspension of payment if the debtor foresees it will not be able to pay all its creditors having due and payable claims[34]. It is not necessary to prove that this criterium is met.

Assuming that the request is properly submitted to a competent court, a provisional suspension of payment is immediately granted by the court without an evaluation of the request by the court on its merits[35]. Such an evaluation only takes place when the court has to decide whether or not to grant the debtor a final suspension of payment[36].

As well as granting a provisional suspension of payment to the debtor, the court:
(1) appoints one or more administrators;
(2) sets a date for a meeting of creditors; and

---

26 See article 2 parapgraph 1 WOR.
27 See article 5a paragraph 1 WOR.
28 See article 1 paragraph 1 sub c WOR.
29 See article 1 paragraph 1 sub d WOR.
30 See article 25 WOR.
31 See article 27 WOR.
32 See article 31 WOR and for the Works Council in bankruptcy, see § 3.5.2.5.
33 See article 218 paragraph 6 Fw.
34 See article 213 paragraph 1 Fw.
35 See article 215 paragraph 2 Fw.
36 See article 218 paragraph 7 Fw.

(3) may also (but has no obligation to do so) appoint a member of the court as a supervisory judge in the suspension of payment[37] .

In practice, a supervisory judge is always appointed.

2.2.2 LEGAL REMEDIES

With regards legal remedies in relation to a suspension of payment, the following are noteworthy:

(1) Legal remedies only exist against a judgment made in respect of final suspension of payment[38];

(2) The legal remedies have no suspensory effect[39];

(3) Where final suspension of payment is denied, the debtor may appeal to the competent court of appeals within eight days following the date of judgment[40];

(4) Where final suspension of payment is allowed, each creditor who has not yet declared to be in favor of the final suspension of payment, may also appeal to the competent court of appeals within eight days following the date of judgment. This includes creditors who have declared nothing and/or creditors who have declared to be neither against nor in favor of a final suspension of payment. In case of an appeal by a creditor, the creditor must give notice to the debtor[41]. In appeal, no new vote is cast on the granting of a final suspension of payment; instead, each creditor is entitled to defend or challenge the judgment rendered[42]; and

(5) Following a judgment rendered in appeal a further appeal to the Netherlands supreme court is open for eight days[43] .

2.2.3 THE INSOLVENCY STAY

The court may – at the request of the debtor or the administrator – issue an order stipulating that, for a period of one month at most, any right of third parties (including secured creditors (§ 3.6.1) and preferential creditors (§ 3.6.3.1)) to:

(1) take recourse against assets belonging to the estate; or

(2) claim assets which are in the control of the debtor or the administrator,

may only be exercised with the authorization of the court or, if appointed, the supervisory judge[44]. This period, in which all means of recourse against the debtor

---

37 See article 215 paragraph 2 Fw.
38 See article 282 Fw.
39 See article 222 paragraph 1 Fw.
40 See article 219 paragraph 1 Fw.
41 See article 219 paragraph 3 Fw.
42 See article 220 paragraph 1 Fw.
43 See article 221 paragraph 1 Fw.
44 See article 241a Fw.

by third parties (including secured creditors and preferential creditors) affected by the suspension of payment are frozen, is called the insolvency stay. The court may extend this period only once for a further period of one month at most.

The insolvency stay in suspension of payment is similar to that in bankruptcy (§ 3.4.1.1). A difference between the two is that in suspension of payment the insolvency stay needs to be requested by the debtor or the administrator while in bankruptcy every interested party, including the supervisory judge *ex officio*, can request for an insolvency stay.

For anticipated amendments to the insolvency stay pursuant to the MDW-Project, see § 2.6.1.1.

Summary
THE STEPS FOR REQUESTING SUSPENSION OF PAYMENT

Petitioner
Only the debtor – together with a competent attorney of record from the appropriate district – may request suspension of payment from the competent district court.

Petition
Depending on whether the debtor is a private person or a company, the petition needs to meet certain requirements.

Concurrence
Where there is a concurrent prior third party request for bankruptcy, the request for suspension of payment will be heard first.

Tests
(1) If the debtor foresees it will not be able to pay all its creditors having due and payable claims.
(2) A provisional suspension of payment is immediately granted by the court without an evaluation of the merits.

Legal remedies
(1) Legal remedies only exist against a judgment made in respect of a final suspension of payment and they do not have suspensory effect.
(2) Appeal within 8 days following the date of the judgment and further appeal within 8 days following the judgment in appeal.

Insolvency stay
(1) During the insolvency stay all means of recourse by third parties (in-
     cluding secured creditors (§ 3.6.1) and preferential creditors (§ 3.6.3.1))
     affected by the suspension of payment are frozen.
(2) The total term of the insolvency stay is 2 months at most.

2.3   The (appointment of the) administrator and the supervisory judge

As already mentioned above (§ 2.2.1), along with the granting of a provisional
suspension of payment, the court appoints one or more administrators and may
also appoint (but has no obligation to do so) a member of the court as a supervisory judge in the suspension of payment[45]. In the following paragraphs the respective positions of the two key, court appointed players in a suspension of payment will be briefly discussed.

2.3.1   THE ADMINISTRATOR

Profile

As is the case for trustees in bankruptcy (§ 3.3.1), an independent third person is
appointed by the competent court to act as an administrator in a suspension of
payment. Generally, in the Netherlands only attorneys (specialized in insolvency
law) are appointed as administrators.

Siamese twins

After the provisional suspension of payment is adjudicated, the administrator and
the debtor are only entitled to continue the business of the debtor and to administer and dispose of the assets of the debtor, with the consent of each other[46]. The
debtor and the administrator become Siamese twins in this respect, whereby the
administrator – in the interest of the creditors of the debtor for whom the suspension of payment has effect – needs to supervise the debtor.

In contrast to the more absolute powers of a trustee in bankruptcy, the position of
an administrator in a suspension of payment could be presumed to have a less active role in comparison. In practice, in suspensions of payment an active administrator is essential (and expected). Remarkably enough, the Fw does not provide
for a procedure to be followed in case disputes arise between the administrator
and the debtor. Strictly speaking, in such cases the following options are available:

---

45   See article 215 paragraph 2 Fw.
46   See article 228 paragraph 1 Fw.

(1) The debtor could – informally – request the competent court to have the administrator replaced; and

(2) The administrator could threaten to have the suspension of payment revoked. Obviously, these remedies will be too heavy-handed for resolving disputes in the majority of cases.

If more than one administrator has been appointed, the consent of the majority of administrators is required in order to make their acts legally binding. In the event of a split vote, a decision of the supervisory judge is required[47]. If no supervisory judge was appointed, a decision by the President of the competent district court is required. An administrator assigned to a specific task under the suspension of payment order has the power to act independently within the limits of his task.

Rights and duties

In respect of the rights and duties of an administrator, the following can be noted:

(1) Similar to that of a trustee in a bankruptcy (§ 3.3.1), an administrator has the duty to set out the state of affairs of the estate in a public report to be filed with the competent court at least every three months or a longer period of time as agreed between the administrator and the supervisory judge (or if no supervisory judge is appointed, by the court)[48]. Such public reports are open for inspection by the public in the competent court were they are filed.

For interested parties in a suspension of payment the public reports by the administrator are oftentimes the only source of information to verify (the motivation for) the conduct of the administrator and to find out what (according to the administrator) the expectations are in the suspension of payment. And in contrast to a bankruptcy (§ 3.3.2), the Fw does not provide for a formal legal basis for creditors or other third parties to order the administrator to perform or refrain from performing a certain act.

(2) During the suspension of payment, an administrator is entitled to:
    (i) request the calling of witnesses who could clarify any circumstances[49] ; and
    (ii) demand an investigation by experts, such as, for example, auditors[50].

(3) In contrast to the rules in a bankruptcy (§ 3.5.2.4), after the commencement of a suspension of payment only the administrator together with the debtor

---

47   See article 224 paragraph Fw.
48   See article 227 Fw.
49   See article 223b Fw.
50   See article 226 Fw. For similar rights of the supervisory judge in bankruptcy, see § 3.3.2.

(not the counter party of the debtor) are entitled to an early termination of rental agreements and leases, as long as a maximum notice period of three months is observed[51].

(4) The same as mentioned above under (3) applies to early termination of both employment agreements and agencies. In respect of employment agreements, the following should further be noted:

   (i)   For employment agreements the maximum notice period to be observed may amount to 26 weeks in a suspension of payment, while in a bankruptcy the maximum notice period may amount to 19 weeks only[52].

   (ii) In contrast to a bankruptcy (§ 3.5.2.5), during a suspension of payment a permission to terminate an employment agreement on the basis of article 6 BBA is still required.

   (iii) Where there is a transfer of business during a suspension of payment, the provisions under Netherlands law preserving the rights following from employment agreements (articles 7:662-7:666 BW) remain applicable, while during bankruptcy they are not[53].

2.3.2   THE SUPERVISORY JUDGE

Role

The role of a supervisory judge in a suspension of payment is basically an advisory one only, whereas in a bankruptcy his role is primarily one of supervising the trustee in bankruptcy (§ 3.3.2)[54]. This difference is clearly evidenced by the following facts:

(1) In a suspension of payment no acts by an administrator are subject to the (prior) consent or permission of the supervisory judge; and

(2) The Fw does not provide for a formal legal basis for creditors or other third parties to order an administrator to perform or refrain from performing certain acts.

Rights

Together with the creditors and (if appointed) other administrators, the supervisory judge is entitled to recommend the dismissal of an administrator[55]. After the

---

51 See article 238 Fw.
52 See article 239 Fw.
53 The non-applicability of the article 7:662-7:666 BW is one of the main reasons for a restart to actually take place in a bankruptcy of the debtor instead of in a suspension of payment of the debtor.
54 See article 223a Fw.
55 See article 224 paragraph 2 Fw.

administrator is heard or properly summoned, the court is competent at all times to dismiss an administrator and replace him or her by someone else.

Summary
ADMINISTRATOR AND SUPERVISORY JUDGE

The administrator
(1) An administrator is a court appointed independent third person (usually attorneys), who is only entitled to continue the business of the debtor and to administer and dispose of the assets of the debtor, with the consent of a debtor and *vice versa*.
(2) An administrator has the right to:
     (i)   call witnesses;
     (ii)   demand investigation by experts;
     (iii) terminate rental agreements and leases (in conjunction with the debtor) early; and
     (iv)   terminate employment agreements and agencies (in conjunction with the debtor) early.
(3) An administrator must file public reports regularly.

The supervisory judge
(1) A supervisory judge is a court appointed judge primarily having a advisory role only.
(2) A supervisory judge is entitled to recommend the dismissal of an administrator.

2.4 The different stages in suspension of payment

The insolvency regime of suspension of payment is divided in:
(1) provisional suspension of payment; and
(2) final suspension of payment.

2.4.1 PROVISIONAL SUSPENSION OF PAYMENT

Duration

As in bankruptcy (§ 3.4.1), provisional suspension of payment takes effect (retroactively) as of 00.00 hours from the day it was declared (for exceptions see § 1.2.1.2)[56]. Provisional suspension of payment commences from the date it was immediately granted by the competent court upon request by the debtor. Provi-

---

56   See article 217 Fw.

sional suspension of payment ends when a final judgment (*i.e.* no longer subject to any appeals) is made by the competent court allowing or denying a final suspension of payment.

Meeting of creditors

In practice, when a provisional suspension of payment is granted, the competent court schedules a meeting of creditors[57]. Such meeting is necessary to enable the court to decide whether or not to grant a final suspension of payment. The date for the meeting is usually two or three months after the provisional suspension of payment is granted.

2.4.2 FINAL SUSPENSION OF PAYMENT

Requirements

The court may grant a final suspension of payment for a period of up to 18 months, provided that:[58]
(1) prospects exist that the debtor will be able – in due course – to satisfy its creditors;
(2) the creditors of the debtor
    (i) holding 1/4 of the total amount of the claims represented at the hearing held before the court; or
    (ii) more than 1/3 in number of its creditors holding such claims
        do not oppose a final suspension of payment; and
(3) there are no grounds for suspecting that the debtor will try to prejudice the creditors during the final suspension of payment[59].

The duration of a final suspension of payment can be extended for a period of up to 18 months each time. If not timely extended, a final suspension of payment terminates automatically after the first 18 months period has lapsed.

Summary
DIFFERENT STAGES IN SUSPENSION OF PAYMENT

Provisional suspension of payment
A provisional suspension of payment is immediately granted without evaluation of the merits.

---

57   See article 215 paragraph 2 Fw.
58   See article 218 paragraph 2 Fw.
59   See article 218 paragraph 4 Fw.

Final suspension of payment
For a final suspension of payment to be granted:
(1) the debtor will have to be able to satisfy its creditors;
(2) the creditors of the debtor
    (i) holding 1/4 of the total amount of the claims represented at the hearing; or
    (ii) more than 1/3 in number of its creditors holding such claims,
      do not oppose to a final suspension of payment; and
(3) there are no grounds for suspecting that the debtor will try to prejudice the creditors during the final suspension of payment.

2.5   The end of a suspension of payment

In this section, the following two ways of bringing a suspension of payment to an end shall be discussed:
(1) Revocation followed by bankruptcy (§ 2.5.1).
(2) Termination by composition (§ 2.5.2).
A third way of ending a suspension of payment is by payment of all debts.

2.5.1   REVOCATION FOLLOWED BY BANKRUPTCY

Grounds for revocation

Upon recommendation of the supervisory judge (if appointed), upon request of the administrator(s), one or more creditors, or *ex officio* by the court, a suspension of payment is revoked by court order when prospects of the debtor being able to satisfy its creditors in due course cease to exist[60]. In that case the court will concurrently declare the debtor to be bankrupt. Other grounds for revocation of suspension of payment followed by bankruptcy of the debtor are[61] :
(1) if the debtor has acted in bad faith in administering the estate during the suspension of payment;
(2) if the debtor attempts to prejudice its creditors;
(3) if the debtor does not act with the consent of the administrator; and
(4) if the debtor fails to do what was imposed upon it by the court at the time or after the suspension of payment was granted or which the administrator requires the debtor to do in the interest of the estate.

---

60 See article 242 paragraph 1 sub 5 Fw and article 283 paragraph 1 Fw.
61 See article 242 paragraph 1 sub 1-4 Fw.

Remedies

Where suspension of payment is revoked, the debtor may appeal to the competent court of appeals within eight days following the date of the court order[62]. Where suspension of payment is not revoked, the party that requested revocation (*i.e.* the administrator(s) or one or more creditors), has a similar right of appeal. From an order rendered in appeal a further appeal to the Netherlands supreme court is open within eight days following the order in appeal[63].

2.5.2   TERMINATION BY COMPOSITION

Proposal

A debtor is entitled to propose a composition to its creditors covered by suspension of payment only once[64]:
(1)   upon submitting a request for suspension of payment; or
(2)   at any date thereafter.

Requirements for acceptance

A composition is accepted when[65]:
(1)   the composition is approved by 2/3 of the admitted and provisionally admitted creditors[66]; and
(2)   such creditors represent 3/4 of the amount of the admitted and provisionally admitted claims.
The approval of an admitted or provisionally admitted creditor having a claim based on a forfeited penalty is not needed.

Ratification

In the meeting in which composition is accepted by creditors, the supervisory judge – or if no supervisory judge is appointed, the competent court – will schedule the date on which the competent court will consider the ratification of the composition[67]. In the following situations, the court will refuse ratification[68]:

---

62   See article 243 paragraph 1 Fw and article 283 paragraph 1 Fw.
63   See article 244 paragraph 1 Fw and article 283 paragraph 2 Fw.
64   See article 252 Fw. See also comment 5 to article 252 Fw by Mr R.J. Verschoof in *"Tekst & Commentaar Faillissementswet"*, Prof. mr B. Wessels/Mr Ph. van Sint Truiden, Kluwer 2nd edition 1999, Deventer, p. 237.
65   See article 268 paragraph 1 Fw.
66   Creditors qualify as "admitted creditors" if the claims they submitted for verification with the administrator have been accepted.
67   See article 269b paragraph 1 Fw.
68   See article 272 paragraph 2 Fw.

(1) if the assets of the estate exceed the amount agreed to in the composition;

(2) if performance of the composition is not sufficiently guaranteed;

(3) if the composition was reached by means of fraudulent acts or the preference of one or more creditors or by other unfair means, regardless of whether or not the debtor or any other party cooperated to that effect; or

(4) if fees and expenses of experts and administrator(s) have not been paid to the administrator(s), nor has security been issued therefore.

In addition, the court may also refuse to ratify the composition on other grounds and *ex officio*[69]. In the same court order in which the court refuses to ratify the composition it may also declare the bankruptcy of the debtor[70].

Binding effect

A ratified composition is binding on all non-preferential or ordinary creditors who were affected by the suspension of payment[71]. The suspension of payment will terminate as soon as the ratification is final and not open to appeal[72]. A ratified composition that is final and not open to appeal creates a title of enforcement[73] for the creditors (whose claims have not been disputed) against the debtor and any guarantors pursuant to a surety who acceded to the composition[74].

Summary
THE END OF A SUSPENSION OF PAYMENT

A suspension of payment can end in the following ways:

(1) *Revocation followed by bankruptcy*
     An appeal is open for 8 days following the date of the court order and a further appeal is open for 8 days following the order of appeal.

(2) *Termination by composition*
     Approval needed of 1/3 of the admitted and provisionally admitted creditors representing 3/4 of the amount of the admitted and provisionally admitted claims.

A third way of ending a suspension of payment is by payment of all debts.

---

69 See article 272 paragraph 3 Fw.
70 See article 272 paragraph 4 Fw.
71 See article 273 Fw.
72 See article 276 Fw.
73 A title of enforcement avoids the need for creditors to obtain a favorable judgement of the court first before they can take recourse against the debtor for their claims.
74 See article 274 Fw.

2.6   Recent developments

The most relevant recent development that may have an effect on suspension of payment is the MDW-Project on modernization of the Netherlands insolvency laws, the main features and potential impact on suspension of payment of which are addressed below.

2.6.1   THE MDW-PROJECT

The MDW-Project aims to investigate whether or not it is possible to enhance the "reorganizational ability" of the Fw, and in particular, the suspension of payment regime. The MDW-Working Group, consisting of representatives of the relevant Ministries (*i.e.* the Ministries of Economic Affairs, Justice, Finance and Social Affairs) with an external chairman in the person of Mr M.J.G.C. Raaijmakers, professor of law at the Catholic University of Brabant, must conduct investigations for this purpose and, in time, will have to develop proposals for amending the Netherlands insolvency laws. The MDW-Project consists of two stages.

The first stage of the MDW-Project

The first stage of the MDW-Project was completed in July 2000, with the submission of Bill 27 244 to the Second Chamber of Parliament. Bill 27 244 primarily suggests changes to the suspension of payment regime. The most important changes to the suspension of payment regime suggested in Bill 27 244 will be briefly addressed below in § 2.6.1.1.

In addition to Bill 27 244, two other bills are currently before Parliament:
(1) Bill 22 942 covering preferential claims and special rights of recourse ("*Wetsvoorstel 22 942 inzake bevoorrechting van vorderingen en bijzonder verhaalsrecht*"); and
(2) Bill 27 199 covering the introduction of simplified bankruptcy proceedings ("*Wetsvoorstel 27 199 tot de invoering van vereenvoudigde afwikkeling van faillissement*").
Bill 22 942 had already been submitted on 30 November 1992 and Bill 27 199 was submitted on 21 June 2000. Neither of the pending bills will be discussed further in this book.

The second stage of the MDW-Project

The second stage of the MDW-Project commenced and is still ongoing. This stage consists of a more in depth consultation by the MDW-Working Group of all interested parties involved in the field of insolvency law. The MDW-Working Group develops its activities based on, *inter alia*, comments, suggestions and scientific research from experts and universities. The MDW-Working Group interviewed experts, judges, lawyers, accountants, and banking professionals in their personal capacity.

The consultation thus far of the different interested parties involved in the field of insolvency law, has resulted in a discussion paper dated 20 February 2001 (the "MDW-Discussion Paper") drafted by the MDW-Working Group. The MDW-Discussion Paper is to serve as the points of departure for (further) consultation of the interested parties involved.

It is further important to note that the consultative procedure in the MDW-Project is conducted with the aid of a website at www.mdw.ez.nl. As well as copies of the MDW-Discussion Paper, Bill 27 244 and other relevant documents in the context of the MDW-Project, which are all posted on and accessible via this website, the website also offers everyone an opportunity to take part in the public debate on further reform of the Netherlands insolvency laws. After public reactions have been collected and analyzed, the MDW-Working Group intends to draw up a final report on potential amendments to the Fw.

The most important issues covered by the MDW-Discussion Paper in respect of suspension of payment regime will be briefly addressed below in § 2.6.1.2.

2.6.1.1   The most important changes to suspension of payment suggested by
           Bill 27 244

The most important changes to suspension of payment suggested by Bill 27 244 can be summarized as follows:

(1)   "Entrance controls" will become tighter and the scope broader;
(2)   Insolvency stay will change and become longer;
(3)   The position of energy providers of the debtor will change;
(4)   The roles of the administrator and the supervisory judge will be greater; and
(5)   A central public register for information concerning suspensions of payment
      will be established.

The main features of each of these issues will be briefly discussed below.

Ad. (1)   "Entrance controls" will become tighter and the scope broader

Aside from a list of assets and liabilities of the debtor, Bill 27 244 requires a request for suspension of payment to be accompanied by[75]:

---

75   See article 214 paragraph 2 of Bill 27 244.

(i)   a statement that continuation of the business of the debtor – in whole or in part – is possible; and

(ii) a draft of a reorganization plan.

Provisional suspension of payment

In the event that one or more documents are missing from a request for suspension of payment, a court will only be able to grant a provisional suspension of payment for 28 days at most (save for an exception mentioned below). In that case, the court grants the debtor a period of up to 21 days to provide it with the missing information[76]. When the missing information is not provided to the court within the set period, the provisionally granted suspension of payment will be terminated by the court[77].

Only if there is sufficient prospect that the business of the debtor shall continue, in whole or in part, can the court grant a provisional suspension of payment to the debtor for a period longer than 28 days or extend the period of 28 days already granted to the debtor[78].

Final suspension of payment

In the event a provisional suspension of payment is granted for a period longer than 28 days, the court orders the registrar to summon all known creditors of the debtor by letter to appear for a hearing prior to making a decision on the granting of a final suspension of payment[79]. A final suspension of payment cannot be granted where[80]:

(i)   good grounds exist for suspecting that the debtor will try to prejudice the creditors during the suspension of payment;

(ii)   insufficient prospect exists that the debtor, in the course of time, will be able to satisfy its creditors; or

(iii) insufficient prospect exists that the business of the debtor will continue to exist, in whole or in part.

Scope of suspension of payment

In § 2.1 it was indicated that under the present rules, a suspension of payment generally takes effect in respect of non-preferential or ordinary creditors not having a claim secured by either mortgage or pledge or any other privileged right. Bill 27 244 suggests broadening the scope of the suspension of payment to preferential claims[81]. As already is the case under the present rules, claims that are secured by pledge, mortgage or right of retention will remain outside the scope of

---

76 See article 215 paragraph 4 of Bill 27 244.
77 See article 215b paragraph 2 of Bill 27 244.
78 See article 215c paragraph 1 of Bill 27 244.
79 See article 215c paragraph 3 of Bill 27 244.
80 See article 218 paragraph 4 of Bill 27 244.
81 See article 232 of Bill 27 244.

suspension of payment, to the extent recourse can be taken for such secured claims on assets of the debtor.

Ad. (2) Insolvency stay will change and become longer

Bill 27 244[82] entitles the supervisory judge in the suspension of payment – at the request of every interested party or *ex officio* – to issue an insolvency stay order for 2 months at most. During that period, any right of third parties – with the exception of estate creditors – to (i) take recourse against assets belonging to the estate or (ii) claim assets which are in the control of the debtor or the administrator, may only be exercised with the authorization of the supervisory judge. The supervisory judge may extend this period once only for another period of 2 months at most. Consequently, pursuant to Bill 27 244:

(i)   an insolvency stay can last for a maximum of 4 months (instead of 2 months under the present rules); and

(ii) not only can the debtor and the administrator request for an insolvency stay, but every interested party, including the supervisory judge *ex officio* may do so.

Some other new features of an insolvency stay pursuant to Bill 27 244 are:

(i)   Third parties who cannot exercise their right to recourse or claim during an insolvency stay are granted reasonable compensation by the supervisory judge[83]. This compensation will rank as an estate claim.

(ii) During an insolvency stay the administrator and the debtor have the right to use, consume or transfer goods covered by the insolvency stay, provided that[84]:

(a)   the debtor had the right to use, consume or transfer such goods;

(b)   the exercise of the right mentioned above under (a) is only used to the extent as is necessary for continuing the normal business of the debtor; and

(c)   they, or one of them, should not reasonably suspect that the estate is insufficient to compensate those who sustained damages as a result of the exercise of the right mentioned above under (a).

Unless otherwise decided by the supervisory judge, this rule even applies where such right terminates as a consequence of a suspension of payment.

(iii) The rule mentioned above in (ii) does not apply to securities, rights in respect of securities and credit claims[85]. In addition, in respect of registered

---

82   See article 241a paragraph 1 of Bill 27 244.
83   See article 241a paragraph 3 of Bill 27 244.
84   See article 241b paragraph 1 read in conjunction with paragraphs 3 and 5 of Bill 27 244.
85   See article 241b paragraph 2 of Bill 27 244.

goods, the debtor and the administrator only have a right to use these goods.

(iv) The rule mentioned above in (ii) does also not apply where the debtor is entitled to transfer a good pursuant to an agreement of mandate to act as intermediary in its own name[86].

(v) The person who sustains damages as a result of the exercise of the right mentioned above in (ii) will be granted reasonable compensation by the supervisory judge[87]. This compensation will also rank as an estate claim.

(vi) A pledgor of an undisclosed pledge is entitled, during an insolvency stay, to disclose its pledge and collect payment[88].

(vii) Unless otherwise decided by the supervisory judge, the Netherlands tax authorities are not entitled, during an insolvency stay, to execute a ground arrest they have made[89].

Ad. (3) The position of energy providers of the debtor will change

In § 1.2.2 factual preference of energy providers has been discussed as an exception to the principle of *paritas creditorum*. Bill 27 244 suggests a change to this position.

Where a debtor fails to pay a debt arisen prior to the suspension of payment, the provider of gas, water, electricity or heating may not suspend, during the suspension of payment, its compliance with the obligation pursuant to its agreement with the debtor to provide gas, water, electricity or heating on a regular basis where it is a first necessity of life[90]. In addition, Bill 27 244 does not entitle such suspension where energy is necessary for the continuation of the business of the debtor.

Moreover, a default by the debtor to pay a debt arisen prior to the suspension of payment is not a valid ground for the energy provider to terminate the agreement with the debtor for the provision of gas, water, electricity or heating[91]. Where there is a clause:

(i)   resulting in an automatic termination of the agreement in the event of a default; or

---

86 See article 241b paragraph 6 of Bill 27 244.
87 See article 241b paragraph 4 of Bill 27 244.
88 See article 241c paragraph 1 of Bill 27 244. For further details on undisclosed pledges, see § 5.2.1.4.
89 See article 241d paragraph 1 of Bill 27 244. For further details on the ground arrest of the Netherlands tax authorities, see § 5.2.3.1.
90 See article 237b paragraph 1 of Bill 27 244.
91 See article 237b paragraph 2 of Bill 27 244.

(ii) indicating that suspension of payment of the debtor is a ground for termination of the said agreement, it can only be invoked by the energy provider with the approval of the administrator[92].

Ad. (4) The roles of the administrator and the supervisory judge will be greater

Bill 27 244 obliges the court – both when granting a provisional suspension of payment[93] and a final suspension of payment[94] – to always appoint one or more supervisory judges. Under the present rules, the appointment of a supervisory judge in a suspension of payment is optional.

In addition, it should be noted that under Bill 27 244 the administrator will – with the consent of the supervisory judge – have the right to give the debtor directions concerning cooperation and the proposal or execution of resolutions, in cooperation with the administrator[95].

Where the debtor is a legal entity and refuses to follow directions given by the administrator, the supervisory judge is entitled – upon request of the administrator or *ex officio* – to suspend one or more directors of the debtor, provided that a final suspension of payment is granted[96].

Finally, Bill 27 244 grants the supervisory judge, in certain circumstances, the right – by way of a court order explaining the grounds – to accept a proposed composition as if it were approved[97].

Ad. (5) A central public register for information concerning suspensions of payment will be established

Bill 27 244 requires the Minister of Justice to establish and operate a central register[98]. In this register all information concerning suspensions of payment, which is currently kept by each district court individually in its own register, is to be compiled. Any person will be able to obtain an extract from this central register upon payment[99].

---

92 See article 237b paragraph 3 of Bill 27 244.
93 See article 215 paragraph 5 of Bill 27 244.
94 See article 218 paragraph 5 of Bill 27 244.
95 See article 228a paragraph 2 of Bill 27 244.
96 See article 228a paragraph 3 of Bill 27 244.
97 See article 268a of Bill 27 244.
98 See article 222b paragraph 1 of Bill 27 244.
99 See article 222b paragraph 3 of Bill 27 244.

2.6.1.2   *The most important issues covered by the MDW-Discussion Paper in respect of suspension of payment*

The MDW-Discussion Paper and an English summary thereof are posted on the website at www.mdw.ez.nl.

In the MDW-Discussion Paper the MDW-Working Group recommends 22 issues for consultation[100]. These issues are further addressed in the MDW-Discussion Paper itself. In essence, these 22 issues relate to both the suspension of payment regime and the bankruptcy regime. For a list of the 22 issues, see § 3.7.1.2.

As a final remark on the MDW-Project, it should be noted that views differ significantly in the Netherlands as to what the actual amendments to the Netherlands insolvency laws (if any) should be[101]. It is therefore not at all clear what will eventually result from the MDW-Project. The public debate is still in progress with no end in sight.

Summary
THE MDW-PROJECT

Bill 27 244
(1) The first stage of the MDW-Project was completed in July 2000, with the submission of Bill 27 244 to the Second Chamber of Parliament.
(2) Bill 27 244 is a proposal to, *inter alia*, amend the Fw, but has not yet been adopted by Parliament.
(3) The most important changes to suspension of payment recommended by Bill 27 244 relate to the following issues:
   (i)   "Entrance controls" will become tighter and the scope broader;
   (ii) Insolvency stay will change and become longer;
   (iii) The position of energy providers of the debtor will change;
   (iv) The roles of the administrator and the supervisory judge will be greater; and
   (v)   A central public register for information concerning suspensions of payment will be established.

The MDW-Discussion Paper
(1) The MDW-Discussion Paper and an English summary thereof are posted on the website at www.mdw.ez.nl.

---

100   See pages 6 and 7 of the MDW-Discussion Paper.
101   For a taste of the range of views on how the future Netherlands insolvency laws is to develop, see the legal literature list included in exhibit 1 to the MDW-Discussion Paper.

(2) For the list of the 22 issues recommended by the MDW-Working Group for consultation, see § 3.7.1.2.

MDW-Project
Public debate on the MDW-Project is still in progress. It is uncertain if and when this will result in any amendments to the Netherlands insolvency laws.

Chapter 3
BANKRUPTCY

Bankruptcy as the principal insolvency regime in the Netherlands will be mapped out in this Chapter. In § 3.1, the purpose, nature, scope and consequences of bankruptcy will be addressed, followed by an explanation of the basic steps for requesting bankruptcy in § 3.2. The following two important court-appointed players in a bankruptcy will be introduced in § 3.3:
(1) the trustee in bankruptcy; and
(2) the supervisory judge in bankruptcy.

Subsequently, in § 3.4, the following three stages will be distinguished:
(1) the preservation stage;
(2) the executorial stage; and
(3) the verification or closing stage.
In § 3.5, special attention will be given to the rights and duties of the trustee in bankruptcy and, in § 3.6, the impact of bankruptcy on the different types of creditors will be addressed.

As in the chapter on suspension of payment, the MDW-Project will be discussed in the last section of this Chapter (§ 3.7). In doing so, the focus will be on the possible consequences on the insolvency regime of bankruptcy.

3.1 Purpose, nature, scope and consequences

Purpose and nature

In § 1.1 the purpose of bankruptcy is described as the (ultimate) liquidation of all assets of the debtor for the benefit of its creditors. To refine this a little further it could be said that a bankruptcy is a collective way of recourse for the benefit of the joint creditors of the debtor including all the property of the debtor[1].

According to the legislator a bankruptcy is a judicial arrest on the total property of a debtor for the benefit of its joint creditors[2]. In recent years, this original idea

---

1   See generally *"De Faillissementscurator: een rechtsvergelijkend onderzoek naar de taak, bevoegdheden en persoonlijke aansprakelijkheid van de faillissementscurator"*, by Mr F.M.J. Verstijlen, W.E.J. Tjeenk Willink 1998, Deventer, pp. 1-449, Chapter III, pp. 23-29.

2   See *"Geschiedenis van de Wet op het Faillissement en de Surséance van Betaling"*, by Mr G.W. van der Feltz, part 2-III, 1896, editors Prof. mr S.C.J.J. Kortmann/Mr N.E.D. Faber, Tjeenk Willink 1995, Zwolle, *MvT*, p.7.

of a bankruptcy being a tool for the satisfaction of the joint creditors of the debtor has become the subject of discussion[3]. The question raised is whether or not, besides the interests of the joint creditors of the debtor, the trustee in bankruptcy also has a duty to observe and look after other interests of a more general nature. The other interests that are mentioned in this context include:

(1) the maintenance of employment;
(2) the continuation of the business of the debtor; and
(3) other community interests.

This issue emerges especially in the context of a restart whereby a bankruptcy is more used as a means to reorganize a business than as a means to liquidate a business. In the case law of the Netherlands supreme court there are indications that these other interests may indeed play a role[4]. Exactly what role they play in shaping the duties of a trustee in bankruptcy is not clear. Much depends on the specific circumstances of the case at hand.

Scope

A bankruptcy comprises all of the property of a debtor – including those assets situated outside the Netherlands (§ 1.2.3) – at the time of declaration into bankruptcy, as well as everything the debtor acquires during the bankruptcy[5]. In the Fw[6] some goods of a personal nature are excluded from a bankruptcy. In case the debtor has legal title to certain goods which are validly encumbered with a property (or proprietary) right for the benefit of a third party only the bare legal title falls within the scope of the bankruptcy of the debtor[7]. Examples of such property (or proprietary) rights are:

(1) a building right;
(2) a leasehold right; or
(3) a right of usufruct.

Consequences

Many of the consequences of the adjudication of bankruptcy follow from the principle of fixation, which was discussed in § 1.2.1. These consequences include:

(1) Limitation periods and terms of forfeiture – which would otherwise lapse during the bankruptcy or within six months after the termination thereof –

---

3   See, for example, *"Crediteurenbelang versus "andere belangen""*, by Mr S.H. de Ranitz in *"De curator, een octopus"*, Prof. mr S.C.J.J Kortmann c.s. (editors), W.E.J. Tjeenk Willink 1996, Deventer, pp. 187-199.
4   See, for example, the Sigmacon II-case (HR 25 February 1996, *NJ* 1996, 472) and the Maclou-case (HR 19 April 1996, *NJ* 1996, 727).
5   See article 20 Fw.
6   See articles 21 and 21a Fw.
7   Such follows from the general structure of Netherlands property law and can be linked to article 20 Fw.

continue to run, by virtue of law, for a period of six months after the termination of the bankruptcy[8].

(2) The Fw provides for extensions in respect of some final terms announced by a counter party of the debtor prior to the bankruptcy of the debtor[9].

(3) The bankruptcy does not take effect in favor of guarantors pursuant to a surety or several and jointly liable co-debtors of the debtor[10]. This means that guarantors pursuant to a surety and co-debtors may be called on their surety or liability, respectively.

(4) Interest accrued after the declaration of bankruptcy of the debtor cannot be verified, unless secured by a pledge or a mortgage[11], in which case the interest will be verified *pro memoria*. In this context, to the extent interest is not covered by the proceeds of the collateral, a secured creditor may not derive any rights from the admission of the interest.

(5) Claims not denominated in the currency of the Netherlands will be expressed in the currency of the Netherlands[12]. For that purpose the exchange rate of the date on which the bankruptcy was adjudicated is used.

(6) The judgment of bankruptcy results in an immediate ending of all judicial execution on any part of the property of the debtor[13].

(7) All arrests made prior to the adjudication of bankruptcy cease to exist and will only spring back into existence as soon as the bankruptcy ends as a consequence of either:
(i) a nullification of the bankruptcy (§ 3.2.2); or
(ii) a discontinuation of the bankruptcy (§ 3.4.3.1).
This rule is, however, subject to the condition that, at that time, the good that was arrested still forms a part of the estate of the debtor[14]. Arrests on registered goods which have been deleted from the relevant public registers will not revive, unless within 14 days after the revival of the arrests a bailiff's notification is filed pursuant to which the debtor is notified of the revival.

(8) In the event that prior to the bankruptcy of the debtor, foreclosure by an arrestor on the goods of the debtor had progressed to such an extent that the day of sale in execution had already been determined, the trustee in bankruptcy may continue the sale for the account of the bankrupt estate[15]. The exercise of this right of the trustee in bankruptcy is subject to the consent from the supervisory judge in bankruptcy. When this right is exercised by the trustee in bankruptcy, the proceeds of the foreclosure will

---

8 See article 36 Fw.
9 See article 36a Fw.
10 See article 160 Fw.
11 See article 128 Fw.
12 See article 133 Fw.
13 See article 33 paragraph 1 Fw.
14 See article 33 paragraph 2 Fw.
15 See article 34 Fw.

be for the benefit of the bankrupt estate, leaving the arrestor without any special rights in respect of such proceeds.

Summary
PURPOSE, NATURE, SCOPE AND CONSEQUENCES OF BANKRUPTCY

Purpose and nature
(1) Bankruptcy is a collective way of recourse for the benefit of the joint creditors of the debtor.
(2) Aside from interests of the joint creditors of the debtor, it is unclear if the trustee in bankruptcy also has to observe other interests.

Scope
A bankruptcy includes all of the property of the debtor (including those assets situated outside the Netherlands) at the time of its declaration into bankruptcy, together with everything the debtor acquires during the bankruptcy.

Consequences
(1) Most of the consequences of the adjudication of a bankruptcy follow from the principle of fixation (§ 1.2.1).
(2) Two important consequences are the following:
      (i) Limitation periods and terms of forfeiture are extended; and
      (ii) Legal recourse to any part of the debtor's property ends and arrests cease to exist.

3.2 Steps for filing bankruptcy

The petitioner

Any debtor can be declared bankrupt by a Netherlands court, provided that:
(1) the debtor resides, or has (had) its place of business, in the Netherlands[16]; and
(2) the debtor either applies for bankruptcy itself, or is subject to a proper petition for bankruptcy filed by a creditor (including the tax authorities)[17], or – for reasons of public interest – by the public prosecutor[18].

---

16 See article 2 Fw.
17 See article 1 paragraph 1 Fw.
18 See article 1 paragraph 2 Fw.

Any creditor, whether foreign or domestic, may file a petition for bankruptcy. Whenever the requirements for the adjudication of bankruptcy under the Fw are fulfilled, a Netherlands court will declare the bankruptcy of a debtor, regardless of a prior adjudication of bankruptcy or similar proceedings in another jurisdiction (§ 1.2.4).

Jurisdiction

A special bankruptcy court does not exist in the Netherlands. Most district courts have so-called bankruptcy chambers presided by judges experienced in insolvency cases. A petition for bankruptcy must be filed in the court of the district in which the debtor resides[19], or, in the case of a company, where it has its (official) seat (as mentioned in its articles of association)[20]. A foreign debtor doing business in the Netherlands can be declared bankrupt by the competent court of the district in which the principal office of the foreign company is situated[21].

3.2.1   THE APPLICABLE TEST(S)

Test(s)

The general test a court will apply prior to declaring a debtor to be in a state of bankruptcy is whether facts and circumstances provide *prima facie* evidence that the debtor has ceased to pay its debts[22]. If, however, the petitioner is a creditor the court will – in addition to the first test – also have to ascertain whether facts and circumstances provide *prima facie* evidence that the creditor-petitioner has a right to claim against the debtor[23].

The petition

A bankruptcy petition has to state facts and circumstances that constitute *prima facie* evidence that the debtor has ceased to pay its debts. This is considered to be the case if there are at least two creditors, one of whom has a claim which is due and payable and which the debtor cannot pay, refuses to pay, or simply does not pay[24]. It should be emphasized that the law does not require that – aside from the petitioner – other creditors support the petition for bankruptcy.

---

19   See article 2 paragraph 1 Fw.
20   See article 2 paragraph 2 Fw.
21   See article 2 paragraph 3 Fw.
22   See article 6 paragraph 3 Fw.
23   See the Amsterdam RAI-case (HR 22 August 1997, *NJ* 1997, 664).
24   See the ADB/Planex-case (HR 7 December 1990, *NJ* 1991, 216).

Where the debtor is a company, the petition for bankruptcy by the debtor itself should include[25]:

(1) a recent official registration of the debtor with the relevant Chamber of Commerce and Industries;
(2) a shareholders' resolution in which the directors of the debtor are ordered to file for the
     bankruptcy of the debtor[26];
(3) a copy of the articles of association of the debtor;
(4) a copy of the shareholders' register of the debtor; and
(5) a recent list of assets and liabilities of the debtor.

In this context it should further be noted that, similar to a suspension of payment (§ 2.2), in respect of larger companies having a supervisory board and to which companies the so-called *"Structuurregeling"*[27] is applicable, the decision of the board of the debtor to file for bankruptcy must be approved by the supervisory board of the debtor[28].

3.2.1.1   Filing for bankruptcy as an abuse of right

The concept of abuse of right

The concept of abuse of right is provided for in article 3:13 BW. This article says:

(1) The holder of a right cannot exercise it to such an extent that he abuses it.
(2) The exercise of a right may, *inter alia*, qualify as an abuse of right when a right is exercised with the sole intention of harming another or for a purpose other than that for which it was granted or, in case of a natural person, the holder could not reasonably have decided to exercise it because the interest served by the exercise of the right is disproportionate to the harm caused thereby.
(3) The nature of the right can be such that it cannot be abused.

From the previous sections of § 3.2 it follows that, aside from the debtor itself, its creditors and the public prosecutor also have the right to file for the bankruptcy of the debtor. Can the exercise by any of them of this right also qualify as an abuse of right?

---

25 See Chapter 1 on bankruptcy petitions from the *"Directives in bankruptcies and suspensions of payment"*, in *Vademecum Advocatuur: Wet & Regelgeving"*, 2001, pp. 486-489.
26 See articles 2:136 BW and 2:246 BW.
27 See articles 2:152-164 BW and articles 2:262-274 BW. See also § 4.3.2.
28 See article 2:164 paragraph 1 sub i BW and article 2:274 paragraph 1 sub i BW.

In recent years with the revival of insolvency law and the increased media attention on bankruptcy, the relevance of this question in practice has become more
apparent. When faced with a need to reorganize in the Netherlands, it is no longer
uncommon to raise the question whether or not a bankruptcy combined with a
subsequent restart[29] can be used as a quick (and therefore cheap) tool to get rid of
unwanted employees[30].

The following three cases will be briefly discussed in order to find some guidance as to when there is a risk that filing for bankruptcy could qualify as abuse of
right:

(1) *The Municipality of Dantumadeel and Provinsje Fryslân-case*[31]
     (§ 3.2.1.1.1).
(2) The *Ammerlaan*-case[32] (§ 3.2.1.1.2).
(3) The *Multi-Terminal Waalhaven*-case[33] (§ 3.2.1.1.3).

In the *Ammerlaan*-case and the *Multi-Terminal Waalhaven*-case, the issue of filing for bankruptcy as an abuse of right is especially considered in light of interests of the employees of the bankrupt debtor.

3.2.1.1.1   The MUNICIPALITY OF DANTUMADEEL AND PROVINSJE FRYSLÂN-case

In this case, two creditors – the Municipality of Dantumadeel (the "Municipality") and Provinsje Fryslân (the "Province") – filed for the bankruptcy of their
debtor ("*B.C. Fashion Beheer B.V.*"). The decision of the district court in which
the debtor was declared bankrupt was set aside in appeal by the court of appeals.
According to the court of appeals, the Municipality and the Province had abused

---

29 For the purposes of this book a restart is described as a continuation of (a part of) the business
    activity of the debtor by another legal entity – which could, but does not necessarily have to, be
    related to the debtor – whereby:
    (1) the debtor ceases to exist after a bankruptcy;
    (2) a part of the debts of the debtor remain unpaid; and/or
    (3) a part of the employees of the debtor, after their employment agreements have been termi-
         nated by the trustee in bankruptcy, remain unemployed and thus are not taken over by the
         other legal entity.
    The concept of "restart" is not discussed further in this book. For a selection of books dealing
    with "restart", see the Further Reading section in the back.
30 See generally "*Doorstarten en onbehoorlijk bestuur*" by Prof. mr R.D. Vriesendorp in
    "*Onbehoorlijk bestuur in het insolventierecht*"", Insolad jaarboek 1997, Prof. mr R.D.
    Vriesendorp (editor), Kluwer 1997, Deventer, pp. 65-82, and the list of further reading con-
    tained in in footnote 3 thereof. See further Verstijlen, *supra* footnote 1, at pp. 160-163 on
    "*Technische faillissementen*".
31 HR 10 November 2000, *NJ* 2001, 249.
32 Court of appeals of the Hague 10 January 1996, *JOR* 1996, 16.
33 HR 29 June 2001, *JOR* 2001, 169.

their right to file for bankruptcy of the debtor because they could not expect any positive result from the bankruptcy. This decision of the court of appeals was, *inter alia*, based on the following:

(1) In his first public report, the trustee in bankruptcy had mentioned that – at first sight – it seemed to him that the bankruptcy of the debtor would not result in any return for the Municipality and the Province;

(2) Pursuant to subordination clauses in the loan agreements, on the basis of which the Municipality and the Province had their claims against the debtor, the claims of the Municipality and the Province were subordinate in rank in the bankruptcy; and

(3) It was established that there were substantial claims in the bankruptcy by a secured creditor and an ordinary creditor, both of which would rank higher than the claims of the Municipality and the Province.

Judgment of the Netherlands supreme court

In this case the Netherlands supreme court came to the following conclusions:

(1) Pursuant to the Fw it is the trustee in bankruptcy who starts an investigation as to:
   (i)   the existence of property of the debtor; or
   (ii) the expectation that such property will be available in the near future.

(2) Such investigation needs to be conducted thoroughly and hence has no place in the fast and brief proceedings in which a request for bankruptcy is made.

(3) Only after examination of the results of the investigation, a court will, in principle, be in a position to deny a request for bankruptcy on the basis that the petitioner abused its right to request for this bankruptcy.

Accordingly, the Netherlands supreme court found that the court of appeals had erred in its decision by placing too much importance on the preliminary findings of the trustee in bankruptcy resulting from his preliminary investigation.

3.2.1.1.2   The AMMERLAAN-case

In this case, a number of former employees instituted legal proceedings against their former employer. The former employer – "*A.V.M. Ammerlaan Diensten B.V.*" ("Ammerlaan") – had filed for its own bankruptcy on 9 November 1995. Prior to this filing for its own bankruptcy, Ammerlaan had filed requests with the cantonal court to have a number of its employment agreements dissolved. At the hearing, the cantonal court judge had made it clear that the requests by Ammerlaan lacked adequate grounds for supporting the requests. Ammerlaan was granted the opportunity to provide the cantonal court judge with more information that would support the requests at a later date. Instead of providing this additional information, Ammerlaan decided to request for its own bankruptcy.

The request was granted by the district court. Soon after Ammerlaan was declared bankrupt, the employment agreements of all employees of Ammerlaan were terminated by the trustee in bankruptcy.

Judgment of the court of appeals of the Hague

In this case the court of appeals of the Hague came to the following conclusions:
(1) The court of appeals held that the applicants (*i.e.* the former employees of Ammerlaan) had rightfully contended that Ammerlaan filed for its own bankruptcy with the preconceived purpose of circumventing the employment law protection to which the applicants were entitled; and
(2) Consequently, the request by Ammerlaan for its own bankruptcy qualified as an abuse of right, resulting in a denial of the request.

3.2.1.1.3   The MULTY-TERMINAL WAALHAVEN-case

In this case, a number of employees and a trade union opposed – by using their right to request for a review[34] – to the decision dated 2 January 2001 pursuant to which the employer – *"Multi-Terminal Waalhaven B.V."* ("MTW") – was declared bankrupt.

In May 1995 MTW had entered into an agreement (the "Agreement") with different trade unions of its employees. MTW had decided to completely terminate its activities, but pursuant to the Agreement MTW agreed to continue to exist until it had found a suitable solution for each of its employees. It was understood that a "suitable solution" in this context meant that MTW would offer each of its employees a suitable job in the port at least twice. It was further understood that a "suitable job" meant a job in the port with a similar job description, with similar working hours and similar pay.

The sole director of MTW – *"Furness Logistics B.V."* – had guaranteed the compliance by MTW of its obligations under the Agreement. In addition, as MTW had decided to terminate all its activities, MTW obtained its financial means from the director and sole shareholder of its director, *"HIM Furness N.V."*.

In 2000, MTW had still not managed to find a suitable solution for all of its employees. In the case of one particular employee, MTW went to the cantonal court with a request to dissolve the employment agreement. In a decision on 24 October 2000 this dissolution was granted and was to be effective from 16 November 2000, subject to the obligation of MTW to pay the employee a compensation of NLG 700,000. MTW withdrew its request for dissolution on 14 November 2000.

---

34   For more details on the right to request for a review, see § 3.2.2.

On 23 November 2000, MTW decided to file for its own bankruptcy. Subsequently, on 6 December 2000 thirteen days after that decision was made HIM Furness N.V. informed MTW that it would be terminating its financial support as of 1 January 2001. On 17 January 2001 the district court of Rotterdam overruled its bankruptcy decision of 2 January 2001. The district court found that there was sufficient *prima facie* evidence that the decision of MTW to request its own bankruptcy was directly related to the employment law protection its employees enjoyed and the financial consequences attached thereto. It concluded that the request by MTW for bankruptcy qualified as an abuse of right because this right was used for a purpose other than that for which it was granted. On 6 March 2001 the court of appeals of the Hague confirmed the decision of the district court. In view of the time span, there was a correlation between the request by MTW to dissolve the employment agreement, the withdrawal thereof and the filing for its own bankruptcy. This led the court of appeals to conclude that MTW wished to avoid the obligations towards its employees by requesting for its own bankruptcy.

Judgment of the Netherlands supreme court

The Netherlands supreme court came to the following conclusions:
(1) The circumstances of the case led the court of appeals to conclude that MTW's filing for its own bankruptcy qualified as an abuse of right. The fact that, in the end, only one of the original 40 employees had not yet been assisted into another job did not obstruct the court of appeals from reaching this conclusion[35]; and
(2) The court of appeals held that MTW exercised its right to request for its own bankruptcy for a purpose other than for which it was granted: via this bankruptcy filing MTW wished to avoid its obligations vis-à-vis its employees and hence abused this right. In deciding the question whether a right is abused because it was exercised for another purpose there is – contrary to what is contended by MTW – no balancing of interests, as follows from adherence to article 3:13 paragraph 2 BW.

3.2.2 THE LEGAL REMEDIES

Remedies in the first instance

The request for bankruptcy has to be handled by a court expediently[36]. The court can and usually will (but is not formally obliged to) allow the debtor to be heard[37]. If the debtor has not been heard, the debtor has the right to request for a

---

35 After MTW's bankruptcy, settlements were reached with all but one employee involving an amount of approximately NLG 2,000,000.
36 See article 4 paragraph 1 Fw.
37 See article 6 paragraph 1 Fw.

review by the same court within 14 days after the judgment of bankruptcy of the debtor is rendered[38]. The creditors of the debtor (with the exception of the creditor-petitioner) and all other interested parties have the same right to request for a review, but they have to exercise their right within a period of 8 days after the judgment of bankruptcy of the debtor is rendered[39]. It should be noted that the interests of the debtor, who was not heard at the bankruptcy request hearing because the debtor was not (properly) summoned, are not considered to be impeded if the debtor has had the opportunity to be heard in review or appeal[40].

Remedies in appeal

Appeals to the court of appeals[41] and subsequently to the Netherlands supreme court[42] can be lodged by the debtor, by the creditors or interested parties against a judgment declaring or refusing to declare the bankruptcy of the debtor. In an appeal to the Netherlands supreme court only questions of law can be addressed; questions of fact fall entirely outside the scope of the Netherlands supreme court's competence[43]. Appeals must be lodged, ultimately, within 8 days after the judgment (which is subject to appeal) was rendered.

Review and subsequent appeals do not have suspensory effect[44] and they are judged by the courts *ex nunc*. This means that the court deciding in review or appeal re-test if the facts and circumstances, known now when judgment is rendered in review or appeal, provide *prima facie* evidence, in the case where the debtor has filed, that the debtor has ceased to pay and, in the case where a creditor-petitioner has filed, that the creditor-petitioner had a right of claim against the debtor when the bankruptcy judgment was rendered. The acts of the trustee in bankruptcy undertaken prior to or on the date on which the nullification of the bankruptcy of the debtor (after the successful use of the legal remedies) has been announced[45], remain valid and binding upon the debtor[46]. However, during the period legal remedies against a judgment of bankruptcy are lodged (and the bankruptcy is thus still subject to change), the trustee in bankruptcy has a duty to take only those irrevocable measures (*e.g.* terminating employment agreements, rental agreements *etc.*) that are strictly necessary and cannot be delayed.

---

38   See article 8 paragraph 2 Fw.
39   See article 10 paragraph 1 Fw.
40   See the Boventoon Dordrecht/Van den Wijk-case (HR 4 October 4 1991, *NJ* 1991, 820).
41   See article 8 paragraph 1 Fw, article 9 paragraph 1 Fw and article 11 paragraph 1 Fw.
42   See article 12 paragraph 1 Fw.
43   See article 419 paragraphs 2 and 3 Rv.
44   See article 4 paragraph 4 Fw.
45   See article 15 Fw.
46   See article 13 paragraph 1 Fw.

Summary
STEPS FOR FILING BANKRUPTCY

Entitlement
The debtor itself, its creditors and the public prosecutor.

Scope
Any debtor that resides or has (had) its place of business in the Netherlands.

Competence
The court of the district in which the debtor resides or, being a company, has its (official) seat.

Test(s)
The applicable tests are:
(1) facts and circumstances provide *prima facie* evidence that the debtor has ceased to pay its debts; and
(2) if a creditor petitioned for the bankruptcy, a further requirement that the creditor-petitioner has a right to claim against the debtor (again, *prima facie* evidence suffices).

Abuse of right
Pursuant to 3:13 BW the exercise of a right may, *inter alia*, be qualified as abuse of right when a right is exercised:
(1) with the sole intention of harming another;
(2) for a purpose other than that for which it was granted; or
(3) in case of a natural person, the holder could not reasonably have decided to exercise it because the interest served by the exercise of the right is disproportionate to the harm caused thereby.
From the (i) the *Municipality of Dantumadeel and Provinsje Fryslân*-case, (ii) the *Ammerlaan*-case, and (iii) the *Multi-Terminal Waalhaven*-case the following guidance can be derived:
(a) Only after a thorough investigation has been conducted by the trustee in bankruptcy will a court be in the position to conclude there was an abuse of right on the basis that no positive result can be expected from the bankruptcy of the debtor; and
(b) A request for bankruptcy could qualify as an abuse of right if it was filed with the preconceived purpose of circumventing employment law protection to which employees of the debtor are entitled.

Legal remedies
Remedies do not have suspensory effect and include the following:

(1) Review by the debtor (if the debtor has not been heard) within 14 days.
(2) Review by interested parties within 8 days; and
(3) Appeal and further appeal within 8 days.

Courts in review and in appeal judge *ex nunc*.

3.3 The (appointment of the) trustee in bankruptcy and the supervisory judge in bankruptcy

Appointments by the court

In a bankruptcy, an independent[47] third person is appointed by the competent court to deal with the existing financial difficulties of the debtor[48]. Such a person is the trustee in bankruptcy and, in the Netherlands, only attorneys are generally appointed as trustees in bankruptcy.

In most cases attorneys of the local bar are appointed as trustees in bankruptcy, but in bankruptcies of a more substantial size, one or more specialized insolvency lawyers will be appointed[49]. The competent court further appoints a judge, the supervisory judge in the bankruptcy, to supervise the activities of the trustee in bankruptcy[50].

3.3.1 THE TRUSTEE IN BANKRUPTCY

The trustee in bankruptcy is entrusted with the administration and liquidation of the bankrupt estate[51].

Payment system of fees and costs

In the Netherlands fees and costs of a trustee in bankruptcy are not paid by the court out of public funds, but out of the proceeds of the bankrupt estate[52]. Furthermore, the fees and the costs of a trustee in bankruptcy have the highest rank

---

47 In practice insolvency lawyers of larger law firms in particular have to decline an appointment as trustee in bankruptcy in a (larger) bankruptcy due to a "conflict of interest" they and their firm may have.
48 See article 14 paragraph 1 Fw.
49 In the Netherlands specialized insolvency lawyers are organized in an association of insolvency lawyers, called "INSOLAD".
50 See article 14 paragraph 1 Fw.
51 See article 68 paragraph 1 Fw.
52 See article 70 paragraph 1 Fw in conjunction with Chapter 9 concerning the determination of fees from the *"Directives in bankrupties and suspensions of payment"*, in *"Vademecum Advocatuur: Wet & Regelgeving"*, 2001, pp. 495-500.

in a bankruptcy and thus are paid out first, prior to all other creditors[53]. This payment system provides the trustee in bankruptcy with a personal incentive to collect as much monies as possible for the benefit of the joint creditors of the debtor, simply because to do otherwise would mean that his fees and costs will not be paid. On the other hand, this system bears the risk that, as soon as the trustee in bankruptcy foresees that the payment of his fees and costs is sufficiently secured, his "eagerness" to generate additional monies for the benefit of the bankrupt estate may be reduced.

Public reports

A trustee in bankruptcy has the obligation to file a public report on the state of affairs of the bankruptcy for the benefit of all interested parties[54]. Unless otherwise agreed with the supervisory judge in bankruptcy, public reports must be made available every three months. Public reports are deposited with the competent court and are open to inspection by the public at no charge[55].

In addition to this ongoing reporting obligation, the trustee in bankruptcy is obliged – shortly after the bankruptcy is adjudicated – to inform the supervisory judge in bankruptcy on the initial state of affairs of the bankrupt estate[56]. If possible this should be done by the trustee in bankruptcy within a period of three weeks after the bankruptcy is adjudicated. Subsequently, an inventory of the bankrupt estate together with a provisional statement of assets and liabilities of the debtor has to be deposited with the competent court by the trustee in bankruptcy[57].

For interested parties in a bankruptcy, public reports by the trustee in bankruptcy are often the only source of information:
(1) to verify the conduct of the trustee in bankruptcy; and
(2) to find out what the expectations in the bankruptcy are, albeit this is from the perspective of the trustee in bankruptcy.
Despite this, public reports are generally brief and only limited to information that is strictly necessary to be disclosed. Nevertheless, with reference to the information included in such public reports, interested parties can ask the trustee in bankruptcy additional questions and/or for a further explanation.

---

53   See the Mr De Ranitz q.q c.s../Ontvanger-case (HR September 28, 1990, *NJ* 1991, 305).
54   See article 73a paragraph 1 Fw.
55   See article 107 paragraph 1 Fw.
56   See Chapter 4 on reports from the *"Directives in bankruptcies and suspensions of payment"*, in *"Vademecum Advocatuur: Wet & Regelgeving"*, 2001, pp. 490-491.
57   See article 97 Fw.

Supervision by the supervisory judge

In addition to his obligation concerning public reports, a trustee in bankruptcy will (and should) inform and consult with the supervisory judge in bankruptcy on a regular basis and in detail about the current state of affairs in the bankruptcy.

The trustee in bankruptcy is required to ask for consent from the supervisory judge in bankruptcy on a number of actions [58]. Such consent can also be given by the supervisory judge in bankruptcy by affirming actions already undertaken by the trustee in bankruptcy[59]. With or without permission from the supervisory judge in bankruptcy, the trustee in bankruptcy is and remains responsible for his actions[60]. In addition, an omission by the trustee in bankruptcy with regard to obtaining the required consent in advance from the supervisory judge in bankruptcy, does not – in itself – render the actions of the trustee in bankruptcy legally invalid and/or not binding.

Examples of actions for which permission from the supervisory judge in bankruptcy is required include the following:
(1) Private sales of assets[61];
(2) Extra-judicial settlements[62];
(3) Termination of agreements with mutual performances, rental agreements and/or employment agreements[63]; and
(4) The continuation of the business of the debtor[64].

Unless otherwise indicated, the correspondence between the trustee in bankruptcy and the supervisory judge in bankruptcy is not public. However, it must be noted that – in principle – the debtor has the right to request the competent court for disclosure of this information. Whether or not such a petition for disclosure by the debtor is granted by the competent court will depend on a valuation by the court of the different interests involved in the specific case at hand[65].

3.3.2 THE SUPERVISORY JUDGE IN BANKRUPTCY

In contrast to a suspension of payment (§ 2.3.2), a supervisory judge in bankruptcy is explicitly entrusted with the supervision of the administration and liqui-

---

58   See, for example, article 65 Fw read in conjunction with article 68 paragraph 2 Fw.
59   See the Bouchar/Dekkers-case (HR 26 November 1982, *NJ* 1983, 442).
60   See article 72 Fw.
61   See article 101 Fw and article 176 Fw.
62   See article 104 Fw.
63   See article 68 paragraph 2 Fw.
64   See article 98 Fw.
65   See the disclosure of bankruptcy file-case (HR 22 September 1995, *NJ* 1997, 339).

dation of the bankrupt estate by the trustee in bankruptcy[66]. In exercising such supervision, the supervisory judge in bankruptcy is entitled to:

(1) hear witnesses who are able to clarify circumstances related to the bankruptcy; and

(2) appoint, if necessary, experts to undertake an investigation[67].

Petition to intervene

Furthermore, each creditor (and also the debtor itself) may file a petition with the supervisory judge in bankruptcy to object to any act by the trustee in bankruptcy or to request the supervisory judge in bankruptcy to order the trustee in bankruptcy to perform or refrain from performing an act[68]. Except for those explicitly excluded in the Fw[69], an appeal by any interested party against any order by the supervisory judge is open for a period of 5 days[70]. Such an appeal must be lodged with the competent court, which will only render a decision:

(1) after hearing the interested parties; or

(2) after the interested parties have been duly summoned.

The decision by the supervisory judge on a request to intervene is subject to appeal.

In practice, however, petitions to the supervisory judge in bankruptcy to intervene are lodged only in very exceptional circumstances. A reason for this may be that supervisory judges in bankruptcy have tended to backup their trustees in bankruptcy. Nevertheless, it is one of the few formal tools creditors in a bankruptcy have for influencing the conduct of a trustee in bankruptcy and therefore they should not be afraid to use it.

> **Summary**
> **THE TRUSTEE IN BANKRUPTCY AND THE SUPERVISORY JUDGE**
>
> *A court appointed trustee in bankruptcy*
> (1) The trustee in bankruptcy is entrusted with the administration and the liquidation of the bankrupt estate.
> (2) The trustee in bankruptcy is the first to be paid out of the proceeds of the estate for his fees and costs.
> (3) The trustee in bankruptcy has a duty to prepare and deposit (generally on a three-monthly basis) public reports.

---

66 See article 64 Fw.
67 See article 66 paragraph 1 Fw.
68 See article 69 paragraph 1 Fw.
69 See article 67 paragraph 2 Fw.
70 See article 67 paragraph 1 Fw.

(4) The trustee in bankruptcy needs authorization of the supervisory judge in bankruptcy for a number of actions.

(5) The correspondence between the trustee in bankruptcy and the supervisory judge in bankruptcy is – in principle – not public.

A court appointed supervisory judge in bankruptcy

(1) The supervisory judge in bankruptcy is entrusted with the supervision of the administration and liquidation of the bankrupt estate by the trustee in bankruptcy.

(2) The supervisory judge in bankruptcy is entitled to hear witnesses and/or appoint experts.

(3) The supervisory judge in bankruptcy is competent to receive requests from creditors to order the trustee in bankruptcy to perform or refrain from performing an act.

3.4 The different stages in a bankruptcy

In a bankruptcy the following three general stages can be distinguished:

(1) The preservation stage (§ 3.4.1);
(2) The executorial stage (§ 3.4.2); and
(3) The verification or closing stage (§ 3.4.3).

In the following paragraphs, the main characteristics of each stage will be dealt with in more detail.

3.4.1 THE PRESERVATION STAGE

Scope and purpose

The preservation stage commences as of the day the bankruptcy is declared and lasts until the day the trustee in bankruptcy finishes his preliminary investigation of the state of affairs of the debtor. In his preliminary investigation, the trustee in bankruptcy must determine and map out the position of the assets and liabilities of the debtor in order to be able to decide whether or not it benefits the bankrupt estate for the business of the debtor to be continued[71]. If the trustee in bankruptcy decides to continue the business of the debtor, the trustee in bankruptcy is both the one to make the business decisions and the one accountable for the business decisions made during that time. If the trustee in bankruptcy decides not to con-

---

71   See article 98 Fw.

tinue the business of the debtor, the trustee in bankruptcy will focus on liquidating the assets of the debtor.

Important consequences

In § 1.2.1 the consequences following from the principle of fixation have been set out. In addition, in § 3.1 the consequences of the adjudication of bankruptcy have also been indicated. For the preservation stage, the following consequences are especially important:

(1) As of 00.00 hours of the day the bankruptcy is declared, the debtor loses its right to administer and dispose of its assets[72]. In the event the debtor is a company, the directors of the debtor also lose that right;

(2) The bankruptcy will immediately be published in both the National Gazette of the Netherlands and – depending on the size of the bankruptcy – a national or local newspaper[73];

(3) Bank accounts of the debtor will be frozen; and

(4) All mail addressed to the debtor will be sent directly to the office of the trustee in bankruptcy[74].

In respect of the consequence mentioned above under (4) it should be noted that more modern modes of communication, such as e-mail, are not explicitly provided for in the Fw. With regard to e-mail, a trustee in bankruptcy must be entitled to ask for the debtor's log-on and password[75]. In order to ensure that the debtor will not (continue to) delete e-mail messages after reading them before the trustee in bankruptcy has had an opportunity to read them, the trustee in bankruptcy can immediately change the password.

As the insolvency stay is typically requested in the preservation stage, it will be addressed in more detail in § 3.4.1.1.

As gathering of information is essential in the preservation stage, there is a duty to render information on the debtor. This duty will be discussed in § 3.4.1.2.

3.4.1.1   The insolvency stay

Scope

Insolvency stay is an important tool the trustee in bankruptcy has to ensure that he is able to conduct a preliminary investigation into the state of affairs of the

---

72   See article 23 Fw.
73   See article 14 paragraph 3 Fw.
74   See article 14 paragraph 2 Fw read in conjunction with article 99 paragraph 1 Fw.
75   See in this respect *"E-mailblokkade"* by Mr M.J. Draaisma in *TvI*, 4, 1997, pp. 101-102.

debtor without being troubled by any creditors of the debtor[76]. At the request of the trustee in bankruptcy (or any other interested party, including the supervisory judge *ex officio*), the supervisory judge in bankruptcy may issue an order stipulating that for a maximum period of one month the right of each third party (including secured creditors (§ 3.6.1)):

(1) to take recourse against any asset falling within the bankrupt estate; or
(2) to claim assets which are in the control of the debtor or the trustee in bankruptcy

may only be executed with the authorization of the supervisory judge in bankruptcy. This regime can only be extended once by the supervisory judge in bankruptcy for a further one month at most.

An order imposing an insolvency stay can be limited to certain third parties only[77]. The supervisory judge in bankruptcy may further attach conditions to:

(1) the extent of the order; and
(2) his authorization to a third party to execute a right against the debtor during the period of the insolvency stay.

At the request of the party petitioning the bankruptcy and/or the debtor itself, the order for an insolvency stay can also be issued by the court declaring the bankruptcy[78].

Consequences

While an insolvency stay is in effect, terms set by or to third parties are extended for a reasonable period of time[79]. However, as far as the other consequences of the insolvency stay are concerned, uncertainty exists[80].

According to the legislator[81] the purpose of the insolvency stay is the following:

> "(...) Especially during the period immediately following the adjudication of the bankruptcy, the trustee in bankruptcy needs time to express an opinion regarding the question of which goods are included in the bankrupt estate, or which goods he, in any event, wants to maintain for the bankrupt estate, for example in connection with a possible continuation or sale of the business. The policy of the trustee in bankruptcy can be severely frustrated if he, during that period, is faced with a "*fait accompli*" by the third parties concerned. That is why there is a need for the possibility to subject them to an insolvency stay, in which they cannot exercise their right without permission

---

76 See article 63a Fw.
77 See article 63a paragraph 2 Fw.
78 See article 63a paragraph 4 Fw.
79 See article 63a paragraph 3 Fw.
80 See generally "*De afkoelingsperiode van de Art. 63a Fw; ondoordachte wetgeving*", by Prof. mr S.C.J.J. Kortmann in "*Financieringen en aansprakelijkheid*", Prof. mr S.C.J.J. Kortmann (editor), W.E.J. Tjeenk Willink 1994, Zwolle, pp. 149-161.

from the supervisory judge in bankruptcy. In this way it prevents – as is currently the situation – third parties coming to remove all kind of goods from the bankrupt estate immediately after a bankruptcy is adjudicated out of fear that other parties – such as the tax authorities – may exercise their rights on those goods. (...)"

The insolvency stay was only introduced in the Fw as of 1 January 1992 and is therefore still a relatively new concept. As a consequence thereof, the scope of its material consequences is not yet fully crystallized. In respect of a substantial number of issues relating to the insolvency stay, a decision by the Netherlands supreme court is awaited. Without attempting to be exhaustive and without going into detail, these issues include the following:

(1) Is a trustee in bankruptcy entitled to use goods during the insolvency stay and if so, what is an adequate compensation for such use and what rank does this compensation have in the bankruptcy?

(2) Should there be compensation for accrued interest during the insolvency stay?

(3) Is it possible during the insolvency stay to collect claims, or to convert an undisclosed pledge into a disclosed pledge (§ 5.2.1.4)?

(4) Is it possible during the insolvency stay to exercise a right of set-off one may have or suspend the performance of one's obligations against the debtor?

(5) Is it possible to terminate agreements during the insolvency stay?

A number of these issues have been addressed in the MDW-Project and amendments to the insolvency stay have been suggested. For more details on the suggested amendments to the insolvency stay pursuant to the MDW-Project, see § 3.7.1.1[82].

3.4.1.2   The duty to render information

The debtor's duty to render information

The need for the trustee in bankruptcy to obtain information about the business of the debtor is great, especially in the preservation stage of a bankruptcy. Therefore, in this first stage of bankruptcy, the trustee in bankruptcy is likely to occupy a great deal of time of (the directors of) the debtor in collecting as much information as possible. To assist the trustee in bankruptcy, the Fw obliges the debtor to provide the trustee in bankruptcy with all information he requests[83]. Where the

---

81   See Van der Feltz 2-III, *supra* footnote 2, at p. 203.
82   See also generally: *"HAASTIGE SPOED... Opmerkingen naar aanleiding van het voorstel tot wijziging van de Faillissementswet"*, by Prof. mr S.C.J.J. Kortmann in *TvI*, 1, 2000, pp. 26-34.
83   See article 105 paragraph 1 Fw.

debtor is a company, a similar duty to render information rests on the present and former directors of the debtor[84].

Means to enforce cooperation

When the debtor is not sufficiently supportive, the trustee in bankruptcy can enforce cooperation by requesting the supervisory judge in bankruptcy to order the debtor to come to court to be heard by the supervisory judge in bankruptcy[85]. If the debtor remains reluctant to cooperate, the debtor may even be ordered to be taken into custody[86]. Where the debtor is a company, the same applies to the directors and the supervisory directors of the debtor[87]. The duty to render information to the trustee in bankruptcy is not unlimited. Like everyone else, the debtor is not required to incriminate itself and has the right to remain silent[88].

Other restrictions

In addition to the duty to render information, the debtor is – from the day of the bankruptcy onwards – not allowed to leave his place of residence, without the prior permission of the supervisory judge in bankruptcy[89]. Again, where the debtor is a company the same applies to the directors of the debtor[90].

Finally it should be noted that, to the extent it is reasonably necessary for the performance of his duties, the trustee in bankruptcy has access to any place. In that context the supervisory judge in bankruptcy is entitled to grant permission pursuant to article 2 of the General Act on entering properties (*"Algemene wet op het binnentreden"*)[91].

Summary
THE PRESERVATION STAGE

Scope
The preservation stage commences as of the day the bankruptcy is declared and lasts until the day the trustee in bankruptcy has finished his preliminary investigation of the state of affairs of the debtor.

---

84   See article 106 Fw.
85   See article 105 paragraph 1 Fw.
86   See article 87 paragraph 1 Fw.
87   See article 106 Fw.
88.   See article 29 Sv in which the right to remain silence is embodied.
89   See article 91 Fw.
90   See article 106 Fw.
91   See article 93a Fw.

Insolvency stay

(1) Insolvency stay can be a useful tool for the trustee in bankruptcy to safeguard his ability to conduct a preliminary investigation without being troubled by creditors who would otherwise be able to exercise:
  (i) their right to take recourse against any asset falling within the bankrupt estate; or
  (ii) their right to claim assets which are in control of the debtor or the trustee in bankruptcy.

(2) All interested parties in a bankruptcy should note that a substantial number of issues concerning (the consequences of) an insolvency stay are not yet fully crystallized.

(3) Amendments to the insolvency stay are suggested pursuant to the MDW-Project (§ 3.7.1.1).

Duty to render information

(1) In the preservation stage it is most likely that the trustee in bankruptcy will exercise its right to request information on the debtor or the directors and the supervisory directors of the debtor.

(2) When there is a lack of cooperation, the debtor or the directors of the debtor can be heard before the supervisory judge in bankruptcy or they can even be taken into custody.

(3) Without the permission of the supervisory judge, the debtor or the directors of the debtor may not leave their place of residence.

(4) To the extent it is reasonably necessary for the performance of his duties, the trustee in bankruptcy has access to any place.

3.4.2   The executorial stage

In practice – compared to the preservation stage – the need of the trustee in bankruptcy for information in the executorial stage of the bankruptcy is a great deal less. Nevertheless, information will still be necessary for the trustee in bankruptcy in order to decide on issues concerning:
(1) invalidation of legal acts by the debtor based on the *actio pauliana*;
(2) corporate liabilities; and
(3) claims based on the concept of wrongful act.
For a detailed discussion of the issues mentioned under (1)-(3), see Chapter 4.

Aside from deciding on the issues mentioned above, the trustee in bankruptcy will also have to address the following two topics in the executorial stage:
(1) recollection of goods by third parties; and
(2) liquidation of the assets of the debtor.

Both topics will be further discussed below in § 3.4.2.1 and § 3.4.2.2 respectively.

3.4.2.1   Recollection of goods by third parties

Determination of assets forming part of the bankrupt estate

Before the trustee in bankruptcy can start a complete liquidation of the assets of the debtor, he first needs to investigate which assets form part of the bankrupt estate[92]. Questions he will need to answer include the following:
(1)   Are there any valid claims by third parties based on reservation of title or ownership[93]?
(2)   Are there any valid security rights (such as pledges and mortgages) vested over any of the assets of the debtor[94]?
(3)   Are there any valid rights to recollect goods held by the debtor[95]?

In order to answer these questions, the trustee in bankruptcy will invite all known creditors of the debtor to prove that they have valid claims against any of the assets of the debtor[96]. The creditors will have to do this[97]:
(1)   on the basis of documents; and
(2)   by specifying exactly which assets of the debtor are subject to their claims.
When the documented claims of the creditors are received by the trustee in bankruptcy, usually one or more days will be scheduled by the trustee in bankruptcy when creditors with valid ownership claims against specific assets of the debtor can (re)collect those assets.

Reservation of title or ownership

In respect of valid claims by third parties based on a reservation of title or ownership, it must be noted that despite the valid creation of such rights, third parties can nevertheless lose their rights as a consequence of:
(1)   mixing of goods; and
(2)   the formation of a new good[98].

Ad. (1)
In case of mixing of goods, the asset that was encumbered with the reservation of title or ownership is mixed with other (similar) assets. As a result of this mixing

---

92   See article 92 paragraph 1 Fw.
93   See article 3:92 BW.
94   For more details on pledges and mortgages, see Chapter 5.
95   See article 7:39 BW.
96   See article 111 Fw.
97   See article 110 Fw.
98   See article 5:15 BW and article 5:16 BW read in conjunction with article 5:14 BW.

the reservation of title or ownership is lost because the encumbered asset can no longer be identified.

Ad. (2)
In case of formation of a new good, the asset that was encumbered with the reservation of title or ownership, has become a part of another newly formed good. This also results in a loss of the reservation of title or ownership because the good that was encumbered with it has ceased to exist as an individual good.

Monies, jewelry, stock and other securities

Unless determined otherwise by the supervisory judge in bankruptcy, all monies, jewelry, stock and other securities are taken in the immediate custody of the trustee in bankruptcy[99]. Cash that is not necessary for the administration and liquidation of the bankrupt estate, shall be invested by the trustee in bankruptcy for the benefit of the bankrupt estate in a manner approved by the supervisory judge in bankruptcy[100]. In practice, cash is usually deposited on an interest bearing payment account, referred to as the bankruptcy account. This account is held by the trustee in bankruptcy in his capacity of trustee in the bankruptcy of the debtor.

3.4.2.2 Liquidation of the assets of the debtor

Sale to a single buyer or multiple buyers

If the trustee in bankruptcy decides not to continue the business of the debtor, the trustee in bankruptcy will have to liquidate the assets of the debtor at the highest price possible. In order to do that, the trustee in bankruptcy will usually have the assets valued by an expert valuation-company. Ideally, the trustee in bankruptcy would wish to sell the assets of the debtor together with the business of the debtor to a single buyer. That will keep life simple, avoids "cherry picking", and oftentimes will generate the highest price. If the single buyer in such a sale aims to continue the business of the debtor, such sale could be referred to as a restart[101].

---

99   See article 102 paragraph 1 BW.
100 See article 102 paragraph 2 Fw.
101 For the purposes of this book a restart is described as a continuation of (a part of) the business activity of the debtor by another legal entity – which could, but does not necessarily have to, be related to the debtor – whereby:
(1) the debtor ceases to exist after a bankruptcy;
(2) a part of the debts of the debtor remain unpaid; and/or
(3) a part of the employees of the debtor, after their employment agreements have been terminated by the trustee in bankruptcy, remain unemployed and thus are not taken over by the other legal entity.
The concept of "restart" is not discussed further in this book. For a selection of books dealing with "restart", see the Further Reading section in the back.

If a sale to a single buyer is not possible, the trustee in bankruptcy will try to sell off the assets in parts to different third parties. This can be done in the following two ways:

(1) Via private sales of (parts of the) assets of the debtor for which authorization of the supervisory judge in bankruptcy is required[102]; and

(2) Via a public auction in which the (remaining) assets of the debtor are sold to the highest bidder.

Reasonable term for foreclosure

An important special right the trustee in bankruptcy has vis-à-vis holders of a valid pledge or mortgage is the right to subject pledgees and/or mortgagees to a reasonable term to foreclose on their collateral[103]. Upon giving such request to the pledgee or mortgagee, the reasonable term set by the trustee in bankruptcy for the foreclosure of the collateral can be extended by the supervisory judge in bankruptcy one or more times.

Why is the right to subject pledgees and/or mortgagees to a reasonable term to foreclose on their collateral such an important right for a trustee in bankruptcy? This right is important for the following reasons:

(1) In the event this reasonable term lapses without the collateral being sold in execution by the pledgee or the mortgagee, the trustee in bankruptcy is entitled to claim the collateral and sell it for the benefit of the bankrupt estate; and

(2) If the collateral is sold by the trustee in bankruptcy in the situation mentioned above under (1), the pledgee or the mortgagee maintains its right of priority over the proceeds of such sale, but it has to share in the allocation of the bankruptcy costs. This means that a distribution of the proceeds of the sale only takes place:

    (i) after an allocation of the bankruptcy costs;

    (ii) after a verification meeting for creditors has taken place[104]; and

    (iii) only on the basis of an approved plan of distribution on which the pledgee or mortgagee is listed as a preferential creditor in respect of the proceeds of the sale of the collateral[105].

From the foregoing it clearly follows that the consequences of the successful exercise by the trustee in bankruptcy of his right to subject the pledgee or mortgagee to a reasonable term are severe. In short, the pledgee or mortgagee loses its

---

102   See article 101 Fw read in conjunction with article 176 Fw.
103   See article 58 paragraph 1 Fw.
104   For more details on the verification meeting, see § 3.4.3.2.
105   See the MeesPierson/Mr Mentink q.q.-case (HR 30 June 1995, *NJ* 1996, 554).

status of *separatist* who can exercise its rights as if no bankruptcy exists[106]. Depending on the level of bankruptcy costs and the amount of monies in the bankruptcy estate, there even is a real risk that the pledgee or mortgagee receives nothing at all out of the proceeds of the sale. This is certainly the case in a negative estate[107].

It should be noted, however, that different rules apply in respect of a mortgage over registered aircraft[108].

Third party protection for debtors of the debtor

Debtors of the debtor are protected against having to pay a second time provided that[109]:
(1) the debt of the debtor is not encumbered with a valid pledge;
(2) the debtor paid its debt pursuant to a pre-bankruptcy obligation directly to the bankrupt debtor;
(3) the payment mentioned under (2) was made after the bankruptcy of the debtor receiving the payment was adjudicated, but prior to the announcement of the bankruptcy; and
(4) it is not proven that the paying debtor had knowledge of the bankruptcy mentioned above under (3).

Where the bankruptcy had already been announced, the paying debtor may still be released from having to pay its debt a second time to the bankrupt estate, provided that[110]:
(1) the paying debtor is able to prove that in his place of residence, the announcement of the bankruptcy declaration could not have been known; and
(2) the trustee in bankruptcy is not able to show that the paying debtor had nevertheless knowledge of the bankruptcy.
A debtor is in any case released from paying its debt for a second time to the bankrupt estate, in as far as its payment to the bankrupt debtor has benefited the bankrupt estate[111].

---

106   See article 57 paragraph 1 Fw.
107   For more details on a negative estate, see § 3.4.3.1.
108   See article 59a Fw.
109   See article 52 paragraph 1 Fw.
110   See article 52 paragraph 2 Fw.
111   See article 52 paragraph 3 Fw.

Summary
THE EXECUTORIAL STAGE

(1) In the executorial stage the trustee in bankruptcy can be expected to focus more on questions concerning invalidating legal acts on the basis of *actio pauliana*, corporate liabilities and claims on the basis of wrongful act. (See Chapter 4 for details on these issues.)

(2) The trustee in bankruptcy will facilitate the recollection of goods to the relevant third parties entitled thereto, provided that:
(i)   the debtor does not hold legal title to those goods; and
(ii) the claims of the third parties are valid and properly documented.
With regard to reservations of title or ownership by third parties especially issues of mixing of goods and the formation of a new good may play an important role.

(3) In order to liquidate the assets of the debtor to the highest bidder, the trustee in bankruptcy could consider:
(i)   a sale to a single buyer of all the assets and the business of the debtor;
(ii) private sales, authorized by the supervisory judge in bankruptcy, of assets or parts thereof to third parties; or
(iii) a public auction to sell the (remaining) assets of the debtor to the highest bidder.

(4) Pledgees and mortgagees should be aware of an important tool with severe consequences the trustee in bankruptcy has to subject them to a reasonable term to foreclose on their collateral. This bears in it the risk that the collateral ultimately is sold by the trustee in bankruptcy for the benefit of the bankrupt estate and the pledgee/mortgagee does not receive any proceeds thereof.

(5) In certain circumstances debtors of the bankrupt debtor are granted protection against a second payment of their debt to the bankrupt estate.

3.4.3   THE VERIFICATION OR CLOSING STAGE

The verification or closing stage is the final stage in a bankruptcy. This stage commences when all assets have been sold and after all legal proceedings that have been started by the trustee in bankruptcy have been finished. According to the Fw, in the verification or closing stage a bankruptcy can terminate in the following three ways:

(1) By liquidation without a verification meeting for creditors, whereby the bankruptcy is discontinued[112];
(2) By liquidation with a verification meeting for creditors, whereby there is a liquidation of the bankruptcy due to the fact that a final plan of distribution has become final and not open to appeal[113]; or
(3) By liquidation by way of composition (*i.e.* a composition with all creditors of the debtor which is ratified and has become final and not open to appeal[114]).

In the liquidations mentioned above under (1) and (2), the debtor is not released from its debts that remain unpaid[115]. If the debtor is a company, it will be dissolved[116]. The debtor may obtain a clean slate only in case of a liquidation by way of composition and the debtor which is a company survives as a legal entity[117]. Each of these three ways of terminating a bankruptcy will be further discussed below.

3.4.3.1 Liquidation without a verification meeting for creditors

Proper discontinuation

As a general rule, a bankruptcy terminates by way of liquidation without a verification meeting for creditors where there is a negative estate[118]. This means that the proceeds of the estate only allow for the pay out – in whole or in part – of the so-called "bankruptcy costs", which consist of:
(1) the fees and costs of the trustee in bankruptcy; and
(2) the total amount of claims by estate creditors[119].

Such a liquidation without a verification meeting for creditors is referred to as a "proper discontinuation" of the bankruptcy.

Improper discontinuation

As an exception to the general rule mentioned above, the bankruptcy will also

---

112   See article 16 Fw.
113   See article 193 paragraph 1 Fw.
114   See article 161 Fw.
115   See article 195 Fw.
116   See article 173 paragraph 1 Fw read in conjunction with article 2:19 paragraph 1 sub c BW.
117   See article 138 Fw read in conjunction with article 160 Fw.
118   See Chapter 7 on discontinuation due to the condition of the estate from the *"Directives in bankruptcies and suspensions of payment"*, in *"Vademecum Advocatuur: Wet & Regelgeving"*, 2001, pp. 492-495.
119   For more details on estate creditors, see § 3.6.2.

terminate without a verification meeting for creditors having to take place in bankruptcies[120]:

(1) in which the bankruptcy costs can be paid in full; and

(2) only the preferential claims of the tax authorities and the social security board can be paid – in whole or in part – from the remainder of the proceeds of the estate.

Such a liquidation without a verification meeting for creditors is referred to as an "improper discontinuation" of the bankruptcy.

Consequences

The above mentioned liquidations without a verification meeting for creditors each have the following two important consequences:

(1) All the preferential creditors (possibly with the exception of the tax authorities and/or the social security board) and all ordinary (non-preferential) creditors will not receive any payment on their claims[121]. Therefore, a presentation of a plan of distribution is not considered necessary; and

(2) After the termination of the bankruptcy the unpaid claims of other creditors continue to exist.

3.4.3.2   Liquidation with a verification meeting for creditors

A liquidation will require a verification meeting for creditors in case the proceeds of the bankrupt estate allow for a partial payment of the preferential creditors of the debtor at the least, in addition to the tax authorities and/or the social security board[122].

Steps to be taken before the verification meeting for creditors

The purpose of a verification meeting for creditors is to list, verify and classify all claims of the creditors of the debtor[123]. Estate creditors are excluded as they will already have been paid at this stage. Before a verification meeting for creditors can take place the following steps need to be taken:

(1) In an order the supervisory judge in bankruptcy determines[124]:

---

120   See also article 19 paragraph 2 Inv.

121   For a more detailed discussion of the different groups of creditors in a bankruptcy, see § 3.6.

122   See Chapter 8 on verification meeting from the *"Directives in bankruptcies and suspensions of payment"* in *"Vademecum Advocatuur: Wet & Regelgeving"*, 2001, p. 495.

123   See article 119 paragraph 1 Fw.

124   See article 108 paragraph 1 Fw.

(i)   the date on which the creditors of the debtor ultimately have to submit their claims against the debtor for verification with the trustee in bankruptcy; and

(ii)   the date, time and location for the verification meeting of creditors to take place.

At least 14 days have to lapse between the date referred to above under (i) and the date referred to above under (ii)[125];

(2) The trustee in bankruptcy is obliged to inform all known creditors of the debtor in writing about the order by the supervisory judge in bankruptcy. He has to do so immediately after the order is rendered by the supervisory judge in the bankruptcy[126];

(3) The trustee in bankruptcy must place all claims he is willing to approve on a list of temporarily admitted claims. All claims he intends to challenge must be placed on a list of temporarily challenged claims, including the grounds for challenging those claims[127]. If, in the opinion of the trustee in bankruptcy, one or more of the claims presented on the lists are secured by a pledge or a mortgage or if a right of retention is executed in respect of a claim, that should be indicated on the lists[128];

(4) A copy of each of the lists mentioned above under (3) must be filed by the trustee in bankruptcy with the competent court and/or cantonal court[129]. These lists must be filed for a period of 7 days prior to the verification meeting for creditors in order to facilitate an examination thereof by any person, at no charge; and

(5) Finally, the trustee in bankruptcy is obliged to[130]:

(i)   inform all known creditors in writing about the filing of the lists as mentioned above under (4); and

(ii)   provide all known creditors with a further notice of the anticipated verification meeting for creditors.

The verification meeting for creditors

At the verification meeting for creditors the supervisory judge in bankruptcy reads the lists of temporarily admitted and challenged creditors[131]. The debtor is,

---

125   See article 108 paragraph 2 Fw.
126   See article 109 Fw.
127   See article 112 Fw.
128   See article 113 Fw.
129   See article 114 paragraph 1 Fw.
130   See article 115 Fw.
131   See article 119 paragraph 1 Fw.

or where the debtor is a company its directors are[132], present at the verification meeting for creditors to render information, where necessary[133]. All claims that are not challenged are transferred to an official report of admitted creditors[134]. If a claim is challenged and the creditor concerned does not agree with the challenge, the supervisory judge in bankruptcy will order that legal proceedings be initiated to determine whether or not the claim can be admitted[135]. Such legal proceedings are referred to as "reference proceedings".

Special situations

In the context of a verification meeting for creditors, the Fw provides for specific rules dealing with the following situations:
– claims that have been submitted too late[136];
– claims that are subject to conditions precedent[137];
– claims that are not (yet) due and payable[138];
– remaining claims of secured creditors that could no be paid out of the collateral[139]; and
– claims with an undetermined value[140].

Steps to be taken after the verification meeting for creditors

After the verification meeting for creditors, the following steps need to be taken in order to terminate the bankruptcy:

(1) After the list of admitted claims has been finalized, the trustee in bankruptcy prepares a plan of distribution[141]. In this plan the percentage that will be paid out in respect of each of the admitted claims of the creditors is indicated. This can be a plan for an interim distribution or a final distribution. Interim distributions to admitted creditors can take place as many times as, in the opinion of the supervisory judge in the bankruptcy, sufficient monies to that extent exist[142];

---

132   See article 117 Fw.
133   See article 116 Fw.
134   See article 121 paragraph 1 Fw.
135   See article 122 paragraph 1 Fw.
136   See article 127 Fw.
137   See article 130 Fw.
138   See article 131 Fw.
139   See article 132 Fw.
140   See article 133 Fw read in conjunction with article 125 Fw.
141   See article 180 paragraph 1 Fw.
142   See article 179 Fw.

(2) The plan of distribution mentioned above under (1) must be approved by the supervisory judge in bankruptcy;

(3) Upon approval, the (final or interim) plan of distribution is filed with the competent court. There it may be examined by creditors during a 10 days period[143];

(4) If no creditors oppose the plan, the bankruptcy – in case of a final distribution – terminates 10 days after the plan is filed and the creditors are paid in accordance with the final plan of distribution[144]. Creditors may oppose the plan by filing a petition showing cause[145]. The decision in first instance with regard to such an opposition by a creditor is subject to appeal to the Netherlands supreme court only[146]; and

(5) Finally, after the lapse of one month after the termination of the bankruptcy, the trustee in bankruptcy is required to account for his acts before the supervisory judge in bankruptcy[147].

Consequences

The above mentioned liquidation with a verification meeting for creditors has as an important consequence that, after the termination of the bankruptcy, the unpaid claims of creditors continue to exist.

3.4.3.3 Liquidation by way of composition

A composition in a suspension of payment is primarily aimed at curing the financial position of the debtor (§ 2.5.2). In contrast, a composition in a bankruptcy is primarily aimed at preventing a judicial liquidation.

The debtor is entitled to propose a composition to its joint creditors[148]. Estate creditors are not included here because they will already have been paid at this stage. In a bankruptcy, the debtor can propose a composition only once prior to the verification meeting for creditors[149]. Requirements as to form and content of a composition proposal in a bankruptcy do not exist. Usually, the proposal is to pay the joint creditors of the debtor a certain percentage of their claims, against final discharge of the debtor for the remaining unsettled part of the claims of the creditors.

---

143   See article 183 paragraph 1 Fw.
144   See article 193 paragraph 1 Fw.
145   See article 184 paragraph 1 Fw.
146   See article 187 paragraph 1 Fw.
147   See article 193 paragraph 2 Fw.
148   See article 138 Fw.
149   See article 158 Fw read in conjunction with article 170 paragraph 1 Fw.

Steps to be taken before the verification meeting for creditors

If a debtor decides to make a composition proposal, he will have to observe the following steps before the verification meeting of creditors:

(1)   The proposal must be filed with the competent district court and/or cantonal court at least 8 days prior to the verification meeting for creditors[150].

(2)   Together with the filing mentioned above under (1), a copy of the composition proposal must be sent to the trustee in bankruptcy and to every member of the temporary commission of creditors, if such a commission has been formed (§ 3.6.4)[151].

The verification meeting for creditors

At the verification meeting for creditors or at a later date in case of postponement[152], a consultation of the creditors will take place, following which the creditors will vote on the proposal[153]. During the verification meeting the debtor is entitled to further explain, defend and even change the composition proposal. In order for a composition to be accepted, consent is required of:
(1)   2/3 of the admitted and provisionally admitted creditors; and
(2)   the creditors mentioned above under (1) must represent at least 3/4 of the amount of the non-preferential admitted and provisionally admitted claims[154].
Creditors having a privileged claim are excluded from voting[155]. This would not be the case if, prior to the commencement of the vote, they waived their right of preference. Such a waiver turns those creditors into non-preferential or ordinary creditors and they will stay that, even when the composition proposal is not accepted[156].

Second vote

A second vote becomes necessary if the two above-mentioned requirements are not met during the first vote. Within 8 days of casting in the first vote, a second vote shall take place in the event that[157]:

---

150   See article 139 paragraph 1 Fw.
151   See article 139 paragraph 2 Fw.
152   See article 141 Fw read in conjunction with article 142 Fw.
153   See article 144 Fw.
154   See article 145 Fw.
155   See article 143 paragraph 1 Fw.
156   See article 143 paragraph 2 Fw.
157   See article 146 Fw.

(1) 2/3 of the creditors present at the verification voted in favor of the composition; and

(2) such creditors represented more than half of the total amount of claims in respect of which a vote can be cast.

For such a second vote no further announcement is required. In addition, nobody is bound by his vote cast in the first vote. Where the required qualified majority is, again, not met, the composition proposal will be considered to be rejected.

Steps to be taken after the composition is accepted

In the event the composition is accepted, the following steps need to be taken in order to come to a termination of the bankruptcy:

(1) Prior to the close of the verification meeting, the supervisory judge in bankruptcy must determine the date for the meeting on which the court will deal with the ratification of the composition[158]. This meeting will be scheduled a minimum 8 and a maximum 14 days after the vote on the composition takes place[159].

During that time, the creditors of the debtor are entitled to indicate in writing to the supervisory judge in bankruptcy the grounds on which they consider a refusal of the ratification of the composition desirable[160]. Grounds on the basis of which the court must refuse ratification of the composition are[161]:

(i)   if the assets of the bankrupt estate considerably exceed the amount agreed to in the composition;

(ii) if performance of the composition is not sufficiently guaranteed; or

(iii) if the composition was reached by means of fraudulent acts or the preference of one or more creditors or by other unfair means, regardless of whether or not the debtor or any other party co-operated to that effect.

In addition to these grounds, the court may also refuse to ratify the composition on other grounds and *ex officio*[162]. Against a judgment in which the composition is ratified or in which the court refused to ratify the composition appeal is open to the competent court of appeals within 8 days following the order by the court[163] and further appeal is open to the Netherlands supreme court within 8 days following the order by the court of appeals[164];

---

158   See article 150 paragraph 1 Fw.
159   See article 150 paragraph 3 Fw.
160   See article 151 Fw.
161   See article 153 paragraph 2 Fw.
162   See article 153 paragraph 3 Fw.
163   See article 154 Fw read in conjunction with article 155 Fw.
164   See article 156 Fw.

(2) A ratified composition is binding on all creditors not having a right of preference without exception and regardless of whether or not they have submitted their claims in the bankruptcy[165];

(3) As soon as the ratification is final and not open to appeal, the bankruptcy will terminate. A final ratified composition creates an entitlement of enforcement for the creditors having admitted claims (that have not been disputed by the debtor) against the debtor and any guarantors pursuant to a surety who acceded to the composition[166]; and

(4) Finally, after the ratification has become effective and final, the trustee in bankruptcy is required to render an account for his acts before the supervisory judge in bankruptcy[167].

Consequences

Depending on the exact terms of the composition, the performance by the debtor of all his obligations pursuant to the composition may result in a clean slate for the debtor.

Dissolution of a ratified composition

In the event the debtor remains in default in the performance of his obligations pursuant to the ratified composition towards a creditor, that creditor is entitled to request a dissolution of the ratified composition[168]. If such a request is made, the competent judge is entitled – also *ex officio* – to grant the debtor a grace period of one month at most to remedy his default[169].

In the judgment in which the dissolution of the composition is declared, a re-opening of the bankruptcy is ordered. In addition, a supervisory judge in bankruptcy is appointed as well as a trustee in bankruptcy and, if there was one previously, a commission of creditors[170]. Acts undertaken by the debtor in between the ratification of the composition and the re-opening of the bankruptcy bind the bankrupt estate, notwithstanding the possibility by the trustee in bankruptcy having to invalidate these acts on the basis of *actio pauliana*[171].

---

165 See article 157 Fw.
166 See article 159 Fw.
167 See article 162 paragraph 1 Fw.
168 See article 165 paragraph 1 Fw.
169 See article 165 paragraph 3 Fw.
170 See article 167 paragraph 1 Fw.
171 See article 169 Fw.

Summary
THE VERIFICATION AND CLOSING STAGE

(1) In the verification and closing stage, the following three ways of terminating a bankruptcy exist:
(i)   By liquidation without a verification meeting for creditors
(a) via a proper discontinuation of the bankruptcy; or
(b) via an improper discontinuation of the bankruptcy;
(ii) By liquidation with a verification meeting for creditors
as a result of a final plan of distribution becoming final and not
open to appeal; or
(iii) By liquidation by way of composition
as a result of a ratified composition becoming final and not open to
appeal.

(2) A liquidation without a verification meeting for creditors as mentioned
above under (1)(i) takes place where the proceeds of the bankrupt estate
only allow for the payment – in whole or in part – of the estate creditors
("proper discontinuation") and the privileged claims of the tax
authorities and/or the social security board ("improper discontinuation").

(3) A liquidation with a verification meeting for creditors as mentioned
under (1)(ii) takes place where the proceeds of the bankrupt estate allow
for at least a partial payment of the preferential creditors other than the
tax authorities and/or the social security board. Reference proceedings,
which may be commenced in case a claim of a creditor is challenged,
may postpone the finalization of this type of liquidation.

(4) A liquidation by way of composition as mentioned above under (1)(iii)
takes place where:
(i)   2/3 of the admitted and provisionally admitted creditors representing 3/4 of the amount of the non-preferential admitted and provisionally admitted claims, consent to a timely submitted composition proposal; and
(ii) the accepted composition is ratified and becomes final and not
open to appeal.

3.5   The rights and duties of a trustee in bankruptcy

As mentioned earlier in § 3.1, a trustee in bankruptcy has to observe many different (sometimes competing) interests. Traditionally, a trustee in bankruptcy was

perceived to primarily represent the interests of the joint creditors of the debtor. However, recent developments in the case law of the Netherlands supreme court[172] indicate that, aside from creditors' interests, a trustee in bankruptcy may in certain circumstances also have to take into consideration:

(1) the maintenance of employment;
(2) the continuation of the business of the debtor; and
(3) other community interests.

In light of this development, the liability of the trustee in bankruptcy for his acts during a bankruptcy will be addressed in § 5.2.1. Subsequently, a number of common situations that a trustee in bankruptcy has to deal with will be discussed in § 5.2.2.

3.5.1 LIABILITY OF THE TRUSTEE IN BANKRUPTCY FOR HIS ACTS

Liability in the capacity as trustee in bankruptcy

With or without the authorization of the supervisory judge in bankruptcy[173], the trustee in bankruptcy is to be held accountable for the acts he undertakes during the course of a bankruptcy. He is held accountable, although not usually personally, but in his capacity as trustee in bankruptcy. This means that the bankrupt estate, which is represented by the trustee in bankruptcy, is liable for the acts of the trustee in bankruptcy[174].

The debtor

As mentioned earlier in § 3.2.2, even if at a later stage – in review or appeal – the bankruptcy of the debtor is nullified, the acts of a trustee in bankruptcy bind the debtor[175].

The standard for personal liability

In the *Maclou*-case[176], the Netherlands supreme court developed a standard to measure whether or not a trustee in bankruptcy can be held personally liable for his acts undertaken during the bankruptcy of a debtor. A trustee in bankruptcy is personally liable for his acts, only if his acts fall short of this standard in the *Maclou*-case. This standard was described as follows:

---

172   See, for example, the Sigmacon II-case (HR February 25, 1996, *NJ* 1996, 472) and the
       Maclou-case (HR 19 April 1996, *NJ* 1996, 727).
173   See article 72 Fw.
174   See article 6:172 BW.
175   See article 13 paragraph 1 Fw.
176   HR 19 April 1996, *NJ* 1996, 727.

"A trustee in bankruptcy should act in such a manner as – in all reasonableness – can be expected from a trustee in bankruptcy having sufficient understanding and experience, fulfilling his duties with dedication and punctuality."

As this standard is a general one, it will have to be specified in each case in which it is applied[177]. In practice the above standard for personal liability is not easily met.

3.5.2   COMMON SITUATIONS FACING A TRUSTEE IN BANKRUPTCY

In this section a number of common situations that a trustee in bankruptcy will have to deal with will be addressed. The focus in the discussion of these situations will be on:
(1)   the rights and duties of the trustee in bankruptcy in such situations; and
(2)   the rights and duties of a counter party in those situations.

From the great variety of situations a trustee in bankruptcy may be confronted with in the course of a bankruptcy, the following common situations will be looked into:

(1)   Lawsuits (§ 3.5.2.1);
(2)   Agreements with mutual performances (§ 3.5.2.2);
(3)   Hire-purchase agreements (§ 3.5.2.3);
(4)   Rental agreements and lease agreements (§ 3.5.2.4);
(5)   Employment agreements and agencies (§ 3.5.2.5); and
(6)   Right of retention (§ 3.5.2.6).

3.5.2.1   Lawsuits

Lawsuits initiated against the debtor

As a consequence of the bankruptcy of the debtor, all lawsuits initiated against the debtor prior to its bankruptcy are suspended by virtue of law, provided that a performance of an obligation by the bankrupt estate is demanded (for example, a payment by the bankrupt estate)[178]. Such lawsuits will only be continued in a reference proceeding where the claim of the plaintiff in the lawsuit against the debtor has been challenged during the verification meeting for creditors. If challenged by a party other than the debtor, that party will replace the debtor as the defendant in the lawsuit.

---

177   See generally Verstijlen, *supra* footnote 1, Chapter XIII, § 7, at pp. 230-237.
178   See article 29 Fw.

Lawsuits initiated against the debtor prior to its bankruptcy concerning claims not subject to verification shall be adjourned upon the request of the plaintiff[179]. Examples of claims not subject to verification are:

(1) claims to recover property; or

(2) claims demanding dissolution of a contract.

The purpose of the adjournment is to give the plaintiff the opportunity to summon the trustee in bankruptcy to take over the lawsuit from the debtor. The plaintiff has to summon the trustee in bankruptcy within a term set by the competent court.

By appearing in court, the trustee in bankruptcy is considered to have taken over the proceedings[180], and the debtor is discharged – by virtue of law – from the proceedings. If the trustee in bankruptcy immediately consents to the claim of the plaintiff, the plaintiff costs of litigation will not be considered to be a claim against the bankrupt estate[181]. However, in the event the trustee in bankruptcy does not appear, the claim of the plaintiff against the debtor will be considered to be a claim against the bankrupt estate which does not have to be submitted for verification[182].

Lawsuits initiated by the debtor

Lawsuits initiated by the debtor prior to its bankruptcy shall be adjourned upon the request of the defendant[183]. The purpose of the adjournment is to give the defendant the opportunity to summon the trustee in bankruptcy to take over the lawsuit from the debtor. The defendant has to summon the trustee in bankruptcy within a term set by the competent court.

Where the trustee in bankruptcy does not respond or does not timely respond to the summons mentioned above, the defendant will be entitled to request for a dismissal. If such a dismissal is not requested by the defendant, the lawsuit will continue between the debtor and the defendant. In this situation, the debtor will be acting on his own and will not be able to burden the bankrupt estate with costs or judgments awarded against it[184].

The foregoing does not change the right of the trustee in bankruptcy to take over the proceedings from the debtor at any time, without being summoned by the defendant[185].

---

179 See article 28 paragraph 1 Fw.
180 See article 28 paragraph 2 Fw.
181 See article 28 paragraph 3 Fw.
182 See article 28 paragraph 4 Fw.
183 See article 27 paragraph 1 Fw.
184 See article 27 paragraph 2 Fw.
185 See article 27 paragraph 3 Fw.

Lawsuits initiated during the bankruptcy

During the bankruptcy of the debtor, claims demanding performance of an obligation by the bankrupt estate can only be brought against the debtor by submitting such claim for verification with the trustee in bankruptcy[186]. Claims against the debtor which are not subject to verification should be initiated against the trustee in bankruptcy[187]. However, in the event such claims have been lodged against the debtor and/or continued against the debtor resulting in a judgment against the debtor, then such judgment will not affect the bankrupt estate[188].

During the bankruptcy, the trustee in bankruptcy is entitled to initiate legal proceedings, provided that the authorization of the supervisory judge in bankruptcy has been obtained[189]. It is important to note that even where there is a negative estate the trustee in bankruptcy is still entitled to commence lawsuits[190]. When doing so, there is no obligation on the trustee in bankruptcy to provide security for the eventuality of the trustee in bankruptcy losing the case and being ordered to pay costs[191].

3.5.2.2   Agreements with mutual performances

Agreements in general
Unless contracted for otherwise, a bankruptcy in itself does not alter the validity or the contents of an existing agreement. However, in respect of certain types of agreements, the Fw provides for special rules. One type of agreement so affected is an agreement with mutual performances.

Scope of article 37 Fw
An agreement qualifies as an agreement with mutual performances where one party agrees to perform an obligation in exchange for the counter party agreeing also to perform an obligation[192]. The special rules for agreements with mutual performances are set forth in article 37 Fw[193]. This article applies where the following requirements are met:
(1)   The agreement must be an agreement with mutual performances;

---

186   See article 26 Fw.
187   See article 25 paragraph 1 Fw.
188   See article 25 paragraph 2 Fw.
189   See article 68 paragraph 2 Fw.
190   For more details on a negative estate, see § 3.4.3.1.
191   See the Stichting Administratiekantoor Hotel Emmen/Geene-case (Court of appeals of Leeuwarden 17 March 1999, *NJ* 2000, 27) and the Badine-case (District court of Breda 19 March 1996, *NJ* 1996, 34).
192   See article 6:262 paragraph 1 BW.
193   Pursuant to article 68 paragraph 2 Fw, the trustee in bankruptcy needs the consent of the supervisory judge in bankruptcy when exercising his right under article 37 Fw.

(2) At the time of declaration of the bankruptcy, the obligations of the debtor under the agreement must be performed only in part or not at all; and

(3) At the time of the declaration of the bankruptcy, the obligations of the counter party of the debtor under the agreement must also be performed only in part or not at all.

In light of the above requirements, it is unclear whether or not a long-term agreement falls within the scope of article 37 Fw if:

(i) the agreement continues to exist after the bankruptcy is adjudicated; and

(ii) the agreement, when the bankruptcy is adjudicated, had been fully performed by both parties thereto.

Rationale behind article 37 Fw

The anticipated goal the legislator had for including the special rules in respect of agreements with mutual performances in the Fw was twofold[194]:

(1) To provide the counter party of the debtor with a means of ending the uncertainty created by the bankruptcy and to clarify its position in respect of the trustee in bankruptcy; and

(2) To give freedom to the trustee in bankruptcy to determine whether or not (further) compliance with the agreement is beneficial for the bankrupt estate, knowing that the obligations pursuant to the agreement will be considered claims against the bankrupt estate.

Content of the special rules pursuant to article 37 Fw

Assuming that an agreement falls within the scope of article 37 Fw, a counter party of the debtor has the right to summon the trustee in bankruptcy in writing to determine, within a reasonable period of time, whether or not he is prepared to comply with the obligations of the debtor under the agreement[195]. In that regard the four possible responses by the trustee in bankruptcy are as follows:

(1) The trustee in bankruptcy does not respond at all;

(2) The trustee in bankruptcy does not respond in time;

(3) The trustee in bankruptcy timely states that he intends not to comply with the agreement; or

(4) The trustee in bankruptcy timely states that he intends to comply with the agreement.

---

194   See Van der Feltz 2-III, *supra* footnote 2, pp. 94-95.
195   See article 37 paragraph 1 Fw.

Situations (1)-(3)

The situations mentioned above under (1)-(3) result in the following consequences:
(i)   The trustee in bankruptcy loses his right to demand compliance with the
      agreement[196];
(ii) The claim for damages by the counter party shall qualify as a non-pref-
      erential or ordinary claim, which has to be submitted for verification to the
      trustee in bankruptcy[197]; and
(iii) The refusal by the trustee in bankruptcy to comply with the obligations
      under the agreement results in a failure attributable to the debtor[198];

It is unclear how claims of the counter party are to be qualified if the counter
party is prepared to perform under the agreement. Should claims that arise
against the debtor where the counter party is prepared to perform his obligations
under the agreement be qualified as claims against the bankrupt estate, notwithstanding the unwillingness of the trustee in bankruptcy to act? One view[199] is that
such a qualification violates the principle of article 37 Fw, unless compliance by
the counter party of its obligations under the agreement would benefit the bankrupt estate[200]. Instead of being claims against the bankrupt estate, these claims
should – following this line of reasoning – be qualified as claims not subject to
verification as bankruptcy only extends in favor of those parties that, at the time
the bankruptcy was adjudicated, were already a creditor of the debtor.

Situation (4)

In the situation mentioned above under (4), the trustee in bankruptcy is required
to provide security within the reasonable period of time set for him[201]. It is not
entirely clear whether or not such security should cover those obligations that result from further performance of the agreement, or whether or not such security
should also cover obligations already in existence prior to the date of the bankruptcy. One view[202] is that the security should cover both categories of obligations, the rationale being as follows: if the trustee in bankruptcy were only
obliged to put up security in respect of obligations that result from further performance of the agreement, the consequence thereof would be that the counter party
of the debtor would still have the right to dissolve the agreement where the un-

---

196   *Id.*
197   See article 37a Fw.
198   See article 6:74 BW.
199   See *"Leasing"*, by Mr J.J. van Hees, W.E.J. Tjeenk Willink 1997, Deventer, p. 166.
200   For a different view, see *"Afwikkeling van de Faillissementsboedel"* by Mr G.A.J. Boekraad,
      W.E.J. Tjeenk Willink 1997, Deventer, pp. 65-66.
201   See article 37 paragraph 2 Fw.
202   See Van Hees, *supra* footnote 199, at p. 164.

settled obligations arisen prior to the date of the bankruptcy qualify as a failure attributable to the debtor. Such a right by the counter party to dissolve the agreement would be in violation of the ethos of article 37 Fw.

With regards assessment of the amount of security to be provided by the trustee in bankruptcy, the following three criteria can be used[203]:

(i)   There should be sufficient coverage for the total risk;
(ii)   Accrued interest and costs should be included, if grounds to that extent exist; and
(iii) The creditor should be able to enforce the security easily.

In respect of the situation as mentioned above under (4), it should further be noted that the counter party of the debtor will have a (non-preferential or ordinary) claim against the bankrupt estate.

Other options in situations (1)-(3)

In respect of agreements with mutual performances in a bankruptcy it should further be noted that in situations (1)-(3), in addition to the rights pursuant to article 37 Fw, the counter party of the debtor (together with the trustee in bankruptcy) also has the following four options:
(i)   Demand (partial) dissolution of the agreement[204];
(ii)   Demand supplementary damages[205];
(iii) Demand performance[206]; or
(iv)   Demand substitute damages[207].

Ad. (i)
In respect of dissolution of the agreement, it should be noted that a dissolution does not have retroactive effect nor does it have consequences of a proprietary nature[208]. A dissolution only results in:
(a)   an obligation to restore the original situation (*i.e.* restore the position parties would have been in had the agreement not been made)[209]; and
(b)   a claim against the debtor for compensation of value[210].
As a consequence of the dissolution, the counter party does *not* acquire a right to recollect assets from the debtor that remain unpaid for.

---

203   See article 6:51 BW.
204   See article 6:265 BW.
205   See article 6:74 BW.
206   See article 3:296 BW.
207   See article 6:87 BW.
208   See article 6:269 BW.
209   See article 6:271 BW.
210   See article 6:272 BW.

Ad. (iii) and (iv)

In the options mentioned above under (iii) and (iv) the trustee in bankruptcy re-acquires all legal options lost as a consequence of article 37 Fw (see above under "Situations (1)-(3)"). The trustee in bankruptcy re-acquires, for example, the right to demand compliance with the agreement.

Goods traded on a commodity market and delivered at a fixed time or within a pre-set period

The declaration of the bankruptcy will always result in an immediate dissolution of an agreement, provided that[211] :
(1) the agreement falls within the scope of article 37 Fw; and
(2) the agreement concerns goods:
      (i) that are traded on a commodity market; and
      (ii) must be delivered at a fixed time or within a pre-set period and such deadline expires after a bankruptcy has been adjudicated.
If these conditions are met, the counter party of the debtor will be entitled to submit a claim for damages for verification with the trustee in bankruptcy as a non-preferential or ordinary creditor. If the bankrupt estate should sustain damages as a consequence of the dissolution, the counter party of the debtor will be required to compensate the bankrupt estate.

International private law aspects

International private law aspects attached to agreements with mutual performances in a bankruptcy will not be discussed[212] .

3.5.2.3   Hire-purchase agreements

Hire-purchase

The general rules of hire-purchase applicable outside a bankruptcy situation with respect to immoveable goods are laid out in a special act[213] and non-registered moveable goods are set forth in the BW[214].

---

211   See article 38 Fw.
212   See *"Grensoverschrijdende aspecten van insolventieprocedures buiten verdrag"*, by Mr R.J. van Galen and Mr J.C. van Apeldoorn in *"Mededelingen van de Nederlandse Vereniging voor Internationaal Recht, number 117: grensoverschrijdende insolventieprocedures"*, Kluwer 1998, Deventer, pp. 109-125.
213   See generally the TWHOZ.
214   See articles 7A:1576h BW-7A:1576x BW.

Hire-purchase has the following two distinctive features:

(1) the emphasis is on the acquisition of goods over time by way of a postponed transfer of legal title to the goods; and

(2) the enjoyment and the use of the goods commences as of the date the goods are factually delivered.

The scope of article 38a Fw

In a bankruptcy context article 38a Fw provides for special rules on hire-purchase agreements. These special rules will apply where the following two requirements are met[215]:

(1) There must be a bankruptcy of the lessee under the hire-purchase agreement; and

(2) The hire-purchase relates to a non-registered moveable good or a registered vessel[216].

Ad. (1)

In case of a bankruptcy of the lessor under a hire-purchase agreement, the rules set forth in article 37 Fw may be applicable provided that the lessor under the hire-purchase agreement has not yet performed all of his obligations under the hire-purchase agreement.

Ad. (2)

In respect of immoveable goods, compulsory law requires judicial interference for a dissolution of a hire-purchase of immoveable goods[217].

The rationale behind article 38a Fw

According to the legislator[218], article 38a Fw aims to provide the trustee in bankruptcy with a right to dissolve a hire-purchase agreement in order to prevent the existence of a situation in which:

(1) the lessor under the hire-purchase agreement will have to be verified for the total remainder of the purchase price; and

(2) the legal title of the good will stay with the lessor under the hire-purchase agreement.

---

215 See article 38a paragraph 1 Fw.

216 The general rules applicable to a hire-purchase of a registered vessel outside of a bankruptcy are set forth in articles 8:800 BW-8:812 BW. Article 7A:1576h paragraph 2 BW provides for the possibility of substantially enlarging the scope of the applicability of article 38a Fw.

217 See article 11 TWHOZ read in conjunction with article 15 TWHOZ.

218 See Van der Feltz 2-III, *supra* footnote 2, p. 102.

The content of the special rules pursuant to article 38a Fw

The content of the special rules pursuant to article 38a Fw can be summarized as follows:

(1) On the basis of article 38a Fw, the trustee in bankruptcy and the lessor under a hire-purchase agreement each have the right to immediately dissolve the hire-purchase agreement at any time[219]. Such a right is only limited to the extent that in the circumstances at hand:
   (i)   the use of the right would qualify as an abuse of right[220]; or
   (ii) the use of the right would, measured by the standard of unreasonableness and fairness, be unacceptable[221];
(2) A dissolution based on article 38a Fw has the same consequences as a dissolution of the hire-purchase agreement based on non-performance by the lessee of his obligations under the hire-purchase agreement[222]. If the lessor under the hire-purchase agreement ends up in a financially better position as a consequence of the dissolution, as compared to if the hire-purchase agreement had been continued, the lessor is required to make full compensation[223]; and
(3) In respect of his unsettled claim against the lessee under the hire-purchase agreement, the lessor is entitled to submit such claim for verification with the trustee in bankruptcy, whereby such claim will be qualified as a non-preferential or ordinary claim[224].

In the event neither the trustee in bankruptcy nor the lessor under the hire-purchase agreement exercises the right to dissolve the hire-purchase agreement, it is not entirely clear what status the unpaid hire-purchase rent arisen prior to the bankruptcy should have. One view[225] is that such outstanding amounts should qualify as claims against the bankrupt estate, the reasoning being that, as no use is made of the right to dissolve the hire-purchase agreement, it must be assumed that the parties intend to continue the hire-purchase agreement. This is because it is highly unlikely that the lessor would be prepared to continue with the agreement when the hire-purchase rent arisen prior to the bankruptcy will not be paid by the trustee in bankruptcy. If, on the other hand, the pre-bankruptcy hire-pur-

---

219   See article 38a paragraph 1 Fw.
220   See article 3:13 BW. For more details on the concept of abuse of right, see § 3.2.1.1.
221   See article 6:2 BW.
222   See article 38a paragraph 2 Fw.
223   See article 7A:1576t BW.
224   See article 38a paragraph 3 Fw.
225   See Van Hees, *supra* footnote 199, at p. 168.

chase rent is to be qualified as a non-preferential or ordinary claim instead of a claim against the bankrupt estate, the trustee in bankruptcy would not be in a position to pay those claims to the lessor under the hire-purchase agreement, until:

(1) a valid verification of those claims has taken place in a verification meeting for creditors; and
(2) the specific rules following from the Fw concerning the distribution of proceeds from the bankrupt estate have all been observed[226].

International private law
International private law aspects of hire-purchase agreements in a bankruptcy will not be discussed[227].

3.5.2.4   Rental agreements and lease agreements

The scope of article 39 Fw

In article 39 Fw special rules are set forth to deal with rental agreements in a bankruptcy. Those rules also extend to lease agreements[228] and are applicable if the following two requirements are met[229]:

(1) There must be a bankruptcy of the lessee under the rental agreement or lease agreement; and
(2) The rental agreement or lease agreement is in respect of an immoveable good.

Ad. (1)
An agreement qualifies as a rental agreement where one party binds itself to provide another party with the enjoyment of a property, for a specified period and for a price, which the latter agrees to pay[230]. A lease agreement can be described as an agreement, notwithstanding its form or name, pursuant to which one party binds itself to another party to provide such other party with the use of a farm or a part of land for purposes of agriculture in return for payment of consideration[231].

---

226   For more details on verification of claims and distribution of proceeds after such a verification, see § 3.4.3.2.
227   See generally Van Galen/Van Apeldoorn, *supra* footnote 212, at pp. 109-125.
228   See article 39 paragraph 2 Fw.
229   See article 34 paragraph 1 Fw.
230   See article 7A:1584 BW.
231   See article 1 sub d Pw.

Ad. (2)
It is not entirely clear whether or not moveable goods should also fall within the scope of article 39 Fw[232].

Rationale behind article 39 Fw

According to the legislator[233] the anticipated purposes of the special rules of article 39 Fw are:

(1) to provide a simple set of rules in which interests of both the bankrupt estate and the lessor under the rental agreement or lease agreement are taken into account;
(2) to provide the trustee in bankruptcy with a possibility of freeing the bankrupt estate from maintaining rented or leased objects when there is no longer a need for those objects; and
(3) to provide the lessor under the rental agreement or lease agreement with the possibility of looking for a new lessee, while having the security that the trustee in bankruptcy will pay the rent or lease price for as long as the agreement runs with the bankrupt estate.

The content of the special rules pursuant to article 39 Fw

The special rules pursuant to article 39 Fw can be summarized as follows:

(1) The lessor under the rental agreement or lease agreement and the trustee in bankruptcy (with the authorization of the supervisory judge in bankruptcy[234]) are entitled to an early termination of the agreement upon observing a notice period in accordance with local practice[235]. A notice period of three months is, in any case, considered to be sufficient; and
(2) In the event rent or lease payments have been made in advance, the rental agreement or lease agreement, as the case may be, can only be terminated as of the day on which the term for which the payments have been made in advance, has lapsed.

---

232   See Van Hees, *supra* footnote 199, at p. 171.
233   See *"Geschiedenis van de Wet op het Faillissement en de Surséance van Betaling"*, by Mr G.W. van der Feltz, part 2-I, 1896, editors Prof. mr S.C.J.J. Kortmann/Mr N.E.D. Faber, Tjeenk Willink 1994, Zwolle, p. 419.
234   See article 68 paragraph 2 Fw.
235   See article 39 paragraph 1 Fw.

Other issues

In addition to the above, a number of other issues exist in respect of rental agreements and lease agreements. These issues are not discussed here, but include, *inter alia*, the following:
-   Eviction;
-   Protection from eviction[236]; and
-   Substitution[237].

International private law aspects

International private law aspects of rental agreements and lease agreements in a bankruptcy will also not be discussed[238].

3.5.2.5   Employment agreements and agencies

The scope of article 40 Fw

The special rules set forth in article 40 Fw apply to:
(1) employment agreements in case of a bankruptcy of an employer; and
(2) agencies in case of a bankruptcy of a principal[239].
These rules are considered to be exceptions to the rules concerning agreements with mutual performances as set forth in article 37 Fw (§ 3.5.2.2).

Ad. (1)
An employment agreement is the agreement pursuant to which one party, the employee, agrees to perform labor in service of the other party, the employer, for wages for a period of time[240].

Ad. (2)
An agency is an agreement pursuant to which one party, the principal, orders the other party, the agent, and the latter agrees, for a fixed term or an indefinite period of time and against payment, to mediate in respect of entering into agreements and, in some cases, of concluding those agreements in the name and for the account of the principal without being in a subordinate position to the principal[241].

---

236   See, for example, the article 28(c)-28(e) Hw and the ADB/Planex-case (HR 7 December 1990, *NJ* 1991, 216).
237   See article 7A:1635 BW.
238   See generally Van Galen/Van Apeldoorn, *supra* footnote 212, pp. 109-125.
239   See article 40 paragraph 3 Fw.
240   See article 7:610 paragraph 1 BW.
241   See article 7:428 paragraph 1 BW.

In the discussion below, the focus will be on employment agreements.

Rationale behind article 40 Fw

With article 40 Fw, the legislator has attempted to balance the following two concerns[242] :

(1) When the business of a debtor is stopped – as is often the case in a bankruptcy – the trustee in bankruptcy must have the possibility of cutting employment costs. This is to avoid, by observing extended notice periods, payments to employees which are financed for a substantial period of time by creditors for which in the majority of cases, no labor is performed in return; and
(2) It is not reasonable to bind an employee for too long to a bankrupt employer. In a bankruptcy of an employer, the normal relationship between an employee and an employer no longer exists.

The content of the special rules pursuant to article 40 Fw

The special rules pursuant to article 40 Fw can be summarized as follows:

(1) Where an employer goes bankrupt, both the employees and the trustee in bankruptcy are entitled to an early termination of the employment agreement, irrespective of whether the agreement was entered into for a fixed term or for an indefinite period of time[243] ;
(2) In exercising his right of early termination pursuant to article 40 Fw, a trustee in bankruptcy needs to have the consent of the supervisory judge in bankruptcy[244] ;
(3) In contrast to suspension of payment (§ 2.3.1), a permit to terminate an employment agreement on the basis of article 6 BBA is not required[245] ;
(4) In exercising the right of early termination pursuant to article 40 Fw, the notice periods generally applicable in employment law[246] or the notice period agreed to in the employment agreement, must be observed. Failure to observe the applicable notice period results in liability for damages. Where the trustee in bankruptcy is in breach, this obligation to pay damages qualifies as a claim against the bankrupt estate.

---

242   See Van der Feltz 2-III, *supra* footnote 2, MvT, at p. 105.
243   See article 40 paragraph 1 Fw.
244   See article 68 paragraph 1 Fw.
245   See article 6 paragraph 2 sub c BBA.
246   See the articles 7:671 BW, 7:672 BW and 7:684 BW.

The observation of a notice period of 6 weeks is, in any case, considered to be sufficient[247]. However, there is an exception in respect of early termination by the trustee in bankruptcy of employment agreements with employees who are older than 45 years, but have not yet reached the age of 65 years, in which case the notice period of 6 weeks may be extended by another period of 13 weeks at most[248].

From the foregoing it follows that the maximum notice period is either 6 weeks or 19 weeks.

Finally, also the rules on the day against which early termination should take place need to be observed[249], unless as a result the above-mentioned maximum notice periods should be exceeded;

(5) The various restrictions in the Netherlands on termination of employment agreements (such as no termination during illness, pregnancy, *etc.*) do not apply in a bankruptcy[250];

(6) In case of an early termination of employment agreements by the trustee in bankruptcy of 20 or more employees, notification and consultation of trade unions is required[251];

(7) During a bankruptcy the Works Council of the debtor maintains its right to advise and its right to agree[252]. As a consequence, it could be argued that the Works Council should be consulted by a trustee in bankruptcy prior to exercising his right of early termination pursuant to article 40 Fw[253];

(8) As of the date the bankruptcy is adjudicated, the wages and the premiums related to the employment agreement, qualify as claims against the bankrupt estate[254]. In practice quite a large variety of claims fall within the scope of the term "wages".

The Mr Frima q.q./Blankers-case[255]

In the *Mr Frima q.q./Blankers*-case, the Netherlands supreme court held that pension claims relating to the financing of the so-called "backservice obligation"[256] also qualify as a claim against the bankrupt estate. The ground for this conclusion was that such claims arise as a consequence of the

---

247 See article 40 paragraph 1 Fw.
248 See article 7:672 paragraph 2 BW.
249 See article 7:670 paragraph 1 BW and the Smits/Mr Bloem q.q.-case (HR 22 May 1970, *NJ* 1970, 419).
250 See article 7:670 paragraphs 2-5 BW.
251 See article 2 paragraph 3 WCO read in conjunction with article 3 paragraph 1 WCO.
252 See especially article 25 WOR. For more details on the Works Council, see also § 2.2.
253 See *"De curator en de medezeggenschap van werknemers"*, by Mr W.P.J. Kroft in *"De curator, een octopus"*, Prof. mr S.C.J.J Kortmann c.s. (editors), W.E.J. Tjeenk Willink 1996, Deventer, pp. 49-62.
254 See article 40 paragraph 2 Fw.
255 HR 12 November 1993, *NJ* 1994, 229.
256 The "backservice-obligation" means the obligation to increase the premium-free claim of the employee in respect of the old-age pension to the level of proportional old-age pension.

exercise by the trustee in bankruptcy of his early termination right pursuant to article 40 Fw.

The LISV/Mr Wilderink q.q.-case[257]

More recently, in the *LISV/Mr Wilderink q.q.*-case, the Netherlands supreme court held that the claim for payment in cash for holidays that have not been used by the employee, also qualifies as a claim against the bankrupt estate;

(9) On the basis of the so-called "Wages Guarantee Arrangement"[258], the social security board takes over – where a valid request to that extent is made – the obligations of the debtor-employer in respect of:

  (i)   unpaid wages for the 13 weeks immediately prior to the declaration of bankruptcy;

  (ii) the payment of wages during the notice period; and

  (iii) unpaid holiday payments and extra holiday allowances for a period of one year at most immediately prior to the declaration of bankruptcy (§ 3.6.1); and

(10) A number of claims of employees that have arisen prior to the bankruptcy of their employer have a preferential rank[259].

Other issues

In addition to what has been mentioned above, a number of other issues arise in respect of employment agreements and their early termination pursuant to a bankruptcy. These issues are not discussed here, but include, *inter alia*, the following:

–   The possible application of the provisions preserving the rights in employment agreements in certain transfer of business cases[260];

–   The consequences of bankruptcy on end-of-term arrangements in employment agreements[261];

–   The consequences of bankruptcy on a non-competition clause in employment agreements;

–   The position of a director/employee in a bankruptcy; and

–   The possibilities, consequences and complications in respect of (temporary) continuation of labor in a bankruptcy.

International private law aspects

The international private law aspects attached to employment agreements and agencies in a bankruptcy will not be discussed[262].

---

257   HR 3 December 1999, *NJ* 2000, 53.
258   See article 61 WW read in conjunction with article 64 WW.
259   See article 3:288 sub(c)-(e) BW.
260   See articles 7:662-7:666 BW.
261   See, for example, the Nebig/Nolen-case (HR 23 May 1980, *NJ* 1980, 502).
262   See Van Galen/Van Apeldoorn, *supra* footnote 212, at pp. 109-125.

3.5.2.6   Right of retention

The scope of the right of retention

The right of retention is the right of a creditor to suspend – in the cases provided for by law – the release of an (moveable or immoveable) asset to a debtor until the claim of the creditor against the debtor is fully paid[263]. The right of retention is an indivisible right. This means that the claim, for the payment in respect of which the creditor is exercising a right of retention, has to be fully paid in order for the right to terminate.

An important requirement for the valid exercise of a right of retention over an asset of the debtor is that, directly or indirectly, the creditor must have factual control over such asset. Whether or not this is indeed the case, is to be determined by:
(1)   common opinion;
(2)   the Code; and
(3)   the circumstances as they appear.
Release is required to return the asset in the factual control of the debtor. For the special rules that exist with respect to immoveable assets, see § 5.3.3.1.

The content of the special rules pursuant to article 60 Fw

A bankruptcy of the debtor does not result in the loss of the right of retention by a creditor[264]. Nevertheless, article 60 Fw provides for some special rules with respect to the right of retention in a bankruptcy of a debtor. These special rules can be summarized as follows:

(1)   A trustee in bankruptcy is entitled (with the authorization of the supervisory judge in bankruptcy)[265] to demand the release of the asset over which the creditor has its right of retention in order to sell the asset[266];

(2)   The proceeds of a sale of such asset by the trustee in bankruptcy fall within the bankrupt estate and the creditor with the right of retention will merely keep its right of priority in respect of those proceeds[267]. After the sale has taken place, the creditor should be aware that he will have to share in the

---

263   See article 3:290 BW.
264   See article 60 paragraph 1 Fw.
265   See article 68 paragraph 2 Fw.
266   See article 60 paragraph 2 Fw.
267   See article 3:292 BW.

allocation of the bankruptcy costs before a (partial) distribution (if any) of the proceeds can be paid to him by the trustee in bankruptcy[268];

(3) To the extent it benefits the bankrupt estate, the trustee in bankruptcy may also return the asset to the bankrupt estate by paying the debt in respect of which the right of retention may be executed[269];

(4) The creditor with a valid right of retention is entitled to set a reasonable period of time for the trustee in bankruptcy to either:
    (i)   exercise his right to demand the asset and sell it; or
    (ii) return the asset to the bankrupt estate by redeeming the claim of the creditor[270].
    At the request of the trustee in bankruptcy such reasonable period of time may be extended several times by the supervisory judge in bankruptcy;

(5) If the trustee in bankruptcy has not sold the asset within a reasonable period of time set by the creditor, the creditor is entitled to sell the asset itself in accordance with the rules of summary execution applicable:
    (i)   to a pledgee, if the asset is a moveable good; and
    (ii) to a mortgagee, if the asset is an immoveable good; and

(6) With regard to a retained registered asset (such as immoveable assets, registered vessels and registered aircraft), the creditor is obliged to notify the trustee in bankruptcy, by bailiff's notification which must be recorded in the relevant public registers, of its intention to proceed with a sale in execution[271]. The notification should be provided to the trustee in bankruptcy within 14 days after the reasonable period of time set by the creditor to the trustee in bankruptcy – as mentioned above in (4) – has lapsed.

Retention of a client file

In the *Mr Middendorf/Mr Kouwenberg q.q.*-case[272], the Netherlands supreme court was asked to decide on the scope of an attorney's right to retain a client file where the client failed to pay the invoice. The client file concerned included information and documents relating to the legal services the attorney had been requested to perform for his client. The question to be resolved was whether an attorney continues to have a right of retention when:

---

268   For more details on sharing in the allocation of the bankruptcy costs, see § 3.4.3.2.
269   See article 60 paragraph 2 Fw.
270   See article 60 paragraph 3 Fw.
271   See article 60 paragraph 4 Fw.
272   HR 15 April 1994, *NJ* 1995, 640.

(1) a client is declared bankrupt;
(2) the client failed to pay the (entire) invoice(s) of the attorney; and
(3) the trustee in bankruptcy needs the client file for the information it contains.

The Netherlands supreme court evaluated the following two competing interests involved:
(i)   The interest of the trustee in bankruptcy to be able to obtain the information contained in the client file of the attorney; and
(ii) The interest of the attorney to continue to exercise his right of retention in order to get his invoice paid.

After evaluating the above competing interests, the Netherlands supreme court held that the continued exercise by the attorney of his right of retention of the client file would be unacceptable when measured by standards of reasonableness and fairness.

Situations of concurrence of rights

In respect of situations of concurrence between a right of retention versus a pledge and a right of retention versus a mortgage, see § 5.2.3.2 and § 5.3.3.1, respectively.

Summary
RIGHTS AND DUTIES OF A TRUSTEE IN BANKRUPTCY

Personal liability
The general standard for measuring the personal liability of a trustee in bankruptcy for his acts during the bankruptcy follows from the *Maclou*-case and must be specified in each case in which the standard is applied.

Lawsuits
(1) All lawsuits initiated against the debtor prior to its bankruptcy are suspended by virtue of law, provided that performance of an obligation by the bankrupt estate is demanded (such as, for example, a payment by the bankrupt estate). During the bankruptcy such lawsuits will only be continued in a reference procedure.
(2) Claims demanding performance of an obligation by the bankrupt estate can only be brought against the debtor by submitting such claim for verification with the trustee in bankruptcy.
(3) Claims not subject to verification should be initiated against the trustee in bankruptcy and, where a lawsuit has already been initiated, the creditor can summon the trustee in bankruptcy to take over the lawsuit from the debtor within a term set by the competent judge.

(4) During the bankruptcy the trustee in bankruptcy is entitled to initiate legal proceedings, provided that the authorization of the supervisory judge in bankruptcy has been obtained.

Agreements with mutual performances
(1) The special rules of article 37 Fw give the trustee in bankruptcy freedom to determine whether or not (further) compliance with the agreement is beneficial for the bankrupt estate.
(2) The counter party of the debtor has the right to summon the trustee in bankruptcy in writing in order to determine whether or not the trustee in bankruptcy is prepared to (further) comply with the obligations of the debtor under the agreement. If the trustee in bankruptcy is so prepared, he is required to provide security within a reasonable period of time set by the counter party.
(3) If the trustee in bankruptcy is not prepared to (further) comply with the obligations of the debtor under the agreement, or he fails to react (in time) to the summons of the counter party as mentioned above under (2), this results in the following 3 consequences:
    (i) The trustee in bankruptcy loses his right to demand compliance with the agreement;
    (ii) The claim for damages by the counter party qualifies as a non-preferential or ordinary claim, which will have to be submitted for verification with the trustee in bankruptcy; and
    (iii) The refusal by the trustee in bankruptcy to further comply with the obligations under the agreement results in a failure attributable to the debtor.

Hire-purchase agreements
(1) The special rules of article 38a Fw only apply in a bankruptcy of the lessee under a hire-purchase agreement.
(2) On the basis of article 38a Fw, both the trustee in bankruptcy and the lessor under the hire-purchase agreement have the right to immediately dissolve the hire-purchase agreement at any time.
(3) In respect of his unsettled claim against the lessee under the hire-purchase agreement, the lessor is entitled to submit such claim for verification with the trustee in bankruptcy, whereupon such claim will be qualified as a non-preferential or ordinary claim.

Rental agreements and lease agreements
(1) The special rules of article 39 Fw only apply in a bankruptcy of the lessee under a rental or lease agreement.
(2) Pursuant to article 39 Fw, the lessor under the rental or lease agreement and the trustee in bankruptcy (with the authorization of the supervisory

judge in bankruptcy) are entitled to an early termination of the agreement as long as they observe a notice period in accordance with local practice. A notice period of 3 months, in any case, will be considered sufficient.

(3) Claims following from the rental or lease agreement after adjudication of the bankruptcy are considered claims against the bankrupt estate.

Employment agreements and agencies

(1) The special rules of article 40 Fw only apply in a bankruptcy of an employer or a principal.

(2) Article 40 Fw provides for a right of early termination of the employment agreement or the agency by both the employee or agent and the trustee in bankruptcy (with the authorization of the supervisory judge in bankruptcy). Depending on the age of the employee involved, the maximum notice period to be observed is either 6 weeks or 19 weeks.

(3) In contrast to a suspension of payment (§ 2.3.1), a permit to terminate an employment agreement on the basis of article 6 BBA is not required.

(4) Claims following from an employment contract or agency arising after adjudication of the bankruptcy are considered to be claims against the bankrupt estate.

(5) The various restrictions in the Netherlands on termination of employment agreements (such as no termination during illness, pregnancy, *etc.*) do not apply in a bankruptcy.

Right of retention

(1) The bankruptcy of a debtor does not result in the loss of a right of retention by a creditor over a (moveable or immoveable) asset of the debtor.

(2) Article 60 Fw provides the trustee in bankruptcy with the right (after the authorization of the supervisory judge in bankruptcy) to demand the release of a retained asset in order to sell it, resulting in a required sharing in the allocation of the bankruptcy costs by the creditor having the right of retention.

(3) In a bankruptcy of his client, an attorney cannot continue to exercise his right of retention in respect of his client file in order to have his invoice paid.

3.6   Creditors in a bankruptcy

Creditors are an important group of players in a bankruptcy who have not yet been properly introduced. Chapter 5 will be entirely devoted to secured creditors holding a valid pledge or a valid mortgage. That is only one group of creditors. Here the focus will be on other groups of creditors, with only a brief introduction to secured creditors. To summarize, the different groups of creditors are as follows:

(1)   The secured creditors (§ 3.6.1).
      This group includes pledgees and mortgagees, who can act as if no bankruptcy exists;

(2)   The estate creditors (§ 3.6.2).
      These creditors fall outside the scope of the specific bankruptcy rules set forth in the Fw[273]. Estate creditors must be paid first from the proceeds of the bankrupt estate, before a distribution can be made to the pre-bankruptcy creditors[274]. In addition, estate creditors have no obligation to submit their claims for verification with the trustee in bankruptcy; and

(3)   The pre-bankruptcy creditors (§ 3.6.3).
      The rules set forth in the Fw are especially addressed to this group of creditors, which will be divided into the following categories[275]:
      (i)   The preferential creditors (§ 3.6.3.1);
      (ii) The non-preferential or ordinary creditors (§ 3.6.3.2); and
      (iii) The subordinated creditors (§ 3.6.3.3).

Finally, the possibility of creating a commission of creditors in a bankruptcy will be briefly addressed in § 3.6.4.

3.6.1   THE SECURED CREDITORS

The scope of the group

In this book, the group of secured creditors has been limited to those creditors who either hold a valid pledge or a valid mortgage over a good over which the debtor holds legal title. The reason for this restrictive definition is that only pledgees and mortgagees qualify as "*separatist*" in a bankruptcy of a debtor. This means that they can foreclose on their collateral as if no bankruptcy exists[276]. In Chapter 5, the pledge and the mortgage will be addressed in substantial detail. Here it suffices to mention only that[277]:

---

273   See article 24 Fw.
274   See article 182 paragraph 1 Fw.
275   From the Mr De Ranitz q.q. c.s./Ontvanger-case (HR 28 September 1990, *NJ* 1991, 305) it follows that a similar distinction of categories can be made in the group of estate creditors in case of a negative estate.
276   See article 57 paragraph 1 BW.
277   See article 227 paragraph 1 BW.

(1) a mortgage can be created over a registered good; and

(2) a pledge can be created over any other good.

Rights of secured creditors

The rights of secured creditors in a bankruptcy of the debtor can be summarized as follows:

(1) They can foreclose on their collateral as if no bankruptcy exists;

(2) They have a right of summary execution (§ 5.1);

(3) They are not obliged to submit their claims for verification with the trustee in bankruptcy; and

(4) They do not have to share in the allocation of the bankruptcy costs[278].

Rights of the trustee in bankruptcy

In respect of secured creditors, the trustee has the following two important rights he may wish to exercise:

(1) The trustee in bankruptcy can avoid a foreclosure by the secured creditors on their collateral by redeeming the unsettled secured claims the secured creditors have against the debtor (including the costs of foreclosure already made by those secured creditors)[279]; and

(2) The trustee in bankruptcy has the right to subject secured creditors to a reasonable term to foreclose on their collateral (§ 3.4.2.2). In the event that this period lapses without the collateral being sold by the secured creditor, the trustee in bankruptcy is entitled to claim the collateral in order to sell it on his own for the benefit of the bankrupt estate. In the case of such a sale of the collateral by the trustee in bankruptcy, the secured creditor maintains its right of preference over the proceeds of such sale. However, a distribution of such proceeds can only take place[280]:

(i)   after an allocation of the bankruptcy costs;

(ii) after a verification meeting for creditors has taken place (§ 3.4.3.2); and

(iii) only on the basis of an approved plan of distribution on which the secured creditor is listed as a preferential creditor in respect of the proceeds of the sale of the collateral.

---

278   See article 182 paragraph 1 Fw.
279   See article 58 paragraph 2 Fw.
280   See the MeesPierson/Mr Mentink q.q.-case (HR 30 June 1995, *NJ* 1996, 554).

3.6.2   THE ESTATE CREDITORS

The scope of the group

When does a claim qualify as a claim against the estate, making the holder of
such a claim an estate creditor? A claim could qualify as a claim against the estate
in the following 3 ways:
(1) by virtue of law;
(2) pursuant to case law of the Netherlands supreme court; and
(3) by meeting the requirements to qualify as such.

Ad. (1)
Examples of claims that qualify as claims against the bankrupt estate by virtue of
law are:
(i)   claims arising after the date the bankruptcy was adjudicated from an agree-
      ment to which the special rules set forth in article 39 Fw apply (§.5.2.4); and
(ii) claims arising after the date the bankruptcy was adjudicated from an agree-
      ment to which the special rules set forth in article 40 Fw apply (§ 3.5.2.5).

Ad. (2)
Examples of claims that qualify as claims against the bankrupt estate pursuant to
case law of the Netherlands supreme court are:
(i)   pension claims relating to the financing of the so-called "backservice ob-
      ligations" pursuant to the *Mr Frima q.q./Blankers*-case[281] (§ 3.5.2.5); and
(ii) claims for payment of cash for holidays that have not been used by em-
      ployees pursuant to the *LISV/Mr Wilderink q.q.*-case[282] (§ 3.5.2.5).

Ad. (3)
If claims do not qualify as claims against the bankrupt estate by virtue of law or
pursuant to case law of the Netherlands supreme court, they still can qualify as
claims against the bankrupt estate if they meet the following two requirements[283]:
(i)   The claim must arise after the date the bankruptcy was adjudicated; and
(ii) The claim must be attributable to acts performed by or on behalf of the
      trustee in bankruptcy to a substantial degree.

Rights of estate creditors

The rights of estate creditors in a bankruptcy of the debtor can be summarized as
follows:

---

281   HR 12 November 1993, *NJ* 1994, 229.
282   HR 3 December 1999, *NJ* 2000, 53.
283   For a more detailed discussion of the rules for measuring the type of a claim, see Boekraad,
      supra footnote 200, at pp. 49-57.

(1) Claims against the bankrupt estate give the estate creditors an immediate right against the bankrupt estate, which should be paid immediately from the proceeds of the bankrupt estate[284]. These are claims against the trustee in bankruptcy in his capacity of trustee in bankruptcy rather than against the debtor;

(2) There is no need for estate creditors to submit their claims for verification with the trustee in bankruptcy; and

(3) Estate creditors are entitled to seek recourse for their unsettled claims during the bankruptcy by:

    (i) commencing a lawsuit against the trustee in bankruptcy[285]; and/or

    (ii) making an arrest on the bankruptcy account of the trustee in bankruptcy.

Ranking

In the *Mr De Ranitz q.q. c.s./Ontvanger*-case[286], the Netherlands supreme court held that in a bankruptcy with a negative estate[287] a ranking similar to that among pre-bankruptcy creditors should be observed among estate creditors (§ 3.6.3). That means that the preferential estate creditors will be paid out prior to the non-preferential or ordinary estate creditors. The fees and costs of the trustee in bankruptcy have the highest rank and will therefore be paid out first.

Characterization of bankruptcy costs

In the Netherlands there is an ongoing discussion about the distinction between[288]:

(1) bankruptcy costs that are general in nature; and

(2) bankruptcy costs that are specific in nature.

In short, bankruptcy costs consist of the total amount paid from the bankrupt estate to the estate creditors. Certain creditors are obliged to share in the allocation of the bankruptcy costs[289]. For that purpose, a percentage of the allocation of the bankruptcy costs needs to be calculated.

Bankruptcy costs that are general in nature must be included in the calculation of the "allocation of bankruptcy costs"-percentage, while bankruptcy costs that are

---

284   See Van der Feltz 2-I, *supra* footnote 233, at p. 384.

285   See article 25 paragraph 1 Fw.

286   HR 28 September 1990, *NJ* 1991, 305.

287   A bankruptcy has a negative estate if there are insufficient proceeds to fully pay all the estate creditors. See also § 3.4.3.1.

288   For more details on this discussion, see Boekraad, *supra* footnote 200, at pp. 84-104.

289   This follows from article 182 Fw.

specific in nature should be excluded[290]. Different views exist on how certain bankruptcy costs should be characterized and consequently should or should not be included in the calculation of the "allocation of bankruptcy costs"-percentage. In practice, these different views can result in different outcomes as to what is distributed to the creditors and therefore have substantial financial consequences. These differing views and their financial consequences in practice will not be discussed further.

3.6.3   THE PRE-BANKRUPTCY CREDITORS

The scope of the group

Pre-bankruptcy creditors are those creditors whose claim against the debtor arose prior to the adjudication of the bankruptcy of the debtor and the application of the resulting principle of fixation[291]. During the course of the bankruptcy of the debtor pre-bankruptcy creditors demanding payment from the bankrupt estate can only bring their claims against the debtor by submitting them for verification with the trustee in bankruptcy[292]. When submitting their claims for verification, the creditors have to include documents evidencing the nature of, the grounds for and the amount of their claim. In addition, they will have to indicate whether they believe they have a preference, priority, pledge, mortgage or right of retention[293]. For further details in respect of the procedure of verification, see § 3.4.3.2.

Below, the following categories of pre-bankruptcy creditors will be briefly addressed:
(1)   The preferential creditors (§ 3.6.3.1);
(2)   The non-preferential or ordinary creditors (§ 3.6.3.2); and
(3)   The subordinated creditors (§ 3.6.3.3).

Creditors having claims that are not subject to verification

A separate category of creditors is formed by creditors:
(1)   having claims that arose after the bankruptcy of debtor was adjudicated; and
(2)   which claims do not qualify as claims against the estate.
These creditors are referred to as "creditors having claims that are not subject to verification". This category of creditors will not be discussed further.

---

290   This has been confirmed by the Netherlands supreme court in the MeesPierson/Mr Mentink q.q.-case (HR 30 June 1995, *NJ* 1996, 554).
291   See Boekraad, *supra* footnote 200, at page 7.
292   See article 26 Fw.
293   See article 110 Fw.

3.6.3.1   Preferential creditors

This category of pre-bankruptcy creditors consists of all those creditors that benefit from a preferential right (or right of privilege). The following general rules of guidance exist in the Netherlands:

(1) Preferential rights arise by virtue of law only[294];
(2) Preferential rights are either:
     (i)   special preferential rights which are attached to certain goods only; or
     (ii) general preferential rights which are attached to all goods that are included in a property;
(3) Unless otherwise provided by law, special preferential rights have priority over general preferential rights[295];
(4) Unless otherwise provided by law, all special preferential rights rank equally[296]; and
(5) General preferential rights are ranked in the way provided by law[297].

Both the tax authorities and the social security board are important preferential creditors in a bankruptcy. For different aspects of their respective positions, see:
–   § 3.4.3.1, for the position of the tax authorities and the social security board in an improper discontinuation of a bankruptcy.
–   § 3.5.2.5, for the position of social security board in respect of employment agreements in a bankruptcy; and
–   § 5.2.3.1, for the fiscal privileged ground right of the tax authorities;
In addition to the tax authorities and the social security board, there are a substantial number of different preferential rights set forth in different laws. All those different types of preferential rights will not be discussed further.

3.6.3.2   Non-preferential or ordinary creditors

The category of non-preferential or ordinary creditors consists of those pre-bankruptcy creditors who do not have the benefit of a preferential right (or right of privilege), but at the same time they have not agreed (or are not subjected) to a subordination of their claims.

Non-preferential or ordinary creditors rank equally among themselves[298]. They rank lower than the preferential creditors (§ 3.6.3.1), but higher than the subordinated creditors (§ 3.6.3.3).

---

294   See article 278 paragraph 2 BW.
295   See article 3:280 BW.
296   See article 3:281 paragraph 1 Fw.
297   See article 3:281 paragraph 2 Fw read in conjunction with article 3:288 BW.
298   See article 3:277 paragraph 1 Fw.

3.6.3.3   Subordinated creditors

Similar to the category of non-preferential or ordinary creditors, the category of subordinated creditors consists of pre-bankruptcy creditors who do not have the benefit of a preferential right (or right of privilege). The difference between them is subordinated creditors have agreed (or are subjected) to a subordination of their claims.

Contractual subordination

According to Netherlands law, a creditor and a debtor are entitled to contractually agree to a subordination[299]. The exact wording of the subordination is very important in determining the exact scope of the subordination. The following two types of subordination can be distinguished:
(1)   proper subordination; and
(2)   improper subordination.

Ad. (1)
A proper subordination is a subordination pursuant to which the claim of the creditor against the debtor will be subordinated in rank to all or certain other creditors of the debtor[300]. In a proper subordination, the subordinated creditor keeps his right of recourse on all goods of the debtor. Only his rank vis-à-vis all or some other creditors is lowered.

Ad. (2)
In an improper subordination the subordination is not limited to rank only, but may also relate to the ability to claim on certain obligations and/or to the right to claim itself.

Subordination by virtue of law

Aside from contractually agreed subordination, subordination by virtue of law also exists. An example is shareholders of the company who are subordinated in relation to the other creditors of the company[301].

Issues relating to subordination

Many issues exist in respect of subordination. An example is whether or not a

---

299   See article 3:277 paragraph 2 Fw.
300   See *"Enkele insolventievragen bij de positie van de achtergestelde crediteur"*, by Prof. mr B. Wessels in *TvI*, 1, 1995, pp. 7-12, at page 8.
301   See article 2:23b paragraph 1 BW.

subordination clause also qualifies as a third party stipulation[302]. These issues will not be listed or addressed here[303].

3.6.4   COMMISSION OF CREDITORS

Commission of creditors is addressed in articles 74-79 Fw. Such a commission of creditors is not set up in the majority of bankruptcies in the Netherlands. Therefore, only the main features of a commission of creditors will be briefly discussed below.

Two types of commissions of creditors in a bankruptcy are distinguished:
(1) temporary commission; and
(2) permanent commission.

Temporary commission

To the extent so required by the importance or the nature of the bankrupt estate, the competent court is entitled to appoint a temporary commission out of the known creditors of the debtor consisting of one to three members[304]. Where a member of the temporary commission does not accept his appointment, resigns or dies, the competent court will fill the vacancy by choosing one of two candidates recommended by the supervisory judge in bankruptcy[305]. A temporary commission can be appointed:
(i)   in the judgment holding the declaration of the bankruptcy of the debtor; or
(ii) pursuant to a later order by the competent court.
The temporary commission can remain in place until a permanent commission is appointed.

Permanent commission

After the completion of the verification at the verification meeting for creditors, the creditors will be consulted by the supervisory judge in bankruptcy about the appointment of a permanent commission from their midst[306]. This consultation takes place irrespective of whether or not a temporary commission has been appointed. If so desired by the creditors, the supervisory judge in bankruptcy will forthwith proceed with the appointment of a permanent commission, which, simi-

---

302   See article 6:253 BW and *"De achtergestelde geldlening nog eens ontrafeld"*, by Prof. mr H.J. Pabbruwe in *WPNR* 6338, 1998, pp. 766-771.
303   See generally *"De achtergestelde vordering, in het bijzonder de achtergestelde lening"*, by Mr A. van Hees, Kluwer 1989, Deventer, pp. 1-170.
304   See article 74 paragraph 1 Fw.
305   See article 74 paragraph 2 Fw.
306   See article 75 paragraph 1 Fw.

lar to the temporary commission, may consist of one to three members. If a member of the permanent commission does not accept this appointment, resigns or dies, the vacancy will be filed by the supervisory judge in bankruptcy[307].

The rights of a commission of creditors

A commission of creditors in a bankruptcy can primarily exercise the following 3 rights:
(1) The right to advise the trustee in bankruptcy;
(2) The right to request the supervisory judge to determine a matter; and
(3) The right to inspect books and documents relating to the bankruptcy.

Ad. (1)
The primary power of both the temporary and the permanent commission is to render advice to the trustee in bankruptcy[308]. The trustee in bankruptcy is required to request for the advice of the commission in – *inter alia* – the following cases[309]:
(i)   Prior to commencing a lawsuit or continuing an already existing lawsuit (with the exception of verification lawsuits);
(ii)   When a decision has to be made whether or not the business of the debtor should be continued;
(iii)   When the trustee in bankruptcy intends to exercise his rights in respect of an agreement pursuant to articles 37, 39 and 40 Fw;
(iv)   When the trustee in bankruptcy intends to exercise his right to redeem a pledge or mortgage;
(v)   When the trustee in bankruptcy intends to sell goods of the debtor;
(vi)   When the trustee in bankruptcy intends to use the services of the debtor in the liquidation of the assets of the debtor[310]; and
(vii) In a broad range of issues in respect of liquidation and realization of the bankrupt estate, including the time and amount of distribution to be made to creditors.
The trustee in bankruptcy meets with the commission in order to obtain advice as frequently as the trustee in bankruptcy deems necessary[311]. The trustee in bankruptcy presides over such meetings and prepares the minutes thereof. If the trustee in bankruptcy has called a meeting of the commission upon adequate notice in order to obtain an advice and such advice is not rendered by the commission, the trustee in bankruptcy may act without the commission's input[312].

---

307   See article 75 paragraph 3 Fw.
308   See article 74 paragraph 1 Fw read in conjunction with article 78 Fw.
309   See article 78 paragraph 1 Fw.
310   See article 177 Fw.
311   See article 77 Fw.
312   See article 78 paragraph 2 Fw.

Ad. (2)

The trustee in bankruptcy is not bound by the advice of the commission[313]. If the trustee in bankruptcy intends not to follow the advice of the commission, he must notify the commission. The commission is then entitled to request the supervisory judge in bankruptcy to determine the matter. If the commission wishes to obtain the decision of the supervisory judge in bankruptcy, the trustee in bankruptcy is obliged to suspend performance of any intended transaction which is contrary to the advice of the commission for 3 days. The omission of the trustee in bankruptcy to request for advice from the commission does not, as regards third parties, render any transaction by the trustee in bankruptcy invalid[314].

Ad. (3)

The commission may, at any time, request to see books and documents relating to the bankruptcy[315]. The trustee in bankruptcy has a duty to provide the commission with all information required by the commission.

Summary
THE CREDITORS IN A BANKRUPTCY

The secured creditors
(1) The group of secured creditors consists of pledgees and mortgagees.
(2) Pledgees and mortgagees can foreclose on their collateral as if no bankruptcy of the debtor exists.
(3) For a detailed discussion of pledgees and mortgagees, see Chapter 5.

The estate creditors
(1) Generally, claims against the bankrupt estate:
    (i)   must arise after the date the bankruptcy was adjudicated; and
    (ii) must be attributable to acts performed by or on behalf of the trustee in bankruptcy to a substantial degree.
(2) Claims can also qualify as claims against the bankrupt estate:
    (i)   by virtue of law; or
    (ii) pursuant to case law of the Netherlands supreme court.
(3) In a bankruptcy with a negative estate a ranking similar to that among pre-bankruptcy creditors should be observed among estate creditors.

The pre-bankruptcy creditors
(1) Preferential creditors have the highest rank among the pre-bankruptcy creditors.

---

313   See article 79 Fw.
314   See article 72 Fw.
315   See article 76 Fw.

(2) Amongst themselves, preferential creditors with a special preferential right rank higher than those with a general preferential right.

(3) Non-preferential or ordinary creditors rank equally among themselves. They rank below preferential creditors and above subordinated creditors.

(4) Between themselves, the individual rank of the subordinated creditors depends on the kind of subordination they have.

The commission of creditors

(1) Both temporary and permanent commissions of creditors can be appointed. In practice this does not take place often.

(2) A commission of creditors in a bankruptcy can primarily exercise the following 3 rights:

    (i) The right to advise the trustee in bankruptcy;

    (ii) The right to request the supervisory judge to determine a matter; and

    (iii) The right to inspect books and documents relating to the bankruptcy.

3.7 Recent developments

Similar to what has been described in § 2.6 for suspension of payment, the most relevant recent development for bankruptcy is also the MDW-Project.

3.7.1 MDW-PROJECT

The MDW-Project aims to investigate whether or not it is possible to enhance the "reorganizational ability" of the Fw. The focus thereby is on suspension of payment. The MDW-Project searches for possibilities of (re)structuring the suspension of payment regime in the Fw in such a way that it once again satisfies its original purpose in practice. Suspension of payment should be requested in view of and result in a continuation of the business of the debtor, after a reorganization. It should not, as is currently too often the case, automatically result in bankruptcy.

Although, the main changes are intended to take place in the suspension of payment regime, the MDW-Project also considers amendments to the bankruptcy regime in the Fw. The first stage of the MDW-Project was completed in July 2000, with the submission of Bill 27 244 to the Second Chamber of Parliament. The most important changes to the bankruptcy regime suggested in Bill 27 244 will be briefly addressed below in § 3.7.1.1.

The second stage of the MDW-Project is still ongoing. Participation in public debate on further reform of the Netherlands insolvency laws in the context of the MDW-Project is encouraged. For that purpose a website has been created at www.mdw.ez.nl where relevant documents can be accessed and reactions and opinions can be posted. Thus far, the second stage of the MDW-Project has resulted in the MDW-Discussion Paper drafted by the MDW-Working Group. The most important issues covered by the MDW-Discussion Paper in respect of bankruptcy will be briefly addressed below in § 3.7.1.2.

3.7.1.1   The most important changes to bankruptcy suggested by Bill 27 244

The most important changes to the bankruptcy regime suggested by Bill 27 244 relate to the following issues:

(1) Insolvency stay will change and become longer;
(2) The position of energy providers of the debtor will change;
(3) The quorum for a composition will change;
(4) The rights and duties of the supervisory judge will change; and
(5) A central public register for information concerning bankruptcies will be established.

The main features of each of these issues will be briefly discussed below.

Ad. (1) Insolvency stay will change and become longer

Bill 27 244[316] entitles the supervisory judge in bankruptcy – at the request of every interested party or *ex officio* – to issue an insolvency stay order for a maximum period of 2 months. During that period any right of third parties – with the exception of estate creditors – to (i) take recourse against assets belonging to the estate or (ii) claim assets which are in the control of the debtor or the trustee in bankruptcy, may only be exercised with the authorization of the supervisory judge. The supervisory judge may extend this period once only for another period of 2 months at most. Consequently, pursuant to Bill 27 244 an insolvency stay can last for a maximum period of 4 months (instead of 2 months under the present rules).

Some other new features of the insolvency stay pursuant to Bill 27 244 are the following:

(i)   Third parties that cannot exercise their right to recourse or to claim during the insolvency stay are granted reasonable compensation by the supervisory judge[317]. This compensation will rank as an estate claim;

---

316   See article 63a paragraph 1 of Bill 27 244.

(ii) During the insolvency stay the trustee in bankruptcy has the right to use, consume or transfer goods covered by the insolvency stay, provided that[318]:

    (a) the debtor had such right to use, consume or transfer such goods prior to its bankruptcy;

    (b) to the extent the exercise of the right mentioned above under (a) is appropriate in the continuation of the normal business of the debtor; and

    (c) the trustee in bankruptcy should not reasonably suspect that the estate is insufficient to compensate those who sustained damages as a result of the exercise of the right mentioned above under (a).

Unless otherwise decided by the supervisory judge, this rule even applies when such right terminates as a consequence of the bankruptcy;

(iii) The rule mentioned above in (ii) does not apply to securities, rights in respect of securities and credit claims[319]. In addition, in respect of registered goods, the trustee in bankruptcy only has a right to use these goods;

(iv) The rule mentioned above in (ii) does also not apply where the debtor is entitled to transfer a good pursuant to an agreement of mandate to act as intermediary in its own name[320];

(v) The person who sustains damages as a result of the exercise of the right mentioned above in (ii), will be granted reasonable compensation by the supervisory judge[321]. This compensation will also rank as an estate claim;

(vi) A pledgor of an undisclosed pledge is entitled, during the insolvency stay, to make a notification to disclose its pledge and collect payments[322]; and

(vii) Unless otherwise decided by the supervisory judge, the Netherlands tax authorities are not entitled, during the insolvency stay, to execute a ground arrest they have made[323].

Ad. (2)   The position of energy providers of the debtor will change

In § 1.2.2 factual preference of energy providers has been discussed as an exception to the principle of *paritas creditorum*. Bill 27 244 suggests a change to this position.

Where the debtor fails to pay a debt arisen prior to the bankruptcy, the provider of gas, water, electricity or heating may not suspend, during the bankruptcy, its

---

317   See article 63a paragraph 3 of Bill 27 244.

318   See article 63b paragraph 1 read in conjunction with paragraphs 3 and 5 of Bill 27 244.

319   See article 63b paragraph 2 of Bill 27 244.

320   See article 63b paragraph 6 of Bill 27 244.

321   See article 63b paragraph 4 of Bill 27 244.

322   See article 63c paragraph 1 of Bill 27 244. For further details on undisclosed pledges, see § 5.2.1.4.

323   See article 63d paragraph 1 of Bill 27 244. For further details on the ground arrest of the Netherlands tax authorities, see § 5.2.3.1.

compliance with the obligation pursuant to its agreement with the debtor to provide gas, water, electricity or heating on a regular basis where it is a first necessity of life [324]. In addition, Bill 27 244 does not entitle such suspension where
energy is necessary for the continuation of the business of the debtor.

Moreover, a default by the debtor to pay a debt arisen prior to the bankruptcy is
not a valid ground for the energy provider to terminate the agreement with the
debtor for the provision of gas, water, electricity or heating[325]. Where there is a
clause:
(i)   resulting in an automatic termination of the agreement in the event of a de-
      fault; or
(ii) indicating that bankruptcy of the debtor is a ground for termination of said
      agreement,
it can only be invoked by the energy provider with the approval of the trustee in
bankruptcy[326].

Ad. (3)   The quorum for a composition will change

As indicated in § 3.4.3.3, the quorum needed for a composition to be accepted
under the present rules is the consent of 2/3 of the admitted and provisionally admitted creditors representing 3/4 of the amount of the non-preferential admitted
and provisionally admitted claims. Bill 27 244 suggests changing this.

Pursuant to Bill 27 244[327] for a composition to be accepted it is required to have
the consent of:
(i)   the normal majority of the admitted and provisionally admitted creditors
      present at the meeting; and
(ii) those creditors must collectively represent at least 1/2 of the amount of the
      non-preferential admitted and provisionally admitted claims.

Ad. (4)   The rights and duties of the supervisory judge will change

In § 3.4.3.2. the concept of reference proceedings was briefly discussed in context of claims of creditors being challenged when submitted for verification in a
bankruptcy. Bill 27 244 requires a supervisory judge in bankruptcy – prior to referring a challenged claim to reference proceedings – to first attempt to reach a
settlement between the parties involved[328].

---

324   See article 37b paragraph 1 of Bill 27 244.
325   See article 37b paragraph 2 of Bill 27 244.
326   See article 37b paragraph 3 of Bill 27 244.
327   See article 145 of Bill 27 244.
328   See article 122 paragraph 1 of Bill 27 244.

Similar to the supervisory judge in a suspension of payment, Bill 27 244 grants the supervisory judge in a bankruptcy, in certain circumstances, the right – by way of a court order explaining the grounds – to accept a proposed composition as if it were approved[329].

Ad. (5) A central public register for information concerning bankruptcies will be established

Bill 27 244 requires the Minister of Justice to establish and operate a central register[330]. In this register all information concerning bankruptcies, which is currently kept by each district court individually in its own register, is to be compiled. Any person will be able to obtain an extract from this central register upon payment[331].

3.7.1.2   The most important issues covered by the MDW-Discussion Paper in
           respect of bankruptcy

The MDW-Discussion Paper and an English summary thereof are posted on the website at www.mdw.ez.nl.

In the MDW-Discussion Paper, the MDW-Working Group recommends the following 22 issues for consultation[332]:

(1) The stigma associated with bankruptcy, viewed in relation to the possibilities to start with a "clean slate";
(2) The purposes of the Fw and the rules of conduct to be observed by the trustees in bankruptcy, the administrators and the supervisory judges need to observe when performing the duties assigned to them are unclear. They have to choose between the following options:
    (i)   continuation of the business and employment;
    (ii) maximalization of the proceeds of the estate in order to satisfy the creditors; or
    (iii) a combination of (i) and (ii) above;
(3) The strict distinction between bankruptcy (which according to the Fw should be aimed at liquidation) and suspension of payment (which is aimed at continuation) is blurred. This seems to result from:
    (i)   the use of bankruptcies for reorganization of businesses (or parts thereof) by way of restart; and
    (ii) the fact that suspension of payment oftentimes results in a bankruptcy.

---

329   See article 146 of Bill 27 244.
330   See article 19a paragraph 1 of Bill 27 244.
331   See article 19a paragraph 3 of Bill 27 244.
332   See pages 6 and 7 of the MDW-Discussion Paper.

This presents the question whether or not both insolvency proceedings should be interwoven and a court should be able to apply – also against the will of the petitioner – a regime other than that which was requested (with the possibility to request for precautionary measures);

(4) Clear rules for restart-procedures are missing (*e.g.* rules concerning the administration and supervision of the business that is continued and rules concerning the maximalization of proceeds for the estate (*e.g.* an auction obligation));

(5) Incentives for a timely filing of requests are missing and consequently requests for bankruptcy and suspension of payment are filed too late. Further, the information duty on the debtor is inadequate (also for a court to be able to judge whether or not the appropriate insolvency proceedings have been requested);

(6) The criteria for judging the timeliness of the filing of a request (and the choice based thereupon) for "insolvency" and "viability of the business" are insufficient;

(7) There is insufficient insight in respect of:
   (i) the (peaceful) preliminary stage of insolvencies; and
   (ii) the ways in which companies are able – with the assistance of financiers and/or other third parties – to resolve their problems (as if they were under a "silent receivership");

(8) Clear principles for workouts are missing;

(9) The influence of the inequality of information for the position of (distinguishable groups of) creditors;

(10) The limited possibilities for extra-judicial settlements and compositions;

(11) The duration of insolvency proceedings, the opportunity for verification and other disputes and the complications this gives rise to, *inter alia*, for (commissions of) creditors;

(12) The limited possibilities to decrease employment costs by way of disposing of redundant employees, considered in view of the "restart" that is commonly used for this purpose;

(13) The determination of which obligations qualify as bankruptcy costs;

(14) The (justification of) the nature and the extent of the privileged positions of the Netherlands tax authorities (especially the fiscal privileged ground right[333]) and of the social security boards;

(15) The influence of the privileged position of certain claims – together with the fiscal privileged ground right of the Netherlands tax authorities – on the recovery rate for non-preferential or ordinary creditors, resulting in the question whether or not this system needs to be reviewed or abolished;

---

333   For more details on the fiscal privileged ground right of the Netherlands tax authorities, see § 5.2.3.1.

(16) The influence of separate foreclosures on the going concern value, resulting in the question whether or not the trustee in bankruptcy should be granted the right to exercise such separate foreclosures on his own;

(17) The position of counter parties in long-term agreements and the consequences of their termination in or prior to an insolvency. Also the question whether or not the law should provide for (further) provisions concerning (mandatory) continuation of financing the provision of goods or services respectively;

(18) Specific rules are missing concerning insolvency of companies that are part of a group of other companies and legal entities;

(19) When invalidating legal acts on the basis of the *actio pauliana*[334], problems exist in respect of the obligation to furnish facts and the burden of proof;

(20) Clear (and harmonized) principles are missing for insolvencies having cross-border effects. In this context it is noted that while the EU Insolvency Regulation becomes effective on 31 May 2002[335], this issue will only concern non-EU member states and Demark;

(21) The expertise of, and specialization and interdisciplinary cooperation within, the judiciary and, to a lesser extent, the legal profession. The judiciary seems to have lost its grip on the application of the insolvency laws as a result of:

    (i) the trend that important parts of the legal profession withdraw from the insolvency practice; and

    (ii) the existence of little interdisciplinary cooperation between the judiciary, the legal profession, accountants, experts in the financial-economical field and interim-managers; and

(22) The rules in respect of creditors with a factual preference[336].

These issues are (partly) further addressed in the MDW-Discussion Paper itself. It would go beyond the scope of this book to provide for a more detailed description of the contents of the MDW-Discussion Paper.

As a final remark on the MDW-Project, it should be noted that views differ significantly in the Netherlands as to what the actual amendments to the Netherlands insolvency laws (if any) should be[337]. It is therefore not at all clear what will eventually result from the MDW-Project. The public debate is still in progress with no end in sight.

---

334 For more details on the *actio pauliana*, see § 4.1.
335 For more details on the EU Insolvency Regulation, see § 1.2.5.1.
336 For an example of a creditor with a factual preference, see § 1.2.2.
337 For a taste of the range of views on how the future Netherlands insolvency laws is to develop, see the legal literature list included in exhibit 1 to the MDW-Discussion Paper.

Summary
THE MDW-PROJECT

Bill 27 244
(1) The first stage of the MDW-Project was completed in July 2000 with the submission of Bill 27 244 to the Second Chamber of Parliament.
(2) Bill 27 244 is a proposal to, *inter alia*, amend the Fw, but has not yet been adopted by Parliament.
(3) The most important changes to bankruptcy suggested by Bill 27 244 relate to the following issues:
  (i)   The insolvency stay will change and become longer;
  (ii) The position of energy providers of the debtor will change;
  (iii) The quorum for a composition will change;
  (iv) The rights and duties of the supervisory judge will change; and
  (v)   A central public register for information concerning bankruptcies will be established.

The MDW-Discussion Paper
(1) The MDW-Discussion Paper and an English summary thereof are posted on the website at www.mdw.ez.nl.
(2) In the MDW-Discussion Paper the MDW-Working Group has recommended 22 issues for consultation.

MDW-Project
Public debate on the MDW-Project is still in progress. It is uncertain if and when this will result in any amendments to the Netherlands insolvency laws.

Chapter 4
IMPORTANT LEGAL CONCEPTS IN INSOLVENCY LAW

This Chapter aims to address the most important legal concepts typical in insolvencies in general and insolvencies in the Netherlands in particular.

In § 4.1 the complex avoiding power of *actio pauliana* will be discussed. The *actio pauliana*, which grants a trustee in bankruptcy special powers to challenge pre-bankruptcy transactions, will be addressed for:
(1) voluntary legal acts conducted by the debtor (§ 4.1.1); and
(2) obligatory legal acts conducted by the debtor (§ 4.1.2).

In § 4.2 the legal concept of set-off will be addressed. First, the general set-off provision pursuant to article 53 Fw will be discussed (§ 4.2.1). Subsequently, the prohibition on using the right of set-off pursuant to article 54 Fw will be dealt with (§ 4.2.2).

In § 4.3 the following different types of corporate liabilities in a bankruptcy will be discussed:
(1) liability of directors (§ 4.3.1), both internal liability (§ 4.3.1.1) and external liability (§ 4.3.1.2);
(2) liability of directors of the supervisory board (§ 4.3.2); and
(3) liability of shareholders (§ 4.3.3).

Finally, in § 4.4 the concept of wrongful act will be briefly touched upon.

4.1 The *actio pauliana*

In § 3.5, the rights and duties of a trustee in bankruptcy have been addressed by looking at a number of common situations for a trustee in bankruptcy to deal with in a bankruptcy. For those situations, the specific rights and duties of a trustee in bankruptcy were set forth. In addition, in § 3.4.2.2, reference was made to the special right a trustee in bankruptcy has vis-à-vis holders of a valid right of pledge or a valid right of mortgage (see also § 3.6.1). Now the focus will be on the special rights granted in the Fw to a trustee in bankruptcy to avoid pre-bankruptcy transactions which are detrimental to the bankrupt estate on the basis of *actio pauliana*.

The actio pauliana outside a bankruptcy

The concept of *actio pauliana* resembles, but is not identical to, concepts of "fraudulent conveyance" and "preferred transaction" known in other jurisdictions. Outside a bankruptcy, creditors have the right to invoke an *actio pauliana* against their debtor. This means that a creditor has the right to invalidate (*i.e.* declare null and void) a voluntary legal act by the debtor if the debtor and his counter party knew or should have known that this act would adversely affect the means of recourse of one or more of the creditors of the debtor[1]. The *actio pauliana* can be invoked by any creditor whose means of recourse against the debtor has been adversely affected, irrespective of whether the claim arose prior to or after the voluntary legal act by the debtor.

As soon as the debtor is declared bankrupt, its creditors lose their right to invoke the *actio pauliana*.[2] Instead, it is now the court appointed trustee in bankruptcy who is granted the exclusive right to invoke the *actio pauliana*. Compared to that of creditors outside a bankruptcy of the debtor, the *actio pauliana* of a trustee in bankruptcy has wider scope; the trustee in bankruptcy not only has the right to invalidate voluntary legal acts by the debtor conducted prior to the bankruptcy of the debtor (§ 4.1.1)[3], but he also has the right to invalidate obligatory legal acts by the debtor performed prior to the bankruptcy (§ 4.1.2)[4].

Voluntary acts conducted by the debtor after being declared bankrupt

The avoiding power of *actio pauliana* of a trustee in bankruptcy does not extend to legal acts (voluntary or obligatory) conducted by the debtor after its bankruptcy. This is not surprising, because – as mentioned in § 1.2.1 – the bankrupt estate is only liable to the extent it benefits from the obligations that have arisen after the declaration of bankruptcy[5].

4.1.1   THE *ACTIO PAULIANA* IN RESPECT OF VOLUNTARY LEGAL ACTS BY THE DEBTOR

Pursuant to article 42 Fw a trustee in bankruptcy is entitled to invalidate – for the benefit of the bankrupt estate – any voluntary legal act (such as the entering into an agreement for which no legal obligation exists) conducted by the debtor prior

---

1   See article 3:45 paragraph 1 BW.
2   This follows (indirectly) from article 49 paragraph 2 Fw.
3   See article 42 Fw.
4   See article 47 Fw.
5   See article 24 Fw.

to the adjudication of bankruptcy, provided that the debtor and his counter party had (or should have had) knowledge that such an act could have an adverse effect on the rights of recourse of creditors of the debtor. In order for the *actio pauliana* to have effect, an extra-judicial statement by the trustee in bankruptcy suffices[6]. In principle, by sending this statement in which the trustee in bankruptcy invokes the *actio pauliana,* the legal act concerned is invalidated, provided that all elements of the *actio pauliana* are met. In practice, where there is disagreement in respect of the validity of the *actio pauliana*, the trustee in bankruptcy will usually bring the matter to court after sending the statement invoking the *actio pauliana*[7]. By doing so the trustee in bankruptcy wishes to achieve the following:

(1) to obtain a declaration of law of the court stating that the invoked *actio pauliana* is valid; and

(2) to ensure that the debtor and the counter party of the debtor fully comply with their obligations resulting from a validly invoked *actio pauliana*.

4.1.1.1   The requirements for a valid *actio pauliana*

Article 42 Fw

For a valid *actio pauliana* in respect of voluntary legal acts by the debtor, the following requirements must be met[8]:

(1) There must be a legal act by the debtor;

(2) Such legal act must be conducted voluntarily;

(3) As a consequence of this legal act the creditors of the debtor must be prejudiced;

(4) The debtor must have had knowledge of this prejudice; and

(5) Where the legal act has been for consideration, the counter party of the debtor must also have had knowledge of the prejudice[9].

Ad. (1)
A legal act requires an intention to procure legal effects, which intention has manifested itself through a declaration[10]. Consequently, factual acts as well as omissions to act cannot be challenged by invoking the *actio pauliana*.

---

6   Please note that the requirements for an extra-judicial invalidation pursuant to article 3:50 paragraph 2 BW, which apply in case of an *actio pauliana* invoked by creditors outside a bankruptcy of the debtor, do not apply to an *actio pauliana* invoked by a trustee in bankruptcy.

7   Please note that, pursuant to article 49 paragraph 1 Fw, legal proceedings in respect of the *actio pauliana* invoked by the trustee in bankruptcy must be lodged by the trustee in bankruptcy. This right can therefore not be transferred to or exercised by creditors of the debtor.

8   These requirements follow from article 42 paragraph 1 Fw.

9   This fifth requirement follows from article 42 paragraph 2 Fw.

10   See article 3:33 BW.

Ad. (2)

For the second requirement it is necessary to assess whether or not the debtor acted voluntarily. This will not be the case if the debtor had a legal obligation to conduct the legal act. In this respect the following rules of guidance may be used:

(i)   If the debtor, in light of the factual circumstances, was "morally obliged" to conduct the legal act that is challenged by the *actio pauliana*, that in itself does not render the legal act *legally* obliged[11];

(ii) The term "legal obligation" must be interpreted in a restrictive manner, meaning that the legal obligation must:

    (a)   be enforceable by the counter party; and

    (b)   concern the performance rendered by the debtor.

In respect of the requirement mentioned under (a) above, it should be noted that compliance with a legal obligation by the debtor that is not yet due and payable is regarded as a voluntary act in this context[12]. Furthermore, in respect of the requirement mentioned under (b) above, it should be noted that where a debtor sells an asset to its creditor in order to be able to set-off the purchase price against other claims owed to that creditor, that sale is considered to be a voluntary legal act for the purposes of the *actio pauliana*[13]; and

(iii) The legal obligation must actually exist, *i.e.* the performance of a legal act by the debtor which performance could be obliged from the debtor but was not yet obliged from the debtor when the debtor performed it, qualifies as a voluntary legal act for the purposes of the *actio pauliana*[14].

Ad. (3)

The third requirement consists of the following two elements both of which have to be met:

(i)   At the time a court needs to decide on the validity of the *actio pauliana* invoked by the trustee in bankruptcy, the actual means of recourse of the creditors must have decreased as a result of the act by the debtor that is challenged[15]; and

(ii) There must be an actual prejudice to one or more creditors.

---

11   This follows from the Mr Van der Feltz q.q./Hoornsche Crediet-en Effectenbank-case of the Netherlands supreme court (HR 8 January 1937, *NJ* 1937, 431) and the Eneca/BACM-case of the Netherlands supreme court (HR 10 December 1976, *NJ* 1977, 617).

12   This follows from the Mr Steinz q.q./Amro-case of the Netherlands supreme court (HR 16 January 1987, *NJ* 1987, 528).

13   This follows from the Kin/Mr Emmerig q.q.-case of the Netherlands supreme court (HR 18 December 1992, *NJ* 1993, 169).

14   This follows from the Ravast/Ontvanger-case of the Netherlands supreme court (HR 22 September 1995, *NJ* 1996, 706).

15   This follows from the Ravast/Ontvanger-case of the Netherlands supreme court (HR 22 September 1995, *NJ* 1996, 706) and has been confirmed by the Netherlands supreme court in the Diepstraten/Mr Gilhuis q.q.-case (HR 9 October 2001, *NJ* 2001, 654).

Ad. (3)(i)

The term "recourse" refers to the possibility of satisfying a monetary (as opposed to a non-monetary) claim for the account of the assets of the debtor. For example, if the debtor delivered an asset to a third party instead of to the buyer of that asset, then the buyer cannot safeguard his claim against the debtor to have the asset delivered (*i.e.* a non-monetary claim) by invoking the *actio pauliana* in respect of the delivery of the purchased asset to the third party. However, if the default by the debtor for not delivering the purchased asset to the purchaser results in a monetary claim for damages against the debtor (for example, as a result of a penalty clause), then that monetary claim *could*[16] be the basis for a valid *actio pauliana*.

Ad. (3)(ii)

For a better understanding of the element of "actual prejudice", the following general rules of guidance could be used:

(a) For prejudice to exist, it is not always necessary that the assets of the debtor available for recourse decrease in value. In certain circumstances, the loss of a right of preference as a result of an legal act by the debtor may also amount to "actual prejudice" for purposes of the *actio pauliana*[17];

(b) From the *Imperial/Waanders*-case[18] of the Netherlands supreme court, it follows that prejudice for the purposes of *actio pauliana* may also exist in circumstances where the act of the debtor has not resulted in a decrease in the size of assets of the debtor. For example, the exchange of a moveable asset of a certain value (*e.g.* a car) for a monetary claim by the debtor against a third party for the same amount may, depending on the incidental circumstances (such as the financial reliability of the third party against whom the claim is, whether or not that third party lives abroad *etc.*), result in "actual prejudice" of the means of recourse of one or more creditors for purposes of the *actio pauliana*; and

(c) From the *Mr Bosselaar q.q./Interniber*-case[19] of the Netherlands supreme court, it further follows that "actual prejudice" for purposes of the *actio pauliana*, may also exist if:

(I) a reasonable purchase price is paid by a purchaser for the purchased and delivered assets of the debtor;

(II) as a result of the payment of the reasonable purchase price, on balance, the total assets of the debtor have not decreased;

---

16 This is provided that the delivery of the asset to the third party prejudiced the purchaser's means of recourse to have its monetary claim for damages satisfied.

17 See explanation of Meijers in respect of Article 3.2.1.1 in the Parliamentary Notes of Book 3 BW, page 215.

18 HR 3 October 1980, *NJ* 1980, 643.

19 HR 22 May 1992, *NJ* 1992, 526. This case is also known as the "Montana caravan"-case.

(III) however, if the trustee in bankruptcy had not invoked the *actio pauliana*, the proceeds of those purchased and delivered assets of the debtor (*i.e.* the reasonable purchase price) would not have been available to the joint creditors of the debtor as a means of recourse.

What happened in the *Mr Bosselaar q.q./Interniber*-case? Caravans were sold by the debtor and the purchase price for those caravans was paid by the purchaser into a bank account of the debtor with a negative balance. Therefore, although the purchase price for the caravans was *per se* reasonable and in accordance with the market price, the proceeds of the sale never became available to the joint creditors.

In addition to the above general rules of guidance, it should further be noted that for the purposes of the *actio pauliana*, prejudice needs to exist at the time a court needs to decide on the validity of the invoked *actio pauliana*[20]), not at the time the challenged act was conducted by the debtor.

Ad. (4) and (5)

For the requirements (4) and (5), knowledge of the prejudice that results from the challenged act is essential. This knowledge needs to be considered in light of the circumstances existing at the time the challenged act was conducted by the debtor. In this context it is not necessary to prove that there was an intention to prejudice. Plain knowledge of prejudice suffices. However, it is insufficient to only prove that the counter party of the debtor was aware of the *chance* of prejudice to the creditors of the debtor[21].

Despite the lowering of the burden of proof for knowledge of prejudice by the fact that actual (*i.e.* subjective) knowledge does not need to be shown and evidence that the debtor and its counter party should have had knowledge (*i.e.* objective) of the prejudice suffices, in practice the requirements (4) and (5) are usually very difficult to meet. Therefore, in order to help the trustee in bankruptcy in this respect, the Fw provides for a number of situations in which knowledge of prejudice is presumed by virtue of law.

4.1.1.2   Situations in which knowledge of prejudice is presumed by virtue of law

In the absence of evidence to the contrary, knowledge of prejudice is presumed

---

20   This follows from the Ravast/Ontvanger-case of the Netherlands supreme court (HR 22 September 1995, *NJ* 1996, 706) and has been confirmed by the Netherlands supreme court in the Diepstraten/Mr Gilhuis q.q.-case (HR 9 October 2001, *NJ*. 2001, 654).

21   This follows from the Ontvanger/Pellicaan-case of the Netherlands supreme court (HR 1 October 1993, *NJ* 1994, 257), which was recently confirmed by the Netherlands supreme court in the Mr Bakker q.q./Katko-case (HR 17 November 2000, *JOR* 2001, 17).

from the debtor and its counter party by virtue of law in a number situations, provided that[22] :

(1) the voluntary legal act concerned, which prejudices creditors, was performed within one year prior to the bankruptcy order; and

(2) the debtor was not already legally bound thereto before the beginning of such period.

The (non-exhaustive) list of situations in which the knowledge of prejudice is presumed by virtue of law includes:

(i) Contracts in which the value of the debtor's obligation considerably exceeds that of the counterpart;

(ii) Legal acts constituting payment of, or security for, a debt not yet payable[23] ;

(iii) Legal acts performed by a debtor, who is a private individual, with or in respect of:

(a) his spouse[24], foster child[25] or a relative by blood or marriage up to the third degree; and

(b) a legal entity in which he, his spouse, his foster child or a relative by blood or marriage up to the third degree, is a director or director of the supervisory board or in which such persons, severally or jointly, participate directly or indirectly as a shareholder of at least half of the issued capital (*i.e.* 50% or more)[26] ;

(iv) Legal acts performed by a debtor, being a legal entity, with or in respect of a private individual:

(a) who is a director or director of the supervisory board of the legal entity, or with or in respect of such person's spouse, foster child or relative of blood or marriage up to the third degree;

(b) who, alone or together with his spouse, foster children and relatives by blood or marriage up to the third degree, participates, directly or indirectly, as a shareholder of at least one half of the issued capital; and

(c) whose spouse, foster children or relatives of blood or marriage up to the third degree, severally or jointly, participate, directly or indirectly, as a shareholder of at least one half of the issued capital;

---

22 See article 43 paragraph 1 Fw.

23 From the Mr Scholten q.q./Van Zwol Wijntjes-case of the Netherlands supreme court (HR 4 February 2000, *NJ* 2000, 192) it follows that this situation of presumed knowledge of prejudice should be interpreted in a restrictive manner.

24 A spouse includes – pursuant to article 43 paragraph 2 Fw – a registered partner or any other life partner.

25 Pursuant to article 43 paragraph 3 Fw a foster child means a child which is raised and brought up as an own child.

26 Pursuant to article 43 paragraph 4 Fw, a director, director of the supervisory board or shareholder includes any person who was a director, director of the supervisory board or shareholder less than one year prior to the act that is challenged by an *actio pauliana*.

(v) Legal acts performed by a debtor, being a legal entity, with or in respect of another legal entity, if[27]:

    (a) one of the legal entities is a director of the other;

    (b) a director, who is a private individual, of one of the legal entities, or his spouse, foster child or relative by blood or marriage up to the third degree, is a director of the other;

(c) a director, a private individual, or a director of the supervisory board of one of the legal entities, or his spouse, foster child or relative by blood or marriage up to the third degree, severally or jointly, participates, directly or indirectly, in the other as a shareholder of at least one half of the issued capital; and

(d) the same legal entity or the same private individual, alone or together with his spouse, foster children and relatives by blood or marriage up to the third degree, participates, directly or indirectly, in both legal entities as a shareholder of at least one half of the issued capital; and

(vi) Legal acts performed by a debtor which is a legal person with or in respect of a group company[28].

Where prejudice is caused by a legal act performed by a debtor for no consideration within one year prior to the bankruptcy order, it is also presumed by virtue of law that the debtor knew or should have known that its creditors would be prejudiced as a result of this act[29].

4.1.1.3   The legal consequences of the *actio pauliana*

Relative effect of the annulment

As a ground for annulment, the *actio pauliana* has retroactive effect and the act targeted by the *actio pauliana* is considered never to have been performed[30]. However, a complicating factor is the so-called "relative effect of the annulment" that follows from a successful *actio pauliana*[31]. This means that the challenged act is only annulled:

(1) for the benefit of the person who invoked the *actio pauliana* (*i.e.* the trustee in bankruptcy); and

(2) to the extent it is necessary to remove the prejudice that person has expe-

---

27 Please note that if the director of a legal entity/director is also a legal entity then – pursuant to article 43 paragraph 5 Fw – the director shall be given and equal status with the legal entity/director.

28 Pursuant to article 2:24b BW a "group company" is defined as legal entities and companies which are united in one group and a "group" is defined as an economic unit in which legal entities and companies are united in one organization.

29 See article 45 Fw.

30 This follows from article 3:53 paragraph 1 BW.

31 This follows from article 3:45 paragraph 4 BW. It is not explicitly mentioned in article 42 Fw, but is understood to be included in the words "for the benefit of the bankrupt estate" in paragraph 1 of article 42 Fw.

rienced as a result of the challenged act in case of an *actio pauliana* outside a bankruptcy and in case of an *actio pauliana* invoked by the trustee in bankruptcy, there is a duty – pursuant to article 51 Fw – to return to the trustee in bankruptcy all assets that have been removed from the property of the debtor as a result of the unvalidated act.

Consequently, the act by the debtor that is successfully challenged on the basis of an *actio pauliana* remains valid and in existence for the rest of the world.

In addition, a successful *actio pauliana* also results in an obligation to restore the original situation. This obligation is further addressed in § 4.1.1.3.1. Finally, in § 4.1.1.3.2 some of the complications attached to the obligation to restore the original situation will be discussed in the context of the *Kuijsters/Mr Gaalman q.q.*-case.

4.1.1.3.1   The obligation to restore the original situation

If the act avoided by the *actio pauliana* invoked by the trustee in bankruptcy has caused assets of the debtor to be removed from the property of the debtor, the parties against whom the *actio pauliana* has effect have the obligation to return such assets to the trustee in bankruptcy, thereby observing the rules on undue payment following from Book 6 BW[32]. When such a return of the removed assets is not possible, a monetary claim for the trustee in bankruptcy against the relevant party is created pursuant to the rules of undue payment. However, in complying with this obligation to restore the original situation, third party rights in respect of the assets are honored provided that the third parties concerned acquired their rights in good faith and for consideration[33].

4.1.1.3.2   The KUIJSTERS/MR GAALMAN Q.Q.-case

In the *Kuijsters/Mr Gaalman q.q.*-case[34] of the Netherlands supreme court the issue was raised whether, in a successful *actio pauliana*, those who have an obligation to restore the original situation are entitled to set-off this obligation with claims they have following from acts of the debtor other than the challenged act.

The facts of the KUIJSTERS /MR GAALMAN Q.Q-case

In the *Kuijsters/Mr Gaalman q.q.*-case the (re)payment of a subordinated loan of NLG 1,000,000 by the debtor, a Netherlands legal entity called "*D.M. de Bruin B.V.*", to Kuijsters, a widow of one of the founders of the debtor, was successfully challenged by Mr Gaalman q.q., the trustee in bankruptcy in the bankruptcy of the debtor. However, prior to the bankruptcy of the debtor, Kuijsters had placed the NLG 1,000,000 she received from the debtor in a deposit account with

---

32   This follows from article 51 paragraph 1 Fw. See also articles 6:203–6:211 BW.
33   This follows from article 51 paragraph 2 Fw. Rights not acquired for consideration are honored only if the third parties can show that, at the time of the declaration of the bankruptcy, they did not benefit from the now challenged legal acts.
34   HR 30 September 1994, *NJ* 1995, 626.

the principal bank of the debtor. Upon the request of the principal bank, Kuijsters had agreed to pledge the amount of NLG 1,000,000 in favor of the principal bank in order to secure the claims the principal bank had against the debtor.

After the debtor was declared bankrupt, the principal bank foreclosed on its pledge over the NLG 1,000,000, as a result of which Kuijsters acquired a claim against the debtor for the total amount that was foreclosed by the principal bank (*i.e.* the NLG 1,000,000). The question that needed to be resolved by the court was whether or not Kuijsters was entitled to set-off the claim she had acquired against the debtor as a result of the foreclosure by the principal bank of the debtor, with the obligation she had as a result of the successful *actio pauliana* by the trustee in bankruptcy to pay back the amount of NLG 1,000,000.

Judgment of the Netherlands supreme court

The Netherlands supreme court denied Kuijsters the right of set-off, as allowing it in the circumstances would violate the purpose and purport of the *actio pauliana* and the obligation to restore the original situation pursuant thereto, and hence destroy *paritas creditorum*[35].

4.1.1.4   Obligation of the trustee in bankruptcy

A successful *actio pauliana* also results in an obligation on the trustee in bankruptcy to return all assets the debtor received pursuant to the challenged act or the value thereof, provided that such assets benefit the bankrupt estate[36]. For any deficit in this respect, the person affected by the successful *actio pauliana* is entitled to submit a claim in the bankruptcy as a non-preferential or ordinary creditor[37]. In practice, assets will generally only benefit the bankrupt estate if they are still in the bankrupt estate. If such is no longer the case, the persons affected by a successful *actio pauliana* will be left with a claim as a non-preferential or ordinary creditor in the bankruptcy of the debtor. Furthermore, claims of non-preferential or ordinary creditors are not often paid in a Netherlands bankruptcy.

4.1.1.5   Liquidation by way of composition and *actio pauliana*

Where a bankruptcy ends by way of ratification of a composition[38], this results in the termination of the legal claims submitted by the trustee in bankruptcy on the basis of *actio pauliana*, unless the composition provides for a renunciation of any

---

35   For more details on the principle of *paritas creditorum*, see § 1.2.2.
36   This follows from article 51 paragraph 3 Fw.
37   In respect of non-preferential or ordinary creditors, see § 3.6.3.2.
38   For further details in respect of liquidation by way of composition, see § 3.4.3.3.

claim against the bankrupt estate, in which case the legal claims may be pursued or lodged by liquidators for the benefit of the creditors[39].

4.1.1.6   Statute of limitations

The limitation period for invoking an *actio pauliana* is three years from when the trustee in bankruptcy discovers the prejudice.[40]

4.1.2   THE *ACTIO PAULIANA* IN RESPECT OF OBLIGATORY LEGAL ACTS BY THE DEBTOR

The scope of article 47 Fw

Pursuant to article 47 Fw, a trustee in bankruptcy is only entitled to invalidate payment (or satisfaction) by the debtor of an obligatory claim which is due if it is proved that:
(1)   the person receiving the payment knew[41] that the bankruptcy of the debtor had already been requested; or
(2)   the payment resulted from a consultation between the debtor and its creditor aimed at preferring the latter over other creditors.

The scope of this type of *actio pauliana* is not restricted to payment (or satisfaction) *by the debtor* of an obligatory claim which is due, but also applies when *a third party* pays into the bank account of the debtor, as a consequence whereof the negative balance of the debtor's bank account (and therefore the claim of the bank against the debtor) decreases[42]. This is to avoid the creation of a special position of banks in this context when credit payments are made.

Furthermore, the *actio pauliana* pursuant to article 47 Fw is not restricted to monetary claims only, but covers all forms of payment (or satisfaction) of obligatory claims that are due. This includes, for example, the obligation to provide fur-

---

39   See article 50 Fw.
40   This follows from article 3:52 paragraph 1 under c BW.
41   Please note that it is not yet entirely clear whether or not knowledge in this context includes subjective knowledge (*i.e.* what the person actually knew) only or also objective knowledge (*i.e.* what the person should have known). In *"Nogmaals artikel 47 Fw"* in *WPNR* 6429, 2001, pp. 33-34, Prof. mr J.B. Huizink argues in favor of for the latter option. A different position is taken by Mr A. van Hees in *"Voorwaarden voor het instellen van de pauliana"* in *"Vragen rond de faillissementspauliana"*, Insolad jaarboek 1998, Prof mr L. Timmerman (editor), Kluwer 1998, Deventer, pp. 1-11.
42   This follows from the Mr Loeffen q.q./Bank Mees en Hope I-case of the Netherlands supreme court (HR 8 July 1987, *NJ* 1988, 104).

ther security rights by preparing lists of pledged claims for purposes of an undisclosed pledge[43].

Requirement for prejudice

As a special application of the "ordinary" *actio pauliana* pursuant to article 42 Fw, the requirement for prejudice[44] will also have to be met in order to successfully invoke the *actio pauliana* pursuant to article 47 Fw. However, in contrast to the requirement of prejudice for an *actio pauliana* pursuant to article 42 Fw, the aim of an *actio pauliana* pursuant to article 47 Fw is more to remedy an interference of the ranking arrangement among creditors of the debtor and not so much to remedy the prejudice to the means of recourse of the creditors of the debtor[45]. Rules of guidance in this context are:

(1) The *actio pauliana* pursuant to article 47 Fw cannot successfully be invoked when the challenged act resulted in the loss of a benefit for the creditors instead of a prejudice to the creditors[46]; and

(2) Prejudice for the purpose of an *actio pauliana* pursuant article 47 Fw does not exist where there is a payment of a debtor's claim by a third party to the debtor's bank, which payment is subsequently set-off by the bank against a claim the bank has against the debtor, and the debtor's claim is also pledged in favor of the bank, because that pledged obligatory claim was never a part of the bankrupt estate that could be used by the other creditors of the debtor to recover their claims[47].

4.1.2.1   Restrictive application

The *actio pauliana* pursuant to article 47 Fw is an exception to the general rule that obligatory legal acts (*i.e.* legal acts that stem from a legal obligation thereto) cannot be challenged by an *actio pauliana* outside bankruptcy. Therefore, the scope of the *actio pauliana* pursuant to article 47 Fw and the situations that fall within that scope are interpreted in a very restrictive manner. The *actio pauliana* pursuant to article 47 Fw and its restrictive application must be understood in light of the following 4 rules of guidance[48]:

---

43   See comment 2 to article 47 Fw by Mr C.R. Christiaans/Mr T.H.M. van Wechem in "*Tekst & Commentaar Faillissementswet*", Prof. mr B. Wessels/Mr Ph. van Sint Truiden, Kluwer 2nd edition 1999, Deventer, p. 60/61. For further details on the creation of an undisclosed pledge, see § 5.2.1.4.

44   See § 4.1.1.1 under Ad. (3).

45   See F.M.J. Verstijlen in "*De Faillissementscurator: een rechtsvergelijkend onderzoek naar de taak, bevoegdheden en persoonlijke aansprakelijkheid van de faillissementscurator*", W.E.J. Tjeenk Willink 1998, Deventer, p. 50 footnote 43.

46   This follows from the Mr Loeffen q.q./Mees en Hope II-case of the Netherlands supreme court (HR 22 March 1991, *NJ* 1991, 214).

47   This follows from the Mr Mulder q.q./CLBN-case of the Netherlands supreme court (HR 17 February 1995, *NJ* 1996, 471).

48   This follows from "*Geschiedenis van de Wet op het Faillissement en de Surséance van Betaling*", by Mr G.W. van der Feltz, part 2-I, 1896, editors Prof. mr S.C.J.J. Kortmann/Mr

(1) The Netherlands legislator was of the opinion that a debtor cannot be blamed when he performs a legal obligation demanded of him;
(2) There is no legal ground to require the recipient benefiting from the debtor's performance to return what he received;
(3) Business practice requires that a creditor should be entitled to enforce its rights when he fears a bankruptcy of his debtor. The granting of credit cannot take place if it cannot be relied upon that the payment obligation will remain inviolable, even if later on (or very soon thereafter) the debtor is declared bankrupt; and
(4) The non-availability of an *actio pauliana* in respect of an obligatory legal act by the debtor does not restrict the right to indirectly challenge this obligatory legal act by challenging (if such a basis exists) the earlier legal act pursuant to which the debtor legally bound himself to perform the obligatory legal act.

4.1.2.2   Knowledge about the request for bankruptcy

If a creditor has certainty about the filing for bankruptcy of the debtor, that creditor would be in violation of the principle of good faith he has to observe vis-à-vis his fellow creditors if he still demands and receives payment from the debtor[49]. In addition, that creditor would also be avoiding the rules of bankruptcy (*i.e.* the "*concursus creditorum*").

It follows from the *Mr Van Dooren q.q./ABN AMRO Bank*-case[50] that for an *actio pauliana* in respect of obligatory legal acts by the debtor, it is not sufficient that the creditor knows that the bankruptcy *will be filed soon* in determining lack of good faith. The decisive factor is whether or not the actual request for the bankruptcy of the debtor has been lodged. If that is not the case at the time the act to be challenged on the basis of the *actio pauliana* took place, the *actio pauliana* cannot be successful on this ground.

4.1.2.3   Consultation between debtor and creditor

The *actio pauliana* pursuant article 47 Fw does not apply to situations in which a debt is lawfully collected and payment is obtained by demanding it, by requesting a court decision, by making an arrest or by foreclosing on assets. The rationale for having this limb of article 47 Fw is to catch those payments that take place on

---

N.E.D. Faber, Tjeenk Willink 1994, Zwolle, pp. 434-437, to which the Netherlands supreme court explicitly refers in the Mr Van Dooren q.q./ABN AMRO Bank-case (HR 16 June 2000, *NJ* 2000, 578, *JOR* 2000, 201).

49 See Van der Feltz 2-I, *supra* footnote 48, at p. 449.
50 HR 16 June 2000, *NJ* 2000, 578, *JOR* 2000, 201. See also the Mr Meijs q.q./Bank of Tokyo-Mitsubishi (Holland)-case (HR 29 June 2001, *NJ* 2001, 662).

the eve of the bankruptcy (oftentimes at the debtor's initiative), *because* the bankruptcy will be filed and while the creditor is fully aware of the state of affairs of the debtor[51].

"Consultation" should be read as "conspire"

In line with the restrictive manner in which the *actio pauliana* pursuant to article 47 Fw should be interpreted, the Netherlands supreme court held that the term "consultation" in article 47 Fw should be read as "conspire"[52]. This means that it is for the trustee in bankruptcy to prove that not only the creditor, but also the debtor had the intention to favor this particular creditor over other creditors by conducting the challenged obligatory legal act.

On the basis of this reading of the term "consultation" in article 47 Fw, it was held to be impossible for the required "consultation" between the creditor and the debtor to have taken place in the *Mr Gispen q.q./IFN*-case[53] because the debtor only gave in and conducted the challenged obligatory legal act under pressure from the creditor threatening to terminate its credit line and filing a criminal complaint.

In cases of group relations whereby the challenged obligatory legal act took place between companies having the same shareholder/board of directors, the "conspiracy" requirement may be more easily presumed by a court[54].

4.1.2.4   The legal consequences of the *actio pauliana*

The legal consequences of the *actio pauliana* as discussed § 4.1.1.3 to § 4.1.1.6 also apply to an *actio pauliana* pursuant to article 47 Fw.

Summary
THE ACTIO PAULIANA

Types
The following two types of *actio pauliana* exist:
(1) *actio pauliana* pursuant to article 42 Fw in respect of voluntary legal acts by the debtor; and

---

51   See Van der Feltz 2-I, *supra* footnote 48, at p. 449.
52   This follows from the Mr Gispen q.q./IFN-case of the Netherlands supreme court (HR 24 March 1995, *NJ* 1995, 628) and was confirmed in the Verkerk/Mr Tiethoff q.q.-case (HR 20 november 1998, *NJ* 1999, 611).
53   See HR 24 March 1995, *NJ* 1995, 628.
54   This follows from the Rokla/Mr Keijser q.q.-case of the court of appeals of Amsterdam dated 9 January 1996 (*JOR* 1996, 26).

(2) *actio pauliana* pursuant to article 47 Fw in respect of obligatory legal acts by the debtor.

Requirements:
(1) For the *actio pauliana* in respect of voluntary legal acts by the debtor, the requirements are:
(i)   there must be a legal act by the debtor;
    (ii)   such legal act must be conducted voluntarily;
    (iii) as a consequence of this legal act the creditors of the debtor must be prejudiced;
    (iv)   the debtor must have had knowledge of this prejudice; and
    (v)   in case the legal act is for consideration, also the counter party of the debtor must have had knowledge of the prejudice
In respect of (iv) and (v) knowledge of prejudice is presumed by virtue of law in a number of situations.
(2) For the *actio pauliana* in respect of obligatory legal acts by the debtor, the requirements are:
    (i)   there must be a legal act by the debtor;
    (ii)   such legal act must be conducted obligatory;
    (iii) as a consequence of this legal act the creditors of the debtor must be prejudiced; and
    (iv)   (a) the person receiving the payment knew that the bankruptcy of the debtor was already requested or (b) the payment resulted from the conspiracy between the debtor and its creditor aimed at preferring the latter over the other creditors.

Legal consequences
The legal consequences of a successful *actio pauliana* are:
(1) an *actio pauliana* is a ground for annulment, but the annulment only has a relative effect;
(2) an *actio pauliana* has retroactive effect; and
(3) an *actio pauliana* results in an obligation to restore the original situation.

Statute of limitations
The limitation period for invoking an *actio pauliana* is 3 years from when the trustee in bankruptcy discovers the prejudice.

4.2   The legal concept of set-off in a bankruptcy

Set-off outside a bankruptcy

Outside a bankruptcy, a debtor has a right of set-off (or compensation) where he has a claim against his counter party for the performance of an obligation which corresponds to a obligation the debtor has towards his counter party and the debtor is entitled to settle the obligation and enforce payment (or satisfaction) of the claim[55]. The requirements for set-off can be summarized as follows:

(1) *Mutual debtorship* – The parties are each other's debtor and creditor.

(2) *The performance corresponds to the claim* – By exercising his right of set-off, the debtor obtains satisfaction of his counter party's obligation.

(3) *Entitlement to payment* – The debtor must be entitled to perform his obligation towards his counter party (*i.e.* that obligation must be due and payable).

(4) *Payment (or settlement) of the claim is enforceable* – The debtor must be entitled to enforce his claim against his counter party.

Where there is a transfer pursuant to particular title of a claim (for example, by way of assignment), the debtor of that claim remains entitled to set-off a counter-claim he had against his original creditor (*i.e.* the transferor of the claim) provided that[56]:

(1) such counterclaim originates from the same legal relationship as the transferred claim; or

(2) the counterclaim had already vested in the debtor and had become due prior to the transfer.

The same rule applies to a claim which has been attached or over which a limited right (such as a pledge) has been established, notice of which has been given to the debtor[57].

General exceptions

General exceptions to the right of set-off are as follows:

(1) When the nature of the claim or obligation involved prevents set-off. For example, an obligation to compensate damages that were intentionally caused by the person wishing to use this obligation in a set-off is not allowed under Netherlands law[58];

(2) When the use of the right of set-off as a defense is overruled by a court. Despite the fact that a defendant invokes a right of set-off, a court may render a judgment in favor of the claimant provided that:

---

55   See article 6:127 paragraph 2 BW.
56   See article 6:130 paragraph 1 BW.
57   See article article 130 paragraph 2 BW.
58   See article 6:135 BW.

(i) the validity of the defense (*i.e.* invoking the right of set-off) cannot eas-
    ily be ascertained; and
(ii) the claim would otherwise be allowable;
(3) the claim and the obligation that are subject to the set-off form part of
    separate estates[59].

Set-off notification

Except for "current-account" situations[60], set-off does not operate by virtue of
law and requires the party having a right of set-off to make a set-off notification[61]. Save for some legal limitations (such as, for example, mandatory rules on
unfair contract terms[62]), parties are entitled to contractually expand, limit or exclude the right to set-off.

In the following paragraphs the legal concept of set-off will be addressed in a
situation of bankruptcy. In § 4.2.1 the general rule on set-off in bankruptcy pursuant to article 53 Fw will be discussed. Subsequently, a special prohibition pursuant to article 54 Fw to use the right of set-off in a bankruptcy will be examined
in § 4.2.2.

4.2.1   THE RIGHT TO SET-OFF PURSUANT TO ARTICLE 53 NETHERLANDS
        BANKRUPTCY ACT

Article 53 Fw

Article 53 paragraph 1 Fw provides that:

> "a person (*private person or legal entity; PJMD*) who is both debtor and creditor of
> the bankrupt debtor may set-off his debt against his claim against the bankrupt debtor
> provided that each (*debt and claim; PJMD*) (1) arose before the bankruptcy of the
> debtor was declared or (2) resulted from acts entered into with the bankrupt debtor
> prior to the declaration of the debtor's bankruptcy."

In contrast to set-off outside a bankruptcy, article 53 Fw extends the possibility to
set-off in a bankruptcy. The requirements (1) (mutual debtorship), (2) (the performance corresponding to the claim) and (3) (entitlement to payment) are the same
for set-off in or outside a bankruptcy. The difference between the two is found in
requirement (4) (payment (or settlement) of the claim being enforceable). For set-
off in a bankruptcy the debt and the claim must:

---

59   See article 6:127 paragraph 3 BW.
60   See article 6:140 paragraph 1 BW, where "current-account" situations are referred to as situa-
     tions "in which – pursuant to law, usage or legal act – monetary claims and monetary obliga-
     tions must be included in one account between two parties".
61   See article 6:127 paragraph 1 BW.
62   See, for example, article 6:236 sub f BW and article 6:237 sub g BW.

(i)   have arisen before the bankruptcy of the debtor was declared; or
(ii) result from acts entered into with the bankrupt debtor prior to the declaration
      of the debtor's bankruptcy.
Another difference between set-off outside and in a bankruptcy relates to the applicable general exceptions. For set-off in a bankruptcy, the general exception relating to the use of the right of set-off as a defense (as discussed in § 4.2 above) is
not available to a trustee in bankruptcy[63].

As article 53 Fw is meant to provide the counter party of the debtor with protection in a debtor's bankruptcy, only the counter party of the debtor can invoke the
right of set-off pursuant to article 53 Fw[64]. Furthermore, article 53 Fw is not applicable to:
(i)   a set-off of estate claims and estate obligations[65]; and
(ii) claims that belong exclusively to the bankrupt estate (*i.e.* claims that
      originate from (legal) acts conducted by the trustee in bankruptcy).
Examples of claims meant above under (ii) are a claim against a third party acquired by the trustee in bankruptcy by way of assignment[66] and a claim lodged
by the trustee in bankruptcy on behalf of the joint creditors of the debtor based on
wrongful act[67].

Contractual modification of the right of set-off

In a bankruptcy, a contractual exclusion of the right of set-off remains, in principle, valid and enforceable, because a bankruptcy does not *per se* alter the contractual obligations the debtor entered into prior to its bankruptcy[68]. However, it
has not yet been clarified by the Netherlands supreme court whether or not a contractual expansion of the right to set-off can be successfully invoked against a
trustee in bankruptcy and, if so, under what circumstances[69].

---

63   See article 53 paragraph 3 Fw.
64   See *"Aspecten van verrekening tijdens faillissement en surséance van betaling"*, by Mr J.T. Jol
     in *"De curator, een octopus"*, Prof. mr S.C.J.J. Kortmann c.s. (editors), W.E.J. Tjeenk Willink
     1996, Deventer, pp. 201-218 at p. 203.
65   See § 3.6.2 for more details on "estate creditors".
66   This follows from the Mr Ruijgrok q.q./AMRO-case of the Netherlands supreme court (HR 25
     May 1990, *NJ* 1990, 605) and the Mr Tripels q.q./Van Rooijen-case (HR 31 May 1963, *NJ*
     1966, 340).
67   This follows from the Mr Peeters q.q./Gatzen-case of the Netherlands supreme court (HR 14
     January 1983, *NJ* 1983, 597).
68   This follows from, *inter alia*, from the ADB/Planex-case of the Netherlands supreme court (HR
     22 July 1991, *NJ* 1991, 748). A similar remark was made in § 3.5.2.2. in relation to the effect
     of a bankruptcy on agreements with mutual performances.
69   See Jol, *supra* footnote 64, at pp. 212/213.

4.2.1.1   Some case law in respect of set-off pursuant to article 53 Netherlands
          Bankruptcy Act

Set-off pursuant to article 53 Fw has resulted in a string of case law. Some rules
of guidance will be drawn from these cases in the following paragraphs. The aim
is not to be exhaustive, and the focus will be limited to the following three topics:
(1) The scope of article 53 Fw (*i.e.* what qualifies as a claim "resulting from
     legal acts entered into with the bankrupt debtor prior to the declaration of the
     debtor's bankruptcy");
(2) The relationship between article 53 Fw and credit payments; and
(3) The relationship between article 53 Fw and undisclosed pledge claims and
     non-possessory pledge assets.
In respect of each of these three topics the following cases of the Netherlands supreme court will be addressed:

Ad. (1)
(i)   The *Mr Tiethoff q.q./NMB*-case[70].
(ii) The *Mr Verhagen q.q./INB*-case[71].

Ad. (2)
(a)   The *Girodienst/Mr Voûte q.q.*-case[72].
(b)   The *Otex/Mr Steenbergen q.q.*-case[73].

Ad. (3)
(I)   The *Mr Mulder q.q./CLBN*-case[74].
(II) The *Mr Van Gorp q.q./Rabobank*-case[75].

4.2.1.1.1   The MR TIETHOFF Q.Q./NMB-case

The facts

In this case, the debtor ("*het Residentieslachthuis*") owned a property that it
rented out, as lessor, to "*de Nederlandsche Middenstandbank N.V.*" ("NMB"), as
lessee. On 17 July 1985, the debtor was declared bankrupt but the rental agreement of the property continued to be in place. NMB continued to pay rent to (the
bankrupt estate of) the debtor until September 1985 whereupon NMB claimed to
be entitled, pursuant to article 53 Fw, to set-off this payment obligation under the

---

70   HR 22 December 1989, *NJ* 1990, 661.
71   HR 15 April 1994, *NJ* 1994, 607.
72   HR 10 January 1975, *NJ* 1976, 249.
73   HR 27 January 1989, *NJ* 1989, 422.
74   HR 17 February 1995, *NJ* 1996, 471.
75   HR 23 April 1999, *NJ* 2000, 158.

rental agreement against claims NMB contended to have against the debtor (amounting to NLG 4,746,344.18) pursuant to a credit facility it had provided the debtor prior to its bankruptcy. The trustee in bankruptcy (Mr Tiethoff q.q,) challenged this right of set-off and claimed payment from NMB in the amount of NLG 73,812.45 plus statutory interest.

Judgment of the Netherlands supreme court

The Netherlands supreme court rendered a decision in favor of Mr Tiethoff q.q. and accepted an exception to the legal concept of set-off pursuant to article 53 Fw. While acknowledging that article 53 Fw also covered pre-bankruptcy obligations and claims which – in short – result from legal acts entered into with the bankrupt debtor prior to the declaration of the debtor's bankruptcy, the Netherlands supreme court further held that a reasonable interpretation of article 53 Fw demanded for an exception in the following case:

(1) an obligation arose after the declaration of the bankruptcy of the debtor (*i.e.* the payment of rent);
(2) the obligation resulted from an agreement that (i) was entered into prior to the bankruptcy of the debtor and (ii) continues to be in place after the declaration of the bankruptcy of the debtor (*i.e.* the rental agreement between the debtor, as lessor, and NMB, as lessee); and
(3) the obligation pursuant to the agreement is the counter-performance for an obligation that, as of the date of the declaration of bankruptcy, must be performed for the account of the bankrupt estate (*i.e.* providing NMB with the quiet enjoyment of the rented property).

When these three requirements are met, a set-off pursuant to article 53 Fw is not available. This exception applies especially if:
(i) the trustee in bankruptcy is obliged, despite the bankruptcy, to continue to perform an obligation (*i.e.* providing NMB with quiet enjoyment of the property); and
(ii) the counter party (*i.e.* NMB) wishes to set-off a claim that is not connected to the agreement (*i.e.* the repayment of the credit facility by the (bankrupt estate of the) debtor to NMB).

The explanation of the Netherlands supreme court for this exception to article 53 Fw is because a different approach would run contrary to the principle of *paritas creditorum*[76]. The Netherlands supreme court further argued that if set-off pursuant to article 53 Fw would be available in this case, then the creditor NMB would be able:

---

76   For more details about the principle of *paritas creditorum*, see § 1.2.2.

(a) to use – in comparison to the applicable law outside a bankruptcy – the relatively favorable set-off rule of article 53 Fw to obtain repayment of its claim against the debtor (*i.e.* the repayment of the credit facility); and

(b) to continue to make use of that which the trustee in bankruptcy needs to provide on the account of the bankrupt estate (*i.e.* the quiet enjoyment of the property), often without providing for an adequate counter-performance.

Accepting set-off pursuant to article 53 Fw in such cases would severely complicate proper administration by the trustee in bankruptcy of the assets included in the bankrupt estate that are subject to long-term agreements (such as the rental agreement in the matter at hand) for the benefit of the joint creditors.

4.2.1.1.2   The MR VERHAGEN Q.Q./INB-case

The facts

In this case the property of the debtor ("*Krevel B.V.*") was destroyed by fire on 25 December 1987. The property was insured by an external insurance company by way of intermediation of the insurance department of the bank (*Internationale Nederlanden Bank N.V.*) ("INB"). Payments by the debtor to the insurance company and payments from the insurance company to the debtor always took place via INB.

On 1 March 1988, the debtor was declared bankrupt and at the end of March 1988 the insurance company paid out on the insurance claim by the debtor in respect of the above-mentioned fire. This payment was made, as per usual, by the insurance company to INB. Instead of paying the monies received from the insurance company on to the bankrupt estate of the debtor, INB claimed to be authorized pursuant to article 53 Fw to set-off this payment obligation against the claim INB contended to have against the debtor pursuant to a current- account relationship that was entered into between INB and the debtor prior to the debtor's bankruptcy. The trustee in bankruptcy (Mr Verhagen q.q.) challenged this right of set-off.

Judgment of the Netherlands supreme court

The Netherlands supreme court rendered a decision in favor of Mr Verhagen q.q. and provided further guidance as to what qualifies as a claim "resulting from legal acts entered into with the bankrupt debtor prior to the declaration of the debtor's bankruptcy" pursuant to article 53 Fw.

In rendering his decision that a set-off pursuant to article 53 Fw is not available to INB, the Netherlands supreme court emphasized the fact that the collection by INB of what the insurance company owed to the debtor took place *after* the debtor's bankruptcy. The Netherlands supreme court ruled that in such a case, the direct cause of the payment obligation of INB against the debtor (*i.e.* the payment of the received monies of the insurance company to the debtor) lay in legal acts performed by third parties (*i.e.* the insurance company) after the declaration of bankruptcy, namely the payments by the insurance company which in itself had no connection to the claim INB contended to have against the (bankrupt estate of the) debtor pursuant to the current-account relationship it had with the debtor. In addition, the Netherlands supreme court held that, as a consequence of the bankruptcy of the debtor, the entitlement of INB to collect the payments of the insurance company (which entitlement was based on proxy[77]) had ceased to exist.

4.2.1.1.3   The GIRODIENST/MR VOÛTE Q.Q.-case

The facts

The debtor in this case ("*Standaardfilms N.V.*") was granted suspension of payment on 1 February 1972 and was declared bankrupt on 29 February 1972. At the time the suspension of payment was granted, the debtor had a giro-account with a negative balance with Girodienst. In the period between the granting of the suspension of payment and the declaration of bankruptcy, Girodienst received orders by third parties to pay a total amount of NLG 806.16 to the debtor. Girodienst accepted these orders and credited the giro-account of the debtor with NLG 806.16, which still left the giro-account with a negative balance.

The trustee in bankruptcy (Mr Voûte q.q.) demanded payment by Girodienst of the NLG 806.16 to the bankrupt estate and contended that, pursuant to article 234 Fw (for suspension of payment) and article 53 Fw (for bankruptcy), Girodienst was not entitled to set-off. Girodienst challenged this position.

Judgment of the Netherlands supreme court

The Netherlands supreme court rendered a decision in favor of Mr Voûte q.q., whereby it was acknowledged that the wording in articles 234 and 53 Fw:

> "resulting from acts performed prior to, respectively, the granting of the suspension of payment and the declaration of the bankruptcy",

indeed opened the possibility of invoking the right of set-off when a creditor of the bankrupt estate has a payment obligation to that estate (*i.e.* the obligation of Girodienst to pay NLG 806.16 to (the bankrupt estate of) the debtor) following from the fulfillment of a legal relationship that was established prior to the declaration of bankruptcy (or the granting of suspension of payment) (*i.e.* the opening

---

77   For more details on other consequences of bankruptcy, see § 1.2.1 and § 3.1.

by the debtor of a giro-account with Girodienst). In light of the legislative history, the Netherlands supreme court held, however, that the scope of this wording may *not* be read to apply to all cases in which a payment obligation arises after the declaration of bankruptcy (or the granting of suspension of payment) seemingly bearing a relationship to an agreement entered into prior to the declaration of bankruptcy (or the granting of suspension of payment).

According to the Netherlands supreme court, the right of set-off pursuant to article 53 (or article 234) Fw is *not* available when:
(1) the direct cause for the existence of the payment obligation follows from a legal act performed by a third party after the declaration of bankruptcy (or the granting of suspension of payment); and
(2) that legal act as such has no connection to the agreement entered into prior to the declaration of bankruptcy (or the granting of suspension of payment) on which the payment obligation is based.
In the matter at hand the orders received by Girodienst from third parties qualified as such legal acts performed by third parties.

4.2.1.1.4   The OTEX/MR STEENBERGEN Q.Q.-case

The facts

In late August 1982, the three debtors in this case (*"Van Kortenhof B.V."*, *"Scheepvaartonderneming Impala B.V."* and *"Scheepvaartonderneming Justo Tempore B.V."*) entered into an agreement with *"Otex Olietransport B.V."* ("Otex"), as a result of which, a current-account relationship came into existence between Otex and each of the three debtors. Earlier, on 27 May 1982, the debtors had granted Otex a proxy to collect on their behalf:
(1) a tax reimbursement claim against the German *Finanzamt*; and
(2) a claim against the Netherlands social security board.

On 27 October 1982, the debtors were declared bankrupt. Subsequently, Otex received an amount of NLG 61,266 from the *Finanzamt* and an amount of NLG 27,714 from the social security board. As the claims Otex had pursuant to the current-account relationship with the debtors were higher than the total amount of the monies Otex received from the *Finanzamt* and the social security board, Otex wished to set-off its obligation to pay these monies against its own claims against Otex pursuant to the current-account relationship. The trustee in bankruptcy (Mr Steenbergen q.q.) challenged this right of set-off.

Judgment of the Netherlands supreme court

The Netherlands supreme court rendered a decision in favor of Mr Steenbergen q.q., using a similar line of reasoning as in the *Girodienst/Mr Voûte q.q.*-case.

The Netherlands supreme court confirmed the decision of the court of appeals that there was an insufficient basis for Otex to invoke a right of set-off in the matter at hand because the direct cause of the existence of the payment obligation by Otex to the debtors (*i.e.* the obligation of Otex to pay the monies received from the *Finanzamt* and the social security board) arose from legal acts performed by third parties after the bankruptcy of the debtors had been declared, which legal acts (*i.e.* the payments by the *Finanzamt* and the social security board) had no connection to the agreements with the debtors invoked by Otex (*i.e.* the agreements underlying the current-account relationship between Otex and the debtors). Therefore, Otex was denied the right of set-off pursuant to article 53 Fw.

4.2.1.1.5   The MR MULDER Q.Q./CLBN-case[78]

The facts

In this case, the debtor (*"Connection Technology B.V."*) had received a credit line from its principal bank, Credit Lyonnais Bank Nederland N.V. ("CLBN"). By an agreement of 30 August 1985, the debtor agreed to assign/transfer by way of security all its existing and future claims to CLBN as security for the complete and timely satisfaction of all its obligations to CLBN. As of 1 January 1992, these assignments/transfers by way of security were converted into undisclosed pledge claims by virtue of law. As of that same date, the debtor periodically pledged its outstanding claims in favor of CLBN by way of registered private deeds[79]. On 6 November 1992, an undisclosed pledge was created by way of registered private deed in favor CLBN on all outstanding claims of the debtor as at 31 October 1992 for a total amount of NLG 1,508,688.09.

On 16 November 1992, the debtor submitted a request for its own bankruptcy and on 17 November 1992, the debtor was declared bankrupt. Prior thereto, on 13 November 1992, CLBN was informed about the debtor's intention to file for its own bankruptcy. On 16 November 1992, CLBN terminated the credit line of the debtor with immediate effect. Save for costs and ongoing interest, the claim of CLBN against the debtor amounted to NLG 4,644,502.80 on the date the debtor was declared bankrupt.

In addition to the above, the following events are important for this case:

(1) In the period between 13 and 16 November 1992 (inclusive), CLBN received payments by third parties in respect of undisclosed pledge claims in

---

78   This case is also briefly addressed in § 5.2.1.4.
79   For further details on undisclosed pledges, see § 5.2.1.4.

the amount of NLG 30,077.20 and DEM 10,408.30 into the bank accounts the debtor held with CLBN.

(2) In the period between 17 and 26 November 1992 (inclusive), CLBN received payments by third parties in respect of undisclosed pledge claims in the amount of NLG 143,875.46 and DEM 5,410.89 into the bank accounts the debtor held with CLBN.

(3) On 25 and 26 November 1992 CLBN notified the debtors of pledge claims about its right of pledge against the debtor.

The trustee in bankruptcy (Mr Mulder q.q.) claimed that CLBN must pay the amounts mentioned in (1) and (2) above to the bankrupt estate and that CLBN was not entitled to invoke the right of set-off. CLBN challenged this and claimed that Mr Mulder q.q. was obliged to pay to CLBN all the amounts that were paid during the bankruptcy by third parties in respect of undisclosed pledge claims to the trustee in bankruptcy in cash or via other bank accounts in the name of the trustee in bankruptcy or the debtor.

Judgment of the Netherlands supreme court

The Netherlands supreme court rendered a decision that was partly in favor of Mr Mulder q.q. and partly in favor of CLBN.

The judgment included decisions on the following issues:

(1) Does CLBN's undisclosed right of pledge over the claims cease to exist as a consequence of the payment made by third parties to the trustee in bankruptcy, or does, after payment, the right of pledge automatically attach to the proceeds (*i.e.* the monies received by the trustee in bankruptcy from third parties)?

(2) If the pledgee is not able to act as *separatist* (*i.e.* as someone who can act as if the bankruptcy of the debtor does not exist)[80], is there another right the pledgee can invoke?

(3) Is there an obligation on CLBN to pay the monies it received from third parties into its bank accounts in respect of undisclosed pledge claims during the period from 13 to 16 November 1992 (inclusive)?

(4) Is there an obligation for CLBN to pay the monies it received from third parties into its bank accounts in respect of undisclosed pledge claims during the period from 17 to 26 November 1992 (inclusive)?

---

80   For further details on "*separatisten*", see § 3.6.1 and § 5.1.

Ad. (1)

The Netherlands supreme court held that as long as notification of the undisclosed pledge is not given, the debtor, as pledgor, is entitled to request payment of the undisclosed pledge claims on its own behalf and collect such payments[81]. As a result of the debtor's bankruptcy, this entitlement is transferred to the trustee in bankruptcy. Consequently, CLBN, as pledgee, had no right to demand payment by the pledgor (or the trustee in bankruptcy) of whatever was received in this manner in respect of the undisclosed pledge claims.

In addition, the Netherlands supreme court held that by payment of an undisclosed pledge claim to a person who is entitled to receive such a payment, the claim ceases to exist and, as a consequence thereof, the right of pledge by which the claim was encumbered also ceases to exist. There is *no* basis for the conclusion that a right of pledge is automatically vested on the proceeds in such a situation.

Ad. (2)

When it was decided to convert all assignments/transfers for security of claims into undisclosed pledges as of 1 January 1992, the following assurances were made by the legislator:
(i)   undisclosed pledges should not give pledgees less protection then assignments/transfers for security; and
(ii) existing financing arrangements should be able to continue without difficulty after the conversion.

In light of these assurances, the Netherlands supreme court was of the opinion that leaving CLBN, as pledgee, completely empty handed would be in breach of these assurances. Therefore, and in order to avoid holders of an undisclosed pledge prematurely giving notification of their right of pledge, the Netherlands supreme court held that when a trustee in bankruptcy has collected undisclosed pledge claims as a consequence of which the pledged claim has ceased to exist, the pledgee continues to have a right of priority over the proceeds.

In respect of this right of priority, the Netherlands supreme court further clarified that for distribution of monies pursuant to this right of priority, the pledgee will have to:
(a)   wait until a plan of distribution has become final and not open to appeal[82]; and
(b)   share in the allocation of the bankruptcy costs over the proceeds.

Only then will the pledgee be able to benefit from its right of priority over the proceeds. However, the unfortunate result is that the pledgee will still be empty

---

81   See article 3:246 paragraph 1 BW.
82   For further details on when a plan of distribution becomes final and not open to appeal, see § 3.4.3.2.

handed if the bankruptcy terminates by way of liquidation without a verification meeting of creditors[83].

Ad. (3) + (4)

The Netherlands supreme court held that in both periods there was no obligation for CLBN to pay to the trustee in bankruptcy the monies received into the debtor's bank accounts with CLBN. In this respect the Netherlands supreme court acknowledged that it had been accepted in previous case law that banks are not entitled to invoke a right of set-off in relation to payments made for the debtor into bank accounts the debtor holds with that bank in the event such payments are received:

(i) when the bank knew the bankruptcy of that debtor was to be expected; or
(ii) after the bankruptcy of that debtor was declared.

However, according to the Netherlands supreme court there are no good grounds to apply these severe rules to a bank setting-off credit payments which are made on the above-mentioned points in time to satisfy claims of the debtor that have been pledged in its favor by way of an undisclosed pledge. The explanation for this position is as follows:

(a) Since the bank, as pledgee, already had priority over the other creditors, it cannot be said that by invoking a right of set-off the bank acquired an exceptional position for itself vis-à-vis the other creditors; and

(b) The legislator made certain assurances (as discussed already in Ad. (2) above) when the decision was made to automatically convert all assignments/transfers for security of claims into undisclosed pledges as of 1 January 1992.

Conclusion

From the foregoing it follows that:

(1) CLBN is entitled to use its right of set-off in respect of:
   (i) payments from third parties received into bank accounts of the debtor with CLBN prior to the debtor's bankruptcy in respect of undisclosed pledge claims; and
   (ii) payments from third parties received into bank accounts of the debtor with CLBN after the declaration of the debtor's bankruptcy in respect of undisclosed pledge claims.

(2) The trustee in bankruptcy does not have an obligation to pay to CLBN, as pledgee, the amounts that have been paid to him during the bankruptcy by third parties in respect of undisclosed pledge claims in cash or via accounts with other banks in the name of the trustee in bankruptcy or the debtor.

---

83   For further details on a liquidation without a verification meeting for creditors, see § 3.4.3.1.

(3) In respect of the payments referred to under (ii) above, CLBN, as pledgee, continues to have a right of priority.

4.2.1.1.6   The Mr Van Gorp q.q./Rabobank-case

The facts

This case resembles in a number of ways the *Mr Mulder q.q./CLBN*-case discussed above. However, while the *Mr Mulder q.q./CLBN*-case involved an undisclosed pledge over claims, this case involves a non-possessory pledge over moveable assets (inventory and stock)[84]. As we will see, this difference had a big influence on the outcome of the case.

In this case the debtor ("*Wollie B.V.*") had assigned/transferred by way of security all its inventory and stock by way of a private deed dated 12 August 1991 in favor of the "*Cooperatieve Rabobank Breda B.A.*" ("Rabobank"), as security for the complete and timely satisfaction of all its current and future obligations against Rabobank. As of 1 January 1992, these assignments/transfers by way of security had been converted by virtue of law into non-possessory pledges over the inventory and stock of the debtor. On 23 November 1994, the debtor entered in a sale and purchase agreement with Mr H.J. Bulten ("Bulten") with the consent of Rabobank. Pursuant to this agreement, the (pledged) inventory was purchased by Bulten for NLG 100,000. This purchase price would be paid by Bulten in the following three installments:
(1) NLG 50,000 on 30 December 1994;
(2) NLG 25,000 on 28 February 1995; and
(3) NLG 25,000 on 31 March 1995.
In was further agreed that all payments by Bulten should be made into the bank account of the debtor with Rabobank and until Bulten had completely satisfied all his obligations, the legal title to the inventory would be reserved to the debtor[85].

The first installment was paid by Bulten on time into the Rabobank bank account of the debtor. On 14 February 1995, the debtor was declared bankrupt. On or about 28 February 1995 NLG 25,000 was paid by Bulten into the Rabobank bank account and on or about 17 March 1995 NLG 17,388 was paid. It is undisputed that by paying the last installment Bulten had satisfied all its obligations vis-à-vis the debtor[86].

---

84   For further details on non-possessory pledges, see § 5.2.1.1.
85   For further details on reservation of title or ownership, see § 3.5.2.6.
86   The third installment was reduced from NLG 25,000 to NLG 17,388 in a separate, unrelated matter.

Rabobank had set-off the amounts it received from Bulten against the negative balance that existed on the Rabobank bank account of the debtor. After this set-off, a negative balance of NLG 315,144.56 (costs and interest not included) remained on the Rabobank bank account of the debtor on 7 April 1995.

The trustee in bankruptcy (Mr Van Gorp q.q.) challenged Rabobank's right of set-off in respect of the amounts paid by Bulten after the debtor was declared bankrupt (*i.e.* in the nominal amount of NLG 42,388) and claimed that Rabobank was obliged to repay those amounts to the bankrupt estate.

Judgment of the Netherlands supreme court

In this case the Netherlands supreme court rendered a decision in favor of Mr Van Gorp q.q., thereby rejecting an analogy with the *Mr Mulder q.q./CLBN*-case.

The Netherlands supreme court held that a right of pledge that is vested over moveable goods not brought in the possession of the pledgee (*i.e.* a non-possessory pledge such as the pledge of Rabobank over the inventory of the debtor) does not automatically transfer to the claim for the purchase price of such moveable goods, where these goods were sold to a third party (*i.e.* Bulten) with the consent of the pledgee (*i.e.* Rabobank). In this case, in giving its consent to the sale of the pledged moveable goods, Rabobank had failed to ask a pledge to be vested over the (the claim for the) purchase price.

In addition, the Netherlands supreme court also held that the payments made by Bulten did not have any relevance to the agreement Rabobank and the debtor entered into prior to the debtor's bankruptcy. Therefore, Rabobank was not entitled to invoke the right of set-off pursuant to article 53 paragraph 1 Fw.

Finally, the Netherlands supreme court deemed it inappropriate in this case to apply an exception, similar to the one in the *Mr Mulder q.q./CLBN*-case, to the rule that banks are not entitled to invoke the right of set-off in relation to payments made for the debtor into bank accounts the debtor holds with that bank where such payments are received after the bankruptcy of that debtor is declared. In support of this position the Netherlands supreme court indicated that, also according to the applicable law prior to 1 January 1992, it was impossible for a person to whom moveable goods of the debtor were assigned/transferred by way of security to have recourse, with priority over other creditors, on the purchase price paid by a third party where these goods were sold by private deed with or without consent of that person, by the debtor to a third party.

Summary
THE RIGHT OF SET-OFF

Right of set-off outside a bankruptcy

Requirements:
(1) mutual debtorship
(2) the performance corresponds to the claim
(3) entitlement to payment
(4) payment (or settlement) of the claim is enforceable

Particular aspects:
(1) The requirement of mutual debtorship may also be met in certain cases of transfer by particular title of a claim.
(2) The nature of a claim may render set-off impossible.
(3) Set-off as a defense may be overruled by a court.
(4) Set-off between a claim and an obligation which form part of separate estates is not possible.
(5) Except for "current-account"-situations, a set-off notification needs to be made.
(6) Save for some legal limitations, parties are entitled to contractually expand, limit or exclude the right of set-off.

Right of set-off in bankruptcy pursuant to article 53 Fw

Requirements:
(1) Requirements (1)-(3) of set-off outside a bankruptcy also apply to set-off in a bankruptcy pursuant to article 53 Fw.
(2) Requirement (4) in a set-off in a bankruptcy pursuant to article 53 Fw requires that the debt and the claim must:
    (i) have arisen before the bankruptcy of the debtor was declared; or
    (ii) result from acts entered into with the bankrupt debtor prior to the declaration of the debtor's bankruptcy.
    This results in an extended possibility to set-off during a bankruptcy.

Particular aspects:
(1) Only the counter party of the debtor can invoke the right of set-off pursuant to article 53 Fw.
(2) Set-off pursuant to article 53 Fw is neither applicable to estate claims and estate obligations nor to claims that exclusively belong to the bankrupt estate.

Guidance following from case law of the Netherlands supreme court:

THE MR TIETHOFF Q.Q./NMB-CASE

Set-off pursuant to article 53 Fw cannot be invoked when the following requirements are all met:

(1) the obligation arose after the declaration of the bankruptcy of the debtor;

(2) such obligation resulted from an agreement that (i) was entered into prior to the bankruptcy of the debtor and (ii) continues to be in place after the declaration of the bankruptcy of the debtor; and

(3) pursuant to the agreement the obligation is the counter-performance that, as of the date of the declaration of bankruptcy, must be performed for the account of the bankrupt estate.

THE MR VERHAGEN Q.Q./INB-CASE – THE GIRODIENST/MR VOÛTE Q.Q.-CASE – THE OTEX/MR STEENBERGEN Q.Q. CASE

The right of set-off pursuant to article 53 (or article 234) Fw is not available where the direct cause for the existence of the payment obligation follows from a legal act performed by a third party after the declaration of bankruptcy (or the granting of suspension of payment), which act has *no connection to* the agreement entered into prior to the declaration of bankruptcy (or the granting of suspension of payment) on which the payment obligation is based.

THE MR MULDER Q.Q./CLBN-CASE

(1) As long as no notification of an undisclosed pledge has been given, the debtor, as pledgor, is entitled to request payment of the undisclosed pledge claims on its own behalf and collect such payments. As a result of the debtor's bankruptcy, this entitlement is transferred to the trustee in bankruptcy. The pledgee has no right to demand payment by the pledgor or the trustee in bankruptcy of whatever was received in this manner in respect of the undisclosed pledge claims.

(2) By payment of an undisclosed pledge claim to a person who is entitled to receive such a payment, the claim ceases to exist, as well as the right of pledge by which the claim was encumbered. There is *no* basis for a conclusion that in such a situation a right of pledge automatically attaches to the proceeds.

(3) When a trustee in bankruptcy has collected undisclosed pledge claims as a consequence of which the pledged claim and related right of pledge has ceased to exist, the pledgee continues to have a right of priority in respect of the proceeds. Only after a plan of distribution has become final and not open to appeal and an allocation of the bankruptcy costs has been made, will the pledgee be able to benefit from its right of priority.

THE MR VAN GORP Q.Q./RABOBANK-CASE

(1) A right of pledge that is vested over moveable goods not brought in the possession of the pledgee (*i.e.* a non-possessory pledge) is not automatically transferred to the claim for the purchase price of such moveable goods in the event that these goods are sold to a third party with the consent of the pledgee.

(2) In such a case an exception, similar to the one in the *Mr Mulder q.q./ CLBN*-case (see above, under (2)), to the rule that banks are not entitled to invoke the right of set-off in relation to payments made for the debtor on bank accounts the debtor holds with that bank where such payments are received after the bankruptcy of that debtor, is not appropriate.

4.2.2   THE PROHIBITION PURSUANT TO ARTICLE 54 NETHERLANDS BANKRUPTCY ACT TO USE THE RIGHT OF SET-OFF

Pursuant to article 54 Fw, set-off pursuant to article 53 Fw is not possible in the following two situations:
(1) A person is not entitled to set-off if he:
  (i)   acquired a claim against the debtor or an obligation (or debt) towards the debtor prior to the bankruptcy of the debtor; and
  (ii) did not act in good faith in respect of such acquisition[87].
(2) Set-off is never permitted for claims or debts acquired after the bankruptcy of the debtor has been declared[88].

In respect of the exception pursuant to article 54 Fw, the following two cases of the Netherlands supreme court will be addressed:
(1) The *Amro/Trustees in bankruptcy THB*-case (§ 4.2.2.1)[89];and
(2) The *NCM/Mr Knottenbelt q.q.*-case (§ 4.2.2.2)[90]

---

87 See article 54 paragraph 1 Fw.
88 See article 54 paragraph 2 Fw.
89 HR 7 October 1988, *NJ* 1989, 449.
90 HR 4 November 1994, *NJ* 1995, 627.

4.2.2.1 The Amro/Trustees in bankruptcy THB-case

In this case, the debtor (*"de Tilburgse Hypotheekbank"*) ("THB") became subjected to the Emergency Arrangement pursuant to the Wtk on 1 July 1982[91]. Earlier on the same day, Amro, a bank with whom THB held a bank account, was
informed by the Central Bank of the Netherlands of its intention to subject THB
to the Emergency Arrangement. At that time the bank account of THB with
Amro had a substantial negative balance (*i.e.* Amro had a substantial claim
against THB in that regard).

On that same day, 1 July 1982, Amro also received a payment order from a third
party to credit the bank account of THB with NLG 2,099,222.01. Amro commenced with the execution of that payment order on that day and completed it the
next day. Consequently, Amro produced a bank statement dated 2 July 1982 on
which the payment was shown. As a result of crediting THB's bank account with
the above-mentioned amount, the balance of the account was still negative but as
the monies paid into the account were all used to set-off the claim Amro had
against THB, the amount of Amro's claim was reduced.

A little later, THB went into bankruptcy and the trustees in bankruptcy claimed
payment of NLG 2,099,222.01 from Amro to the bankrupt estate. The trustees in
bankruptcy contended that by executing the payment order of the third party (*i.e.*
setting-off the amount of the payment order against Amro's claim against THB
for the negative balance of THB's bank account with Amro) on the day Amro
knew that THB would be subjected to the Emergency Arrangement, it violated
article 235 Fw (which provision is similar to article 54 Fw for cases of bankruptcy).

Judgment of the Netherlands supreme court

The Netherlands supreme court rendered a decision in favor of the trustees in
bankruptcy.

In a time where credit payments are the rule, not the exception, the Netherlands
supreme court held that it would *not* be in accordance with the system laid out in
the Fw if credit payments would provide credit institutions with an exceptional
position pursuant to which they – by way of set-off and in view of the debtor's
bankruptcy or suspension of payment – separately could take recourse on that
which they owed to the debtor. Therefore, such a set-off is considered to be in
violation of articles 54 and 235 Fw when:

---

91 For a brief discussion of the Emergency Arrangement, see the introduction to Chapter 1.

(1) a debtor of the (insolvent) debtor (*i.e.* a third party of THB) satisfies its debt by paying into the account of the (insolvent) debtor with a credit institution (*i.e.* Amro); and

(2) the credit institution was not acting in good faith when crediting the bank account of the debtor, as a result of which the credit institution itself becomes a debtor of the (insolvent) debtor (*i.e.* by crediting the account of THB, Amro becomes a debtor of THB for the amount credited).

In addition, the Netherlands supreme court clarified that in interpreting the phrase "not acting in good faith" pursuant to article 54 and 235 Fw, it is in any case sufficient that the party acquiring the claim against the debtor (*i.e.* Amro when it acquired the payment order of the third party) knew at the time of acquisition of the claim that the debtor was in such a situation that its bankruptcy or suspension of payment respectively was to be expected.

4.2.2.2   The NCM/MR KNOTTENBELT Q.Q.-case

In this case, the debtor (*"Houthandel Janssen B.V."*) was granted suspension of payment on 20 November 1985 and was subsequently declared bankrupt on 6 December 1985. Prior to those events, on 20 December 1983, the debtor had entered into an agreement with, *inter alia*, *"de Nederlandsche Credietverzekering Maatschappij N.V."* ("NCM") pursuant to which the debtor agreed to assign by way of security[92] all its claims against third parties to, *inter alia*, NCM to secure the full and timely payment of, *inter alia*, all claims NCM had or would acquire against the debtor. On 8 November 1985, all existing claims of the debtor as at 31 October 1985 were assigned in that way to, *inter alia*, NCM. At that time NCM itself did not have a claim against the debtor nor was this the case when the suspension of payment was granted or when the bankruptcy of the debtor was declared.

In addition to the 20 December 1983 agreement, NCM also had entered into credit insurance agreements with a number of creditors of the debtor. In case of insolvency or possible insolvency of the debtor, those creditors could claim payment from NCM pursuant to those credit insurance agreements for damages those creditors sustained resulting from the (possible) insolvency of the debtor. In turn, these creditors were obliged to assign their claims against the debtor to NCM when damages were paid out to them by NCM.

---

92 Pursuant to article 3:84 paragraph 3 BW, an assignment by way of security of claims, as mentioned in this case, is no longer allowed. Pursuant to article 86 paragraph 6 Ow, all arrangements to that extent have been converted into undisclosed pledges. For more details on undisclosed pledges, see § 5.2.1.4 and also see the discussion of the Mr Mulder q.q./CLBN-case in § 4.2.1.1.5.

Pursuant to the payment received from third parties under the 8 November 1985 assignment, NCM received a total amount of NLG 1,104,245.08. The trustee in bankruptcy (Mr Knottenbelt q.q.) demanded payment by NCM of this amount to the bankrupt estate and contended that NCM was not entitled, pursuant to article 54 Fw, to set-off the NLG 1,104,245.08 against the claims NCM received pursuant to the agreements of credit insurance. NCM challenged this position of the trustee in bankruptcy.

Judgment of the Netherlands supreme court

The Netherlands supreme court rendered a decision in favor of Mr Knottenbelt q.q.

According to the Netherlands supreme court, NCM was *only* entitled to have recourse against the amount it received from the assigned claims of the debtor to pay NCM's claims against the debtor it had at the commencement of the suspension of payment. Claims against the debtor arising *after* the commencement of the suspension of payment:
(1) could not be used as secured obligations for recourse against the NLG 1,104,245.08 NCM received in respect of the assigned claims; and
(2) could not be set-off, pursuant to articles 234-235 Fw in a suspension of payment and pursuant to articles 53-54 Fw in a bankruptcy, against amounts NCM owed to the bankrupt estate for monies that had been acquired through collection of the assigned claims and should be paid by NCM to the trustee in bankruptcy.

NCM argued that the claims against the debtor it received pursuant to the credit insurance agreements should be considered to be acquired by NCM at the time of the suspension of payment because:
(1) as a consequence of the suspension of payment, NCM became obliged to compensate the creditors of the debtor that had entered into credit insurance agreements with NCM; and
(2) after being compensated for their damages, those creditors were obliged to assign their claims against the debtor to NCM.
Therefore, NCM should be considered to have conditional claims against the debtor as of the date of the suspension of payment.

This line of reasoning was not followed by the Netherlands supreme court, because from this line of reasoning it followed that NCM could not have derived conditional claims against the debtor that already existed *prior to* the suspension of payment, if the claims of the debtor's creditors with whom NCM entered into agreements of credit insurance arose only as a consequence of the suspension of payment.

Summary
ARTICLE 54 NETHERLANDS BANKRUPTCY ACT

Scope of article 54 Fw:
(1) A person is not entitled to set-off if he:
   (i) acquired a claim against the debtor or an obligation (or debt) to-wards the debtor prior to the bankruptcy of the debtor; and
   (ii) did not act in good faith with respect to such acquisition.
(2) Set-off is never permitted for claims or debts acquired after the bankruptcy of the debtor has been declared.

Guidance following from case law of the Netherlands supreme court:

The Amro/Trustees in bankruptcy THB

(1) A set-off is considered to be in violation of articles 54 and 235 Fw, respectively, when:
   (i) a debtor of the (insolvent) debtor (*i.e.* the third party in respect of THB) satisfies its debt obligation by paying into the account of the debtor with a credit institution (*i.e.* Amro); and
   (ii) the credit institution was not acting in good faith when crediting the bank account of the debtor, as a result of which the credit institution itself becomes a debtor of the (insolvent) debtor (*i.e.* by crediting the account of THB, Amro becomes a debtor of THB for the amount credited).
(2) In respect of "not acting in good faith" pursuant to article 54 and 235 Fw, it is in any case sufficient that the party acquiring the claim against the debtor (*i.e.* Amro when it acquired the payment order of the third party) knew at the time of acquisition of the claim that the debtor was in such a situation that its bankruptcy respectively suspension of payment was to be expected.

The NCM/Mr Knottenbelt q.q.-case

Claims against the debtor received by NCM *after* the commencement of the suspension of payment:

(1) could not be used as secured obligations for recourse against the amount NCM received in respect of assigned claims (regardless of the fact that these claims were the collateral of a security given to NCM prior to the commencement of the suspension of payment); and
(2) could not be set-off with amounts NCM owed to the bankrupt estate for monies that had been acquired through collection of the assigned claims and should be paid by NCM to the trustee in bankruptcy.

4.3 Corporate liabilities in a bankruptcy

In the revival of insolvency law in the Netherlands, corporate liabilities in a bankruptcy have also come more into the public eye. In this section the basic aspects of corporate liabilities will be addressed in the context of a bankruptcy of a corporate debtor.

In § 4.3.1 there will be a discussion of the liability of directors. Both internal liability (§ 4.3.1.1) and external liability (§ 4.3.1.2) will be looked at. Subsequently, in § 4.3.2, the liability of directors of a supervisory board will be addressed. The liability of shareholders will be dealt with in § 4.3.3.

4.3.1 LIABILITY OF DIRECTORS

The task of the board of directors of a company can be described as management of the company[93]. In managing a company, limits can be found in the statutory provisions, the articles of association of the company and the objects clause included in those articles of association[94].

The BW contains a number of rules, pursuant to which a director of a bankrupt company can be held liable for either damages pursuant to a specific transaction which was detrimental to the bankrupt company, or the total deficit of the bankrupt estate. Under Netherlands law a distinction can be made between internal and external liability of directors:
(1) Internal liability of directors concerns their liability towards the company (§ 4.3.1.1); and
(2) External liability of directors concerns their liability towards third parties (§ 4.3.2.2).

4.3.1.1 Internal liability of directors

Article 2:9 BW
The relevant article in respect of internal liability of directors vis-à-vis their company is article 2:9 BW:

> "Each director shall be responsible to a legal entity for the proper performance of the duties assigned to him. If a matter of the board falls within the scope of responsibility of two or more directors, each shall be jointly and severally liable for any shortcoming, unless he proves that it is not attributable to him and that he was not negligent in acting to prevent its consequences."

---

93 See articles 2:129/2:239 BW.
94 See article 2:7 BW.

Article 2:9 BW contains the obligation of directors for the proper fulfillment of their duties. They can be held liable towards the company, when they act contrary to such obligations and the company sustains damages pursuant thereto. A trustee in bankruptcy may – on behalf of the bankrupt company – require the payment of damages by the directors.

Contractual and corporate law position of directors

Aside from the contractual law position of a director towards his company evidenced by an employment agreement or an agreement of engagement, the director also has a corporate law position. This latter concept forms the basis for the internal liability provision of article 2:9 BW. However, it is also argued by some that the liability following from the contractual law position of the director is entirely dictated by article 2:9 BW[95]. An element of objectivity is included in the qualification "proper performance of the duties assigned to him".

"Seriously to blame"

A director performs his duties in a proper way if he does what can reasonably be expected of him. The Netherlands supreme court made it clear, particularly in the *Staleman/Van de Ven*-case[96], which will be discussed in greater detail below, that a director must be "seriously to blame" in order for him to be liable pursuant to article 2:9 BW. Needless to say, in performing the duties assigned to him, a director is granted a certain degree of freedom of management. His acts can only qualify as improper performance of his duties as a director of the company within the meaning of article 2:9 BW, if his acts would not have been performed by any reasonably acting director in the same circumstances. Whether or not that is the case will therefore always have to be judged on a case-to-case basis, taking into account all relevant facts and circumstances.

Burden of proof

It follows from article 2:9 BW that directors' internal liability is primarily considered a liability of the board of directors as a collective body. Therefore, each director is, in principle, jointly and severally liable for the total amount of damages. The burden of proof for liability pursuant to article 2:9 BW rests primarily with the company or the trustee in bankruptcy, in a bankruptcy of the company. This may be different when the board of a company consists of only one director[97]. If

---

95   See *"Aansprakelijkheid van bestuurders"* by Mr J.W. Wezeman, Kluwer 1998, Deventer, pp. 66-67.

96   HR 10 January 1997, *JOR* 1997, 29.

97   See the Van Waning/Van der Vliet-case (HR 3 April 1992, *NJ* 1992, 411) and the Romme/ Bakker-case (HR 10 June 1994, *NJ* 1994, 766) and see also Prof. mr L. Timmerman in

it is proven that the board of directors of a company is seriously to blame for the improper performance of the duties assigned to it, and therefore liable pursuant to article 2:9 BW, each individual director has the possibility of exculpating himself. Each individual director can avoid personal liability pursuant to article 2:9 BW if he can prove:

(1) that the matters in which there has been a shortcoming of the board did not fall within his scope of responsibility in the board and he was not negligent (*i.e.* "seriously to blame") in acting to prevent the consequences of such shortcoming; or

(2) that the matters in which there has been a shortcoming of the board did fall within his scope of responsibility together with one or more other directors, but that the shortcoming is not attributable to him and that he was not negligent in acting to prevent its consequences.

Here, the burden of proof rests with the director.

4.3.1.1.1   Statute of limitations

The limitation period for a claim pursuant to article 2:9 BW is 5 years[98]. This term starts to run from the day subsequent to the day the aggrieved party has become aware of both the damages and the identity of the party liable for the damages. The long-stop is 20 years after the event giving rise to the damages took place.

4.3.1.1.2   Discharge

A claim pursuant to article 2:9 BW may not be successful if it relates to activities for which the board of directors has already been granted a discharge by the company[99]. Such discharge cannot be granted in advance[100]. The BW does not contain a rule with respect to discharge, but oftentimes, discharge provisions are included in the articles of association of a company. It is common to have an automatic discharge of the acts of directors and supervisory directors when the annual accounts and the annual report of a company are adopted or approved[101]. It

---

"*Bewijslastverdeling bij doorbraak van aansprakelijkheid*", in *TVVS*, 9, 1993, p. 234 and Mr M.C.M. van Dijk in "*Stelplicht en bewijslast in zaken van bestuurdersaansprakelijkheid*", in *NbBW*, 2, 2001, pp. 14-19.

98   See article 3:310 paragraph 1 BW.

99   This follows from article 2:25 BW read in conjunction with the "discharge" provisions of the articles of association of the company. See also Wezeman, *supra* footnote 95, at pp. 78-79.

100   See article 3:40 BW.

101   In respect of discharge a bill exists ("*Wetsvoorstel Décharge (Tweede Kamer no 27 483)*"), pursuant to which there will no longer be an automatical discharge upon adoption of the annual report. In this respect see also "*Het spookbeeld van de décharge herrezen*" by Mr E.A. de Jong in "*Ondernemingsrecht*" 2001-8, pp. 232-235.

should, however, be noted that, unless complete disclosure of all the facts has been provided during the adoption or approval of the annual accounts and the annual report of the company, the discharge only covers those facts that are disclosed in the annual accounts or the annual report and only applies to the term covered by those annual accounts or the annual report[102].

As soon as a director becomes aware of a discharge decision and does not immediately object to this decision, the discharge has immediate effect[103]. Such discharge decision could still be invalidated if it is in violation of the principle of reasonableness and fairness[104]. Such may, for example, be the case if the discharge decision was the result of an abuse of right. In a bankruptcy of a company, the trustee in bankruptcy also has to respect a valid discharge decision, unless he is, for example, able to successfully invalidate the discharge decision on the basis of *actio pauliana*[105].

4.3.1.1.3   The STALEMAN/VAN DE VEN-case

In this case, legal action was instituted for mismanagement against two directors, Mrs J.C. Staleman and H.G.A. Richelle (hereinafter referred together as "Staleman"), by 3 companies in which they were the only directors, "*Van de Ven Automobielbedrijf Venlo*", "*Venlease B.V.*" and "*Venrent B.V.*" (hereinafter referred together as "Van de Ven"). The mismanagement allegations by Van de Ven were denied by Staleman, who referred to a discharge granted to them by Van de Ven.

Only two of the issues in respect of which the Netherlands supreme court was requested to render judgment will be addressed below. There will be no further discussion of the factual details of the *Staleman/Van der Ven*-case. Those two issues are:

(1)   When is mismanagement sufficiently serious in nature for a director to be held liable pursuant to article 2:9 BW?
(2)   What is the scope of the discharge granted by Van de Ven to Staleman?

Ad. (1)
The supreme court held that the level of mismanagement that is required pursuant to article 2:9 BW to hold a director liable must be such that the director is "seri-

---

102   See the Deen/Parlak-case (HR 17 June 1921, *NJ* 1921, 737), the Truffino-case (HR 20 June 1924, *NJ* 1924, 1107), and the Staleman/Van de Ven-case (HR 10 January 1997, *JOR* 1997, 29).
103   See article 6:160 paragraph 2 BW.
104   See article 2:15 paragraph 2 BW. In this respect please note the 1 year time limit of paragraph 5 of article 2:15 BW. See also article 2:8 BW.
105   For more details on the rules of *actio pauliana*, see § 4.1.

ously to blame". Whether or not this conclusion can be reached needs to be determined by taking into account all facts and circumstances of the case. The circumstances to be taken into account in this context include, *inter alia*, the following:

(i)   the nature of activities performed by the legal entity (*i.e.* Van de Ven);
(ii) the risks that generally result from such activities;
(iii) the allocation of tasks within the board;
(iv) any possible guidelines that may apply to the board;
(v)   the information the director had or should have had at the time the – now challenged – decisions were made or activities were performed; and
(vi) the understanding and care that can be expected from a director who is suitable for his duties and performs these with punctuality.

Ad. (2)
In respect of the scope of a discharge – irrespective of whether it follows, pursuant to the articles of association from the company, from the adoption of the annual accounts and the annual report or whether it is explicitly granted by the general meeting of shareholders when the annual accounts and the annual report are adopted – the supreme court held a discharge should not extend to include:

(i)   information that has become available to an individual shareholder in another capacity, outside the context of the general meeting of shareholders; or
(ii) information which does not follow from the annual accounts or the annual report and is not otherwise disclosed to the general meeting of shareholders prior to the adoption of the annual accounts by it.

4.3.1.2   External liability of directors

WBF
Pursuant to the so-called Third Act on Abuse ("*Derde Misbruikwet*")[106], which Act came into effect on 1 January 1987, the trustee in bankruptcy was granted a number of new rights to hold directors and supervisory directors of a bankrupt company liable for the debts of a company. In practice, this Act is also referred to as the "WBF". The core of the WBF consists of almost identical articles 2:138 and 2:248 BW relating to NVs and BVs, respectively.

WBA
Aside from external liability of directors pursuant to articles 2:138 and 2:248 BW, liability of directors towards third parties may also result from:

---

106   Act of 16 May 1986 (*Staatsblad* 1986, 275), concerning the amendment of provisions of the Civil Code and the Bankruptcy Act in order to prevent the abuse of legal entities.

(1) acts conducted by directors for and on behalf of a company that is not yet incorporated[107]; or

(2) a misleading annual report of a company[108].

These types of external liability of directors will not be addressed. The same applies to external liability of directors following from the Second Act on Abuse ("*Tweede Misbruikwet*")[109], which also came into effect on 1 January 1987 and in practice is referred to as the "WBA". The WBA introduced rules pursuant to which directors of companies could be held liable on the basis of apparent mismanagement for unpaid premiums relating to social insurances, unpaid contributions concerning the mandatory participation in corporate pension funds, unpaid wages tax and unpaid VAT[110].

In § 4.3.1.2.1, the discussion of external liability of directors will be restricted to only the external liability of directors in case of bankruptcy of the company pursuant to article 2:248 BW. External liability of directors will resurface when the concept of wrongful act is addressed in § 4.4.

4.3.1.2.1 Article 2:248 Netherlands Civil Code

Article 2:248 BW provides the following basis of liability of directors in a bankruptcy of a BV[111]:

(1) In a bankruptcy of a BV, each director shall be jointly and severally liable to the estate for the amount of the obligations to the extent that these cannot be satisfied out of the liquidation of the assets, provided that the board has apparently performed its duties in an improper way and it is plausible that this is an important cause of the bankruptcy.

(2) If the board of directors has not complied with its obligations under articles 2:10 BW *(in respect of maintaining an adequate administration of the company; PJMD)* or 2:394 BW *(in respect of timely publication of the*

---

107 See articles 2:93/2:203 BW and see also the Food Processing Machinery B.V/Clara Candy Lt.-case (HR 8 July 1992, *NJ* 1993, 116), the Stichting Diva/Meijs c.s. -case (HR 24 January 1997, *JOR* 1997, 18), the Hoekstra/Holma B.V.-case (HR 28 March 1997, *NJ* 1997, 582) and the Rabobank/Mr Niezink q.q.-case (HR 11 April 1997, *NJ* 1997, 583).

108 See articles 2:139/2:249 BW.

109 Act of 21 May 1986 (*Staatsblad* 1986, 276) concerning further amendments of certain Acts on social security, the Act concerning mandatory participation in a corporate pension fund and certain tax laws in respect of abuse of legal entities.

110 For further details in respect of the WBA, see Wezeman, *supra* footnote 95, Chapter 3, at pp. 129-271 and "*Bestuurdersaansprakelijkheid ingevolge de Tweede Misbruikwet*" by Mr J. C. van Oven in "*Onbehoorlijk bestuur in het insolventierecht*", Insolad jaarboek 1997, Prof. mr R.D. Vriesendorp (editor), Kluwer 1997, Deventer, pp. 1-14.

111 For a similar provision for a NV, see article 2:138 BW.

annual accounts and annual reports of the company; PJMD), it has performed its duties in an improper way and it shall be presumed that this constitutes an important cause of the bankruptcy. The same shall apply if the company is a fully liable partner in a general partnership or a limited partnership and the obligations under article 15a of Book 3 BW were not performed. Any immaterial default shall not be taken into account.

(3) A director shall not be liable if he proves that the improper performance of duties by the board of directors is not attributable to him and that he has not been negligent in taking measures to prevent the consequences thereof.

(4) A court may reduce the amount for which the directors are liable if it considers the same excessive, having regard to the nature and seriousness of the improper performance of duties by the board of directors, the other causes of the bankruptcy and the manner in which the company is liquidated. Furthermore, the court may reduce the amount of the liability of an individual director if it considers the same excessive, having regard to the time during which the director was in office in the period during which the improper performance of duties took place.

(5) If the extent of the deficit is not yet known, the court may determine that a statement of the deficit shall be prepared pursuant to the provisions of the Sixth Title of the Second Book of the Rv and order the directors to pay the amount of such deficit, whether or not paragraph (4) above is applied.

(6) An action may be instituted only on the grounds of improper performance of duties in respect of duties performed during the period of three years preceding the bankruptcy. The institution of an action shall not be barred by any discharge granted to a director.

(7) Any person who has determined, or jointly determined, the policy of the business of a company as if he were a managing director shall, for the purposes of this article, be treated as a managing director. No action may be instituted against an administrator appointed by the court.

(8) This article shall be without prejudice to the power of the trustee in bankruptcy to institute an action on the grounds of an agreement with a director or on the grounds of article 2:9 BW.

(9) If a director is liable pursuant to this article but is not in a position to meet such liability, the trustee in bankruptcy may, by means of an extra-judicial statement, on behalf of the estate, nullify any legal actions which the director was not under a duty to perform and as a result of which the possibility of

recourse against him is diminished, provided that it is likely that such acts were performed wholly or almost wholly with the intent of diminishing such recourse. Article 45, paragraphs 4 and 5 of Book 3 BW (*rules in respect of actio pauliana by creditors outside a bankruptcy; PJMD*[112]) shall apply *mutatis mutandis*.

(10) If the assets of an estate are insufficient for the institution of a legal action on the grounds of this article or of article 2:9 BW or for the institution of a prior inquiry as to the possibility thereof, the trustee in bankruptcy may apply to Our Minister of Justice for the necessary funds by way of an advance. Our Minister may make rules for the consideration of the justification of the application and for the parameters within which the application may be granted. The application must state the grounds on which it is based and a reasoned estimate of the costs and the extent of the inquiry. To the extent that the application concerns the institution of a prior inquiry, it shall require the approval of the supervisory judge.

4.3.1.2.2   The requirements for liability pursuant to article 2:248 Netherlands Civil Code

For a successful liability claim on the basis of article 2:248 BW there must be:
(1) a bankruptcy of a company (*i.e.* a BV);
(2) apparent mismanagement of the board of directors of the BV; and
(3) *prima facie* evidence that the apparent mismanagement was an important cause of the bankruptcy.
Each of these 3 requirements will be briefly discussed below.

4.3.1.2.2.1   Bankruptcy of a company

Representation of the trustee in bankruptcy

A liability claim pursuant to article 2:248 BW can only be invoked by the trustee in bankruptcy[113] and, as a result of the special nature of this claim, it cannot be transferred[114]. One view[115] in this context is that when a claim on the basis of article 2:248 BW is submitted, the trustee in bankruptcy acts as representative of the interests of the joint creditors of the bankrupt company. Others[116], however,

---

112   For more details on the rules of *actio pauliana*, see § 4.1.
113   See Wezeman, *supra* footnote 95, at p. 323.
114   This follows from the Bowling Kralingen-case of the Netherlands supreme court (HR 7 September 1990, *NJ* 1991, 52).
115   See Wezeman, *supra* footnote 95, at p. 323.
116   See *"De faillissementscurator: vertegenwoordiger of niet?"* by Prof. mr. S.C.J.J. Kortmann and Mr N.E.D. Faber in *"De curator, een octopus"*, Prof. mr S.C.J.J. Kortmann c.s. (editors), W.E.J. Tjeenk Willink 1996, Deventer, pp. 139-172, at pp. 154-159.

challenge this view and argue that the claim based on article 2:248 BW should not be considered as an external liability claim, but an internal liability claim. They reason – in short – that the obligation for the directors to properly perform their duties is, strictly speaking, only an obligation towards the bankrupt company and not towards the creditors of the company.

4.3.1.2.2.2 Apparent mismanagement

Hard and fast rules do not exist on what constitutes "apparent mismanagement" within the meaning of article 2:248 BW. An indication of how the term should be viewed is given below by an extract from the parliamentary notes to article 2:248 BW.

The parliamentary notes

Whether or not there is a case of apparent mismanagement must be judged at the moment when the acts of management were conducted, without hindsight. The parliamentary notes indicate by way of further explanation the following[117]:

> "(...) It must be decided whether the acts of management that are challenged (or omissions to act) qualify as mismanagement when the act or omission occurred. In considering this question a court must, obviously, take into account all the facts and circumstances of the matter at hand and the court must come to a reasonable and fair judgment. The court cannot be asked to take the seat of the entrepreneur. Aside from that, one must be conscious of the fact that the line dividing mismanagement from management that may have been detrimental for the company and its creditors, but cannot qualify as mismanagement, is not always easy to draw. A so-called "grey area" exists. The recognition of this fact, however, must not result in the test for mismanagement becoming blurred and liability of directors only being concluded in cases of *exceptional* mismanagement. There is no good reason to use such a "difficult to meet"-criterium (*"zo weinig dwingend criterium"*) in an Act that aims to prevent abuse. In the old text the terms "willful misconduct" and "gross negligence" were used. Exactly because these criteria make the limits to liability of directors so great, we have now looked for a term with a broader content. However, the reason for the addition of the word "apparent" is to make it absolutely clear that the improper nature of the act or omission of the board must be obvious and that in case of doubt (the "grey area") no liability arises. (...) However, mismanagement must definitely be distinguished from "unprofessional", "thoughtfulness" or "unwise" management or other management that may be detrimental to the (creditors of the) company, but does not in itself need to be improper. The term "improper" must be read especially to include an element of blame. In this context, improper conduct towards the creditors is especially important because the creditors are the victims of the bankruptcy that is caused by that conduct to a great extent. (...)"

From this extract it follows that the test for apparent mismanagement is not easily met. In order to help the trustee in bankruptcy in meeting this test, two legal presumptions are included in article 2:248 BW, each of which will be addressed below.

---

117   MvT, Tweede Kamer, 16 631, no. 6, p. 4.

4.3.1.2.2.2.1   Legal presumptions in article 2:248 Netherlands Civil Code

Two legal presumptions

When the board of directors of a bankrupt company has not fully fulfilled either its obligations to maintain an adequate administration of the company pursuant to article 2:10 BW or its obligations to timely publish the annual accounts and annual report of the company pursuant to article 2:234 BW, there is by virtue of law:
(1) an irrebuttable presumption of apparent mismanagement by the board of directors; and
(2) a rebuttable presumption that this apparent mismanagement was an important cause of the bankruptcy.

Article 2:10 BW

Pursuant to article 2:10 paragraph 1 BW the board of directors of a company is obliged to administer to the financial condition of the company and everything relating to its activities in such a way as the activities may require, and keep the books, records and other carriers of information pertaining thereto in a manner so that the rights and obligations of the company can be ascertained at any time[118]. Books, records and other carriers of information need to be retained for 7 years.[119]

Article 2:394 BW

Pursuant to article 2:394 paragraph 3 BW the board of directors of a company is obliged to publish the annual accounts and the annual report of the company within 13 months from the end of the fiscal year[120]. Publication is made by depositing a copy prepared entirely in Dutch, or, if no Dutch version is prepared, a copy in French, German or English, at the trade register kept by the competent Chamber of Commerce and Industries[121].

4.3.1.2.2.2.2   Immaterial default

In respect of the obligations discussed above pursuant to article 2:10 BW and 2:394 BW it should be noted that an "immaterial default" is not taken into ac-

---

118   For more details on the administration obligation pursuant to article 2:10 BW in the context of the WBF, see Wezeman, *supra* footnote 95, at pp. 296-318.
119   See article 2:10 paragraph 3 BW.
120   For more details on this issue, see *"Curator, jaarrekening, en voortzetting van het bedrijf"* by Mr J.W. Winter in *"De curator, een octopus"*, Prof. mr S.C.J.J. Kortmann c.s. (editors), W.E.J. Tjeenk Willink 1996, Deventer, pp.37-48 at pp. 40-42.
121   See article 2:394 paragraph 1 BW.

count pursuant to paragraph 2 of article 2:248 BW. From case law it further follows that in respect of the publication obligation of article 2:394 BW, overstepping the 13 months-period by a few days is considered to be an immaterial default. In the *Kempers en Sarper*-case[122] it was held that missing the 13 months-period by 12 days constituted an immaterial default while in the *Pfennings/Mr Niederer q.q.*-case[123], missing the deadline by 17 days without providing for a reasonable excuse, was held to be a material default.

As a general rule of guidance, it is safe to say that the longer the 13 months-period is exceeded by, the more important the circumstances of the case will have to be to justify it[124].

4.3.1.2.2.2.3   Three year limit

From paragraph 6 of article 2:248 BW it follows that only mismanagement performed during the period of three years preceding the bankruptcy is relevant for a claim based on article 2:248 BW. The purpose of this three year limit is to prevent article 2:248 BW from operating too harshly on directors and former directors[125]. However, it is important to note that even if mismanagement occurred more than three years preceding the bankruptcy, a claim based on article 2:248 BW may still be successful if the situation that was created by that mismanagement is continued by the board of directors of the bankrupt company during the 3 year time span because that, in itself, may result in apparent mismanagement within the meaning of article 2:248 BW[126].

4.3.1.2.2.3   Apparent mismanagement is an important cause of the bankruptcy

The requirements for article 2:248 BW are not met when the bankruptcy was primarily the result of external factors, beyond the control of the directors. The parliamentary notes to article 2:248 BW provide the following guidance on this requirement[127]:

> "(...) The bill (*including article 2:248 BW; PJMD*) is aimed at easing the position of the directors in this respect by the choice of the term "an important cause". This term says exactly what is meant, not more and not less. In comparison to the old text, it is clear that "important" includes more than partially, meaning that the conduct of the

---

122   HR 11 June 1993, *NJ* 1993, 713.
123   HR 2 February 1996, *NJ* 1996, 406.
124   For more details in respect of the qualification of "immaterial default" within the meaning of article 2:248 BW, see Wezeman, *supra* footnote 95, at pp. 316-318.
125   MvT, Tweede Kamer, 16 631, no. 3, p. 6.
126   See the Mr Luchtman q.q./Van Gils c.s.-case (District court of Breda 10 June 1997, *JOR* 1997, 95).
127   MvA, Eerste Kamer, 16 631, no. 27b, pp. 8-9.

board of directors in light of the causes *(for the bankruptcy; PJMD)*, must take a noticeable place. It is insufficient if the conduct has, to a certain extent, contributed to the bankruptcy, but, in comparison to other causes, played a minor role. On the other hand, one cannot equal "important" with "to a predominant degree" (*"in overwegende mate"*). (...) We have not opted for the term "to a predominant degree" but for the less difficult to meet term (*"de minder ver gaande term"*) "important". As a necessary consequence thereof, we believe that conduct which has not caused the bankruptcy to a predominant degree, but which conduct has been noticeably meaningful for the creation of the situation *(of bankruptcy; PJMD)*, should be considered to be an important cause of the bankruptcy. (...)."

4.3.1.2.3   Exculpation and mitigation under article 2:248 Netherlands Civil Code

Exculpation

The liability that may follow from article 2:248 BW is primarily imposed on the *collective body* of the board of directors. However, in light of the possibility of exculpation that is provided in paragraph 3 of article 2:248 BW, the conduct of each director individually is also important. Where a director is prevented by his co-directors from proper management, the director can invoke the third paragraph of article 2:248 BW and release himself from liability by showing that he was not to blame for the mismanagement. Whether or not an exculpation will be granted to the director will greatly depend on the specific facts and circumstances of the matter at hand. In such a situation, the appeal for exculpation will be more acceptable if the director has resigned or resisted the improper conduct of the board of directors in other ways [128].

Mitigation

The liability pursuant to article 2:248 BW is aimed at recovering the deficit in the bankruptcy. It is possible that the deficit exceeds the damages that have resulted from the apparent mismanagement. In such a situation it is considered unreasonable to hold a director liable for a higher amount than the amount of damages that could have resulted from the mismanagement[129], and a court may *ex officio* use the mitigation possibility provided in paragraph 4 of article 2:248 BW. In mitigating liability the court can take into account[130]:
(1) the part that mismanagement has contributed to the total of causes that resulted in the bankruptcy;

---

128   MvA, Tweede Kamer, 16 631, no. 6, p. 19. See also Wezeman, *supra* footnote 95, at pp. 295-296.
129   MvT, Tweede Kamer, 16 631, no. 3, p. 5.
130   MvT, Tweede Kamer, 16 631, no. 3, p. 5. See Wezeman, *supra* footnote 95, at pp. 346-351.

(2) the manner in which the bankruptcy has been liquidated by the trustee in bankruptcy; and

(3) where both new and former directors are held liable, the period of time when the mismanagement of the board of directors took place.

4.3.1.2.4 The scope of article 2:248 Netherlands Civil Code

Article 2:248 BW is primarily addressed to current and former statutory directors of the bankrupt company[131]. However, in paragraph 7 the scope of article 2:248 BW is extended to those persons who determine or co-determine the policy of the business of the company as if they were a director of the company (hereinafter referred to as: "Par. 7-directors"). When does a person qualify as a Par. 7-director? The question is not easy to answer. Hard and fast rules do not exist. Below, a search for guidelines as to when a person qualifies as a Par.7-director will be conducted by having a closer look at the following three elements of paragraph 7 of article 2:248 BW:

(1) (co-)determinator of the policy of the business of the company (§ 4.3.1.2.4.1);

(2) policy (§ 4.3.1.2.4.2); and

(3) acting as if one were a director (§ 4.3.1.2.4.3).

Parliamentary notes

From the following extract of the parliamentary notes to article 2:248 BW[132], it is clear that in this context the facts and circumstances of the matter at hand are very important in determining who is a "Par. 7-director"[133]:

> "(...) I *(the Minister; PJMD)* deem a further clarification of paragraph 7 as suggested by the members *(of parliament; PJMD)* not possible. In that case, danger exists that one has to revert to a more or less case-by-case description which will not clarify the provision. We are dealing here with a concept that must obtain its content by application of the statutory provision to specific cases in practice. (...)"

4.3.1.2.4.1 (Co-)policy-determinator

The parliamentary notes to article 2:248 BW[134] provide the following guidance on the term "(co-)policy- determinator":

> "(...) I have been asked to further clarify what is meant by (co-)policy-determinators. In this respect, one could think of persons inside the company, for example a (major-

---

131 MvT, Tweede Kamer, 16 631, no. 3, p. 5.

132 MvA, Tweede Kamer, 16 631, no. 6, p. 19.

133 For further details, see Wezeman, *supra* footnote 95, at pp. 195-212.

134 MvA, Tweede Kamer, 16 631, no. 6, pp. 42-43.

ity) shareholder or a director of the supervisory board, who has a factual position of power and there from they control the board of directors and (co-)determine its policy. A complete list of the persons that must be considered as policy-determinators can, however, not be given. It will depend, for a great deal, on the circumstances of the case. One cannot anticipate all situations that can arise. It is true that a parent company may also, under certain circumstances, qualify as a policy-determinator. In my opinion, it is not advisable to regulate, in the statutory provision itself, that advisors, credit providers and the like cannot qualify as policy-determinators. Such a list could result in the incorrect assumption that others who are not included therein, do qualify as policy-determinators. On the other hand, circumstances are imaginable in which advisors or credit providers make use of their position – thereby exceeding the limits of their assignment or service providing – to take control and act as policy-determinators. In that case, the statutory provision should not protect them. (...)".

4.3.1.2.4.2   Policy

The parliamentary notes to article 2:248 BW[135] clarify the term "policy" as follows:

"(...) I have been asked what is meant by "policy". I believe that this term should be interpreted in an extensive manner, meaning that it not only includes consistency of behavior following from a series of management acts, but also, in some circumstances, one management decision evidencing a serious lack of a notion of responsibility or even a dishonest intention (...)."

4.3.1.2.4.3   Acting as if one were a director

The parliamentary notes to article 2:248 BW[136] explain the concept of "acting as if one were a director" as follows:

"(...) The addition "as if he were a director" aims to draw a certain line between persons inside a company (the enterprise), who in fact perform the management task without being formal directors, and others, who may have influence on policy making, but stand outside the company (the enterprise). In the explanatory notes, credit institutions, advisors, and government-appointed observers were mentioned as examples of the latter category. Setting conditions for credit provision, providing corporate advice, and providing certain directions, does not, in general, qualify as policy-determination "as if one were a director". When a board of directors accepts such conditions or follows such advice or directions and acts accordingly, it is the board that acts, not the credit institution or the external advisor. When a director of the supervisory board acts within the boundaries of his statutory and corporate powers, he is not acting as a director. However, if he, by using his factual position of power within the company, has control, attracts the management power and imposes his will on the formal directors,

---

135   MvA, Tweede Kamer, 16 631, no. 6, p. 24.
136   MvA, Tweede Kamer, 16 631, no. 6, pp. 23-24.

he qualifies as a policy-determinator within the meaning of paragraph 7 *(of article 2:248 BW; PJMD)*. The same applies to advisors or credit providers when they leave their position of being an outsider and in fact take over the management task. A parent company can also, without being a formal director of its daughter company *(subsidiary; PJMD)*, act as a policy-determinator when it in fact, as a result of its position of power, takes over the leadership of the daughter company and directly imposes its will on the formal directors (...)."

Practice and case law[137] show that one qualifies as a Par. 7-director only in very exceptional cases.

Directors of the supervisory board

Aside from being applicable to formal directors and Par. 7-directors, article 2:248 BW also applies to directors of the supervisory board of a bankrupt company[138].

Summary
LIABILITY OF DIRECTORS

INTERNAL LIABILITY

Article 2:9 BW:
(1) demands from the director proper performance of the duties assigned to him;
(2) provides for liability of the board as a collective body with an individual exculpation possibility for each director; and
(3) results in personal liability for the director if he is "seriously to blame" for mismanagement.

Statute of limitations:
The limitation period is 5 years from the aggrieved party becoming aware of both damages and the identity of the party to be held liable for the damages.

---

137   See, *inter alia*, the Koster/Mr Van Nie q.q.-case (HR 20 May 1988, *NJ* 1989, 676), the Mr Van Essen q.q./Aalbrecht c.s.-case (HR 30 May 1997, *JOR* 1997, 111), the Kandel/Koolhaas Verzekeringen N.V.-case (HR 7 November 1997, *NJ* 1998, 269), Mr Luchtman q.q./Van Gils c.s.-case (District court of Breda, 10 June 1997, *JOR* 1997, 95). the Montedison/Mr De Liagre Böhl q.q. (Court of appeals of Amsterdam 26 November 1998, *JOR* 1999, 10), the Mr Van Essen q.q./Aalbrecht c.s. II-case (Court of appeals of Amsterdam 10 June 1999, *JOR* 2001, 23), the Mr Libosan q.q./Van Roij-case (Court of appeals of the Hague 26 September 2000, *JOR* 2001, 24).
138   See article 2:259 BW for a BV and article 2:149 BW for a NV. For further details on the liability of directors of the supervisory board, see § 4.3.2.

Discharge:
A discharge may be used to avoid a successful claim pursuant to article 2:9 BW, but it may be invalidated on the basis of (i) a violation of the principle of reasonableness and fairness or (ii) *actio pauliana.*

The STALEMAN/VAN DE VEN-case:
(1) includes a non-exhaustive list of circumstances that need to be taken into account when determining liability pursuant to article 2:9 BW; and
(2) provides rules of guidance on the scope of a discharge.

EXTERNAL LIABILITY

The requirements of article 2:248 BW:
(1) Bankruptcy of a BV;
(2) Apparent mismanagement of the board of directors; and
(3) *Prima facie* evidence that the apparent mismanagement is an important cause of the bankruptcy.

Ad. (1)
A claim based on article 2:248 BW can only be invoked by the trustee in bankruptcy.

Ad. (2)
Presumptions exist by virtue of law where the board of directors has not fully fulfilled either its obligations to keep an adequate administration of the company pursuant to article 2:10 BW or its obligations to timely publish annual accounts and annual report of the company pursuant to article 2:234 BW. But an immaterial default is not taken into account.

Only mismanagement performed during the period of three years preceding the bankruptcy is relevant for a claim based on article 2:248 BW.

Ad. (3)
There is no liability of directors on the basis of article 2:248 BW when the bankruptcy was primarily the result of external factors beyond the control of the directors.

Exculpation
When a director is prevented by his co-directors from proper management, the director can invoke the third paragraph of article 2:248 BW and release himself from personal liability by showing that he was not to blame for the mismanagement. Whether or not exculpation will be granted to the director will greatly depend on the specific facts and circumstances of the matter at hand.

Mitigation

It is possible that the deficit in a bankruptcy exceeds the damages that have resulted from the apparent mismanagement. In such a situation it is considered unreasonable to hold a director liable for a higher amount than the amount of damages that could have resulted from the mismanagement and there is a possibility of mitigating the liability of the director(s).

Scope of article 2:248 BW

Article 2:248 BW covers:

(1) current and former directors of a BV;
(2) persons who determine or co-determine the policy of the business of the company as if they were a director of the company ("Par. 7-directors"); and
(3) current and former directors of the supervisory board of a BV.

4.3.2 LIABILITY OF DIRECTORS OF A SUPERVISORY BOARD

In the Netherlands, the adoption of a two-tier-system of corporate governance requiring the installation of a supervisory board is required pursuant to the so-called *"Structuurregeling"*[139]. However, companies can also voluntarily elect to establish a supervisory board.

The duties of the directors of a supervisory board can be described as supervision of the policy of the board of directors of the company, the general course of affairs of the company and the enterprise connected therewith[140]. A director of the supervisory board assists the board of directors with advice. In fulfilling his duties, a director of the supervisory board shall be guided by the interest of the company and the enterprise connected therewith.

Similar to directors of a company, directors of the supervisory board of a company can be held liable on the basis of article 2:9 BW, and in a bankruptcy of the company, on the basis of article 2:248 BW[141]. For more details on a liability claim based on article 2:9 BW, see § 4.3.1.1 and for more details on a liability claim based on article 2:248 BW, see § 4.3.1.2.

---

139 For more details on the *"Structuurregeling"*, see Section 6 of Book 2 BW concerning the supervisory board in a large NV (articles 2:152-2:165 BW) and Section 6 of Book 2 BW concerning the supervisory board in a large BV (articles 2:262-2:275 BW). It should further be noted that changes to the current *"Structuurregeling"* are in progress. For more details in that respect, see bill 25 732.

140 See articles 2:140/2:250 paragraph 2 BW.

141 See articles 2:149/2:259 BW. As indicated in § 4.3.1.2, in case of a bankrupt NV claims will have to be based on article 2:138 BW instead of article 2:248 BW.

When applying articles 2:9 and 2:248 BW to directors of the supervisory board, the measuring-rule will be the duties (as described above) that are imposed on the supervisory board. As a consequence, articles 2:9 and 2:248 BW have a different application for directors of the supervisory board than for directors of the company, because the duties of the two types of directors are different.

4.3.2.1   The BODAM YACHTSERVICE-case

The Netherlands supreme court provided the following rules of guidance in the *Bodam Yachtservice*-case[142] for the application of the rules of article 2:248 BW to directors of a supervisory board:

(1) The directors of the supervisory board are not themselves required to comply with the obligations set forth in article 2:248 paragraph 2 BW in respect of keeping an adequate administration pursuant to article 2:10 BW and the timely publication of the annual accounts and the annual report of the company pursuant article 2:394 BW, even if the board of directors fails to (fully) comply with these obligations[143];

(2) It is the duty of the supervisory board to supervise the compliance by the board of directors of the above obligations; and

(3) In fulfilling their duty, each director of the supervisory board has an obligation:
   (i)   to be adequately informed by the board of directors;
   (ii) to advise the board of directors in respect of the compliance with their obligations; and
   (iii) to intervene (if necessary), for example, by advancing the suspension or the dismissal of one or more directors of the board.

From the foregoing it follows that under Netherlands law, in order to avoid personal liability, an active approach of the directors of the supervisory board is required.

Summary
LIABILITY OF DIRECTORS OF A SUPERVISORY BOARD

(1) Similar to directors of a company, directors of the supervisory board of a company can be held liable:
   (i)   on the basis of article 2:9 BW; and
   (ii) in a bankruptcy of the company by the trustee in bankruptcy on the basis of article 2:248 BW.

---

142   HR 28 June 1996, *NJ* 1997, 58.
143   See also § 4.3.1.2.2.2.1. on legal presumptions in article 2:248 BW.

(2) Articles 2:9 and 2:248 BW have a different application for directors of a supervisory board than for directors of a company, because the duties of the two types of directors are different.

(3) From the *Bodam Yachtservice*-case it follows that an active approach of the directors of a supervisory board is required in order to avoid personal liability.

4.3.3 LIABILITY OF SHAREHOLDERS

Limited liability of shareholders

The shareholders of a company are only liable to pay up the nominal amount of the shares they subscribed for[144]. No other obligation may be imposed upon a shareholder against its will, not even by amending the articles of association of the company[145]. Aside from providing capital to the company by paying up their subscribed shares, the general meeting of shareholders of the company has – within the limits set by the law and the articles of association of the company – any powers not conferred upon the board of directors of the company or other persons in the company[146]. In addition, the board of directors and the supervisory board of the company have a duty to render the general meeting of shareholders with all the information the shareholders request, unless this conflicts with a substantial interest of the company[147].

From the foregoing it follows that – as a general rule of Netherlands company law – the shareholders of a company are neither personally liable for acts performed in the name of the company nor are they liable to contribute to the losses of the company in excess of the amount they paid up on the shares they subscribed for. Nevertheless, in practice, liability of shareholders remains an issue, especially in cases where a parent company is the sole shareholder of the bankrupt company. Therefore, in the coming paragraphs the following grounds of extended liability for shareholders will be addressed:

(1) Extended liability based on the so-called "403-declaration" (§ 4.3.3.1);
(2) Extended liability based on article 2:248 paragraph 7 BW (§ 4.3.3.2); and
(3) Extended liability based on specific circumstances derived from case law (§ 4.3.3.3).

---

144   See article 2:80/2:191 BW.
145   See articles 2:81/2:192 BW.
146   See articles 2:107/2:217 paragraph 1 BW.
147   See articles 2:107/2:217 paragraph 2 BW.

4.3.3.1   Extended liability pursuant to the 403-declaration

Article 2:403 BW

Provided that certain conditions are met, article 2:403 BW gives a company, which forms part of a group, the possibility of presenting its annual accounts in a more simplified way than it would otherwise have to if it presented its annual accounts in accordance with the provisions of law. The financial information in respect of a company that wishes to benefit from article 2:403 BW must already have been consolidated by another company in its annual accounts[148]. Typically, a parent company will consolidate the financial information of its subsidiary or subsidiaries in its annual accounts. One of the most important conditions attached to article 2:403 BW is a financial condition, which – in practice – is also referred to as the "403-declaration". Only this condition will be addressed further[149].

The 403-declaration

The 403-declaration can be described as the obligation of a parent company (*i.e.* the company in whose annual accounts the financial information is consolidated in respect of its subsidiaries) to declare in writing that it assumes joint and several liability for any obligations arising from legal acts of its subsidiary or subsidiaries (*i.e.* the company that wishes to benefit from article 2:403 BW)[150]. Such 403-declaration must be filed with the trade register of the Chamber of Commerce and Industries where the subsidiary or subsidiaries are required to be registered[151].

Scope

Legal authors in the Netherlands are divided as to what the exact scope of the 403-declaration should be[152]. The dominant view seems to be that a 403-declaration can cover both existing and future liabilities. It is further argued that a parent company can use the 403-declaration to specify which liabilities it wishes to cover by, for example, limiting itself to liabilities that arise or become due and payable after a certain date. If nothing to that effect is mentioned in the 403-declaration, the date the 403-declaration is filed with the trade register of the competent Chamber of Commerce and Industries will be considered to be the com-

---

148   See article 2:403 paragraph 1 sub c BW.
149   For a detailed discussion of the conditions of article 2:403 BW, see *"De jaarrekening-vrijstelling voor afhankelijke groepsmaatschappijen: Een analyse van artikel 2:403 BW en zijn voorgangers"* by Prof. mr H. Beckman, Kluwer 1995, Deventer, pp. 1-812 and *"Aansprakelijkheid in concernverhoudingen"*, by Mr L.G.H.J. Houwen/Mr drs. A.P. Schoonbrood-Wessels/Mr J.A.W. Schreurs, Kluwer 1993, Deventer, pp. 815-857.
150   See article 2:403 paragraph 1 sub f BW.
151   See article 2:403 paragraph 1 sub g BW.
152   See Beckman, *supra* footnote 149, at pp. 294-297.

mencement date of the declaration. In that case, however, it remains uncertain whether or not liabilities that were already due and payable on the commencement date are also covered by the 403-declaration[153].

Withdrawal

A withdrawal of the 403-declaration is possible by filing a statement to that effect with the trade register of the Chamber of Commerce and Industries where the 403-declaration was initially filed[154]. As a result of such a filing, the parent company will no longer be liable for liabilities arising *after* the filing of the statement of withdrawal. Nevertheless, the liability of the parent company shall continue to exist in respect of the obligations that arise from legal acts performed *before* the withdrawal could be invoked against creditors of the subsidiary[155]. This remaining liability towards creditors only ceases to exist if the following conditions are satisfied[156]:

(1) the subsidiary no longer forms part of the group (of the parent company);
(2) a notice of the intention to terminate has been made available for inspection at the Chamber of Commerce and Industries at which the subsidiary company is registered for at least two months;
(3) at least two months have lapsed since the publication in a nationally distributed daily newspaper of a notice that such information is available and where it may be inspected; and
(4) creditors have not timely opposed such intention or their opposition has been withdrawn or declared unfounded by an non-appealable decision of a competent court.

From the foregoing it follows that before a company decides to file for its own bankruptcy, it should be investigated whether or not a 403-declaration exists. If a 403-declaration exists and it has not yet been withdrawn, a bankruptcy of the subsidiary will have substantial consequences for the parent company. Even if a 403-declaration was filed in the past but has already been withdrawn, it is important for the parent company to assess whether or not it still can incur some liability.

4.3.3.2 Extended liability pursuant to article 2:248 paragraph 7 Netherlands Civil Code

As discussed in more detail above in § 4.3.1.2.1, article 2:248 BW provides the

---

153 For a detailed discussion of the different views in this respect, see Beckman, *supra* footnote 149, at pp. 497-536.
154 See article 2:404 paragraph 1 BW.
155 See article 2:404 paragraph 2 BW.
156 See article 2:404 paragraph 3 BW.

trustee in bankruptcy with a liability claim against the directors of the board of a bankrupt BV for the deficit of the bankrupt estate[157]. Pursuant to paragraph 7, the scope of article 2:248 BW is extended to those persons who determine or co-determine the policy of the business of the company as if they were a director of the company. In § 4.3.1.2.4 these persons were defined as "Par. 7-directors". Under certain circumstances the shareholders of the bankrupt company may also qualify as Par. 7-directors.

It is difficult to say when exactly a shareholder will qualify as a Par. 7-director. In assessing this, the following three important elements of paragraph 7 of article 2:248 BW must be borne in mind:
(1) (co-)determinator of the policy of the business of the company;
(2) policy; and
(3) to act as if one were a director.
For further details on each of these three elements see guidelines in § 4.3.1.2.4.1 – § 4.3.1.2.4.3.

4.3.3.3   Extended liability based on specific circumstances derived from case law

Which specific circumstances derived from case law may result in an extended liability of shareholders? Guidance can be found in a string of landmark cases in the Netherlands dealing with liability in situations of insolvency or near insolvency. Below, the most important cases will be addressed. The facts of each case will not be discussed in great detail and the conclusions that can be derived from the case will be summarized.

4.3.3.3.1   The OSBY-case[158]

In this case, the Netherlands subsidiary (*"Osby-Nederland N.V."*) of a Swedish parent company (*"Osby-Pannan A/B"*) filed for its own bankruptcy in the Netherlands in March 1970. Subsequently, one of the creditor of the bankrupt Netherlands subsidiary (*"Las Verkoopmaatschappij B.V."*) held the Swedish parent company liable for an unpaid claim it had against the bankrupt Netherlands subsidiary. The Swedish parent company challenged this claim by referring to the limited liability of shareholders. The creditor, however, argued that the circumstances of this matter must result in an extended liability for the Swedish parent company as sole shareholder of the bankrupt Netherlands subsidiary. In short, the Netherlands supreme court was asked whether in the circumstances of this case, the solvent parent company could be held liable by a creditor of the Netherlands subsidiary.

---

157   For a bankrupt NV, see article 2:138 BW instead of article 2:248 BW.
158   HR 25 September 1981, *NJ* 1982, 443.

Judgment of the Netherlands supreme court

The Netherlands supreme court reached the following conclusions:

(1) A parent company can, under certain circumstances, be held liable against creditors of its subsidiary on the basis of wrongful act, provided that:
   (i)   the parent company holds all the shares in the subsidiary;
   (ii) the parent company has granted the subsidiary a credit;
   (iii) the parent company subsequently acquires all or almost all of the assets of the subsidiary (including future assets) in security ownership[159];
   (iv) the subsidiary is not able to provide recourse to the creditors that gave the subsidiary credit after the transfer to the parent company took place; and
   (v)   the parent company omits to take into account the interests of those new creditors.
(2) Liability of the parent company can be concluded especially when the parent company had insight in and control over the policy of the subsidiary to such an extent that:
   (i)   at the time of its acts, the parent company knew or should have foreseen that new creditors would be prejudiced by lack of recourse, in view of:
         –   the amount of parent company's claim (against the subsidiary);
         –   the amount of the transfer of security ownership;
         –   the course of affairs in the business of the subsidiary; and
   (ii) despite that, the parent company omits to take care that the creditors are satisfied.

4.3.3.3.2   The ALBADA JELGERSMA-case[160]

In this case, a company (*"Wijnalda Kuntz B.V."*) was declared bankrupt in March 1981. Subsequently, a creditor of the bankrupt company (*"Intercooperatieve Zuivelfabriek van Antwerpen"*) held the parent company (*"Albada Jelgersma Holding B.V."*) of the (bankrupt) subsidiary liable for an unpaid claim it had against the subsidiary.

Prior to acquiring the shares of the subsidiary, the parent company sent a letter to a great number of creditors of the subsidiary. In this letter its intention to acquire the shares in the subsidiary was announced together with a guaranty that all outstanding unpaid claims would be satisfied in the normal way on the conditions

---

159   As of 1 January 1992, the concept of security ownership has been converted into the concept of non-possessory pledge. For further details on the concept of non-possessory pledge, see § 5.2.1.1.
160   HR 19 February 1988, *NJ* 1988, 487.

that (i) no recourse would be taken by the creditors against the subsidiary for unpaid deliveries and (ii) new deliveries would continue to be made by the creditors to the subsidiary.

Judgment of the Netherlands supreme court

The Netherlands supreme court reached the following conclusion:

In light of the following circumstances, the parent company acted in a wrongful manner towards the creditor by not preventing the company from buying more goods from the creditor or alternatively, by not taking care of the payment of the continued deliveries made by the creditor to the company:

(1) The parent company had generated a great deal of publicity in respect of its acquisition of the subsidiary as a result of which an expectation was created among the creditors of the subsidiary that the parent company would succeed in making the subsidiary financially healthy again;

(2) After the acquisition, the parent company was closely and intensively involved in the subsidiary and had control over its business policy; and

(3) Having knowledge of the poor financial situation of the subsidiary, the parent company foresaw or could have foreseen that the continued deliveries by the creditors would prejudice them due to lack of recourse.

4.3.3.3.3   The NIMOX/MR VAN DEN END Q.Q.-case[161]

In this case, the subsidiary (*"Auditrade B.V."*) was declared bankrupt on 7 August 1984. In a general meeting of shareholders on 20 December 1983, the parent company (*"Nimox N.V."*) decided to pay out an amount of NLG 1,124,000 by way of dividend. Subsequently, this claim for dividend payment was converted into a loan for the same amount by the parent company to the subsidiary. As security for repayment of the loan, the parent company demanded transfer in security ownership[162] of all stock and claims of the subsidiary. After the subsidiary was declared bankrupt, the trustee in the bankruptcy, Mr Van den End q.q., instituted legal action against the parent company.

Judgment of the Netherlands supreme court

The Netherlands supreme court reached the following conclusion:

In light of the following circumstances, the parent company acted in a wrongful

---

161   HR 8 November 1991, *NJ* 1992, 174.
162   As of 1 January 1992, the concept of security ownership has been converted into the concept of non-possessory pledge. For further details on the concept of non-possessory pledge, see § 5.2.1.1.

manner against the other creditors of the subsidiary by voting in favor of the resolution to pay out a dividend of NLG 1,124,000:
(1) The dividend resolution resulted in a payout of all reserves of the subsidiary, leaving an equity of only NLG 100,000;
(2) At the time of the dividend resolution, the parent company had the certainty that, as a consequence of the dividend resolution, no reserves would be left in the subsidiary unless the Transonic-project[163] would result in the spectacular improvement of the financial condition of the subsidiary, as expected by the parent company;
(3) The risk that this expectation would not materialize should have been borne by the parent company by, in that case, making its claim in respect of payment of the dividend subordinate to the claims of other creditors of the subsidiary;
(4) By omitting to bear this risk the parent company had not taken sufficient account of the interests of the other creditors of the subsidiary; and
(5) The risk had materialized: the bankruptcy of the company was caused by the total failure of the Transonic-project.

4.3.3.3.4   The NBM/Securicor-case[164]

The subsidiary company ("*Van Luijk Moerdijk B.V.*") filed for its own bankruptcy on 17 January 1990. The key question in this case was whether or not the parent company ("*Nederlandse Bezol Maatschappij B.V.* ("NBM")") could be held liable for damages sustained by a creditor of the subsidiary company ("*Securicor Nederland B.V.* ("Securicor")") following from unpaid invoices amounting to NLG 29,581.57 for service provided in the period from 1 January to 5 February 1990.

Judgment of the Netherlands supreme court

The Netherlands supreme court reached the following conclusion:

In light of the following circumstances, NBM acted in a wrongful manner against Securicor and must be held liable for the damages sustained by Securicor:
(1) Prior to Securicor's agreement to arrange security services for the subsidiary, a representative of Securicor was informed by a representative of NBM and a representative of the subsidiary company, that the subsidiary company planned to terminate its activities, but in doing so, the representative of Securicor was assured that "the creditors of the subsidiary company would be treated in a proper manner";

---

163   The Transonic-project was a project involving hi-fi equipment to be sold by the subsidiary.
164   HR 18 November 1994, *NJ* 1995, 170.

(2) Securicor obtained comfort and could have obtained comfort from the statements made by the representative of NBM and, therefore, Securicor could expect NBM to pay for the security services Securicor agreed to arrange for the subsidiary company; and

(3) In view of the justified expectation by Securicor, it is understandable that Securicor saw no reason to secure itself, for example, by demanding security from NBM against the risks attached to accepting performance of services for the subsidiary company that was about to terminate its activities.

4.3.3.3.5   The BATO's ERF-case[165]

This case deals with, in particular, the (im)possibility of a direct "piercing of the corporate veil"[166] on the basis of close connection resulting in difficulties in identification of companies. Soil pollution had occurred from operating a brick company for a long time on certain premises. The State of the Netherlands (*"Staat der Nederlanden"*) had a claim against the party responsible for the pollution for the costs of cleaning up. In this case, it was not clear who was to be considered as the party responsible for the pollution. The parent company (*"Bato's Erf Beheer Nijmegen B.V."*) was held liable by the State of the Netherlands as the responsible party, but the parent company challenged that claim on the basis that it was its subsidiary (*"Steenfabriek Bato's Erf B.V."*) that operated the brick company and therefore should be considered to be the party responsible for the pollution.

Judgment of the Netherlands supreme court

The Netherlands supreme court reached the following conclusion:

The fact that a parent company, either by having its directors also act as directors of its subsidiary or as a director and/or sole shareholder of its subsidiary, determines the policy in respect of the business activities of the subsidiary, gives guidance, or influences the policy, does *not* lead to the conclusion that such business activities become the business activities of the parent company as a consequence, as this would mean that a parent company would be, in any event, liable for all activities that appear to be wrongful.

---

165   HR 16 June 1995, *NJ* 1996, 214.

166   For a detailed discussion of the concept of "piercing the corporate veil" in the Netherlands, see *"Identificatie in het rechtspersonenrecht: Rechtsvergelijkende beschouwingen over "Piercing the corporate veil" in het interne en internationale privaatrecht van Nederland, Duitsland, Zwitserland, New York en Texas "* by Mr. R.C. van Dongen, Kluwer 1995, Deventer, pp. 1 -362.

4.3.3.3.6 The Roco/Staat der Nederlanden-case[167]

In this case, the State of the Netherlands had a claim against the party responsible for soil pollution for the costs of the clean-up. Early in 1984, after investigations by a expert company, this pollution was discovered on the premises used by Mr J.P. Rouwenhorst ("Rouwenhorst") and his father to operate a family business in oil, fat and the like since 1922. Only in 1990 did the State of the Netherlands clean-up the discovered pollution.

In the meantime, Rouwenhorst and his wife, Ms. Hoekstra ("Hoekstra"), decided to establish the following two BVs in October 1984:
(1) Hoekstra Holding B.V., having Hoekstra as its sole director; and
(2) Roco B.V. ("Roco"), having Hoekstra Holding B.V. as its sole shareholder and Rouwenhorst as its sole director.

At the same time, the family business of Rouwenhorst and his father (including employees) was sold and transferred by Rouwenhorst to Roco. This sale and transfer took place with the exception of "all immoveable goods and debts, charges and other obligations attached thereto". This exception was a specific condition of Rouwenhorst's bank for continuing its relationship with Rouwenhorst.

In order to recover the clean-up costs, the State of the Netherlands commenced legal proceedings against both Rouwenhorst and Roco.

Judgment of the Netherlands supreme court

The Netherlands supreme court reached the following conclusions:

(1) The relevant question in this matter is *not* in which cases, generally, the difference of identity between a legal entity and one or more other (legal) persons involved with the legal entity may be ignored (resulting in the attribution of certain acts of the other (legal) persons to the legal entity), but whether or not the court of appeals could have concluded the liability of another (*i.e.* Roco) and not the original debtor by applying the "concept of identification";

(2) The Netherlands supreme court understood the application of the concept of identification by the court of appeals in this matter to work as follows:
   (i) The court of appeals considered the (former) enterprise of Rouwenhorst and the enterprise operated by Roco to be in fact one and the same (continued) enterprise;
   (ii) This consideration was made in the light of the "close involvement" of

---

167 HR 3 November 1995, *NJ* 1996, 215.

Rouwenhorst with (the incorporation of) Roco and the interest of Rouwenhorst as sole director in Roco;

(iii) The legal consequence of this consideration was that the debt, which
arose from wrongful acts committed by Rouwenhorst prior to the incorporation of Roco, had been transferred to Roco as the new owner/opera-
tor of the enterprise, because this debt was connected to the transferred
enterprise; and

(3) This use of the legal concept of identification by the court of appeals was
inappropriate in a civil law system (*as opposed to a common law system;
PJMD*) in respect of transfer of debts, arisen in the context of an enterprise,
to a person other than the original debtor.

Despite this conclusion under (3) the Netherlands supreme court rendered a decision in favor of the State of the Netherlands because the following statements of
the State of the Netherlands supported the decision of the court of appeals and
were not (sufficiently) disputed by Roco and Rouwenhorst:

(I)   The continuation of the activities by Roco had the apparent aim of avoiding
possible claims by third parties, such as the State of the Netherlands; and

(II) The State of the Netherlands is prejudiced because the liability relating to the
clean-up costs remained with Rouwenhorst, while Rocco continued the
enterprise on a different location, leaving behind the heritage of the polluted
old location.

4.3.3.3.7   The CORAL/STALT-case[168]

In this case, a creditor (*"Texan Coral Navigation Company Inc.* ("Coral")") of the
subsidiary company (*"Forsythe International NV/SA* ("Forsythe")") held the parent company (*"Stalt Holding B.V.* ("Stalt")") liable for an unpaid claim amounting to US 454, 681.76 arising from an agreement between Coral and Forsythe for
the transport of oil. Forsythe had already terminated its activities and in that context transferred a 100%-participation in another group company (*"Forsythe International Cyprus Ltd."*) (the "Cyprus-shares") to Stalt.

Judgment of the Netherlands supreme court

The Netherlands supreme court reached the following conclusion:

In light of the following circumstances (on the validity of which no decision was
given), Stalt acted in a wrongful manner towards Coral by facilitating or allowing
Forsythe to act in a wrongful manner towards Coral by subordinating the claim
of Coral:

---

168   HR 12 June 1998, *NJ* 1998, 727.

(1) The proceeds of the Cyprus-shares had been used exclusively to satisfy an intercompany claim;

(2) Forsythe had intentionally subordinated Coral in relation to its other creditors;

(3) Stalt had been intensively involved in the course of affairs at Forsythe, including the termination of the business activities of Forsythe;

(4) Stalt had facilitated, or at least allowed that, with the exception of Coral, all trade creditors of Forsythe had been satisfied;

(5) After the trade creditors were satisfied, the remaining assets of Forsythe had been used to satisfy, as much as possible, the claims of sister companies of Forsythe; and

(6) When satisfying the trade creditors and the sister companies, the board of directors of Forsythe knew or should have known that nothing would remain to pay the claim of Coral.

Summary
LIABILITY OF SHAREHOLDERS

General rule:
As a general rule of Netherlands company law, the shareholders of a company are:
(1) neither personally liable for acts performed in the name of the company;
(2) nor liable to contribute to the losses of the company in excess of the amount they paid up on the shares they subscribed for.

Extended liability pursuant to the 403-declaration:
(1) In short, the 403-declaration can be described as the obligation of the parent company to declare in writing that it assumes joint and several liability for any obligations arising from legal acts of its subsidiary or subsidiaries.
(2) The dominant view in the Netherlands is that a 403-declaration can cover both existing and future liabilities.
(3) As a result of the filing of a statement of withdrawal:
  (i) the parent company will no longer be liable for liabilities arising *after* the filing of the statement of withdrawal; and
  (ii) the liability of the parent company shall continue to exist in respect of the obligations which arise from legal acts performed *before* the withdrawal could be invoked against creditors of the subsidiary.

Extended liability pursuant to article 2:248 paragraph 7 BW:
Under certain circumstances shareholders of the bankrupt company may also qualify as persons who determine or co-determine the policy of the business

of the company as if they were a director of the company (*i.e.* "Par. 7-directors").

Extended liability based on specific circumstances derived from case law:
In order to better understand which circumstances may result in an extended liability of shareholders, the following landmark cases have been briefly discussed for rules of guidance:

- The *Osby*-case
- The *Albada Jelgersma*-case
- The *Nimox/Mr Van den End q.q.*-case
- The *NBM/Securicor*-case
- The *Bato's Erf*-case
- The *Roco/Staat der Nederlanden*-case
- The *Coral/Stalt*-case

From the above cases it follows that the following circumstances may increase the risk of an extended liability of shareholders and, consequently, require shareholders to extra take into account the interests of other creditors of the company:

(1)   A high level of insight in and control over the policy of the company;
(2)   Taking security rights from the company for the provision of credit to the company to such an extent that the company is no longer able to provide recourse to its other creditors;
(3)   Creating expectations as to (a) the improvement in the financial condition of the company by generating publicity on a large scale about one's involvement in the company or (b) the treatment of claims of the (other) creditors of the company;
(4)   Voting in favor of a dividend resolution that will result in a pay out of all reserves of the company, leaving the company with only a low level of equity to continue its business; and
(5)   Facilitating or allowing the company to satisfy all its trade creditors, with the exception of one or more specific creditors.

In addition, it further follows, especially from the *Bato's Erf*-case and the *Roco/Staat der Nederlanden*-case, that only a very restrictive use of the concept of identification (also referred to as "piercing the corporate veil") is accepted in the Netherlands.

4.4   The concept of the wrongful act

Article 6:162 BW

The general prohibition on committing a wrongful act can be found in article 6:162 BW:

(1) A person who commits a wrongful act against another which is attributable to him, is obliged to repair the damage suffered by the other in consequence thereof.
(2) Except where there are grounds for justification, the following qualifies as a wrongful act: a violation of a right and an act or omission in breach of a duty imposed by law or a rule of unwritten law pertaining to proper social conduct.
(3) A wrongful act can be attributed to the person committing the act when it is due to his fault or to a cause for which he is accountable by law or generally accepted principles.

The concept of wrongful act is certainly not restricted to situations of insolvency, but has a much wider scope. Below, only the two following insolvency related questions concerning the concept of wrongful act will be addressed:
(1) Is the trustee in bankruptcy entitled to institute a legal claim on the basis of wrongful act?
(2) What is the standard for liability of directors based on the concept of wrongful act?
The first question will be discussed in § 4.4.1 by looking at the *Mr Peeters q.q./ Gatzen*-case[169] and the second question in § 4.4.2 by looking at the *Romme/ Bakker*-case[170].

4.4.1   THE MR PEETERS Q.Q./GATZEN-CASE

In this case, the trustee in bankruptcy, Mr Peeters q.q., commenced legal proceedings against Ms. M.C.M. Gatzen ("Gatzen"), contending that Gatzen had committed a wrongful act against the joint creditors of the bankrupt debtor ("*Mr. C. van Rooy*") by facilitating the completion of a transaction prior to the bankruptcy of the debtor as a result of which the joint creditors were prejudiced. Pursuant to this transaction the debtor sold and transferred his house to a third party (*"Seco-Vastgoed Maatschappij B.V."*) at a below-market purchase price. Subsequently, the third party sold the house on to Gatzen.

---

169   HR 14 January 1983, *NJ* 1983, 597.
170   HR 10 June 1994, *NJ* 1994, 766.

Judgment of the Netherlands supreme court

The Netherlands supreme court reached the following conclusions:

(1) The position of the court of appeals was understood to be that the trustee in bankruptcy would only be allowed to bring a claim against Gatzen based on a wrongful act committed by her against the creditors of the debtor prior to its bankruptcy if, after the debtor was declared bankrupt, such claim formed part of the bankrupt estate (*i.e.* a claim of the debtor against Gatzen).

(2) In contrast to this position of the court of appeals, the Netherlands supreme court held that:

  (i) a trustee in bankruptcy is also allowed to attend to the interests of the creditors when they are prejudiced by the debtor; and

  (ii) in that case there may also be room, under certain circumstances, for the trustee in bankruptcy to bring a claim based on wrongful act against a third party involved in the prejudice of the creditors, even if the debtor obviously did not have such a claim himself.

The claim mentioned under (2)(ii) above is also referred to as the "Mr Peeters q.q./Gatzen-claim".[171]

The MR PEETERS Q.Q./GATZEN-claim in practice

The fact that no statutory legal basis exists for the "Mr Peeters q.q./Gatzen-claim" has given rise to a number of questions in practice, on the answers to which different views exist[172]. These different views will not be discussed, but some of the questions raised by the Mr Peeters q.q./Gatzen-claim are:

---

171   In the Sobi c.s./Hurks c.s.-case (HR 21 December 2001, *RvdW* 2002, 6 / *JOR* 2002, 38) the Netherlands supreme court held that the existence of the "Mr Peeters q.q./Gatzen"-claim of the trustee in bankruptcy, irrespective of whether or not the trustee in bankruptcy chooses to bring this claim, does not form an obstacle for creditors of the debtor to make the claim for damages based on wrongful act - similar to the "Mr Peeters q.q./Gatzen"-claim- against the third party who was involved in the prejudice of the creditors by the debtor, even if the debtor obviously did not have such a claim himself. The Netherlands supreme court further explained that, because this concerns a claim of prejudiced creditors against a third party, an interference of the principle to be observed in a bankruptcy of *"paritas creditorum"* (§ 1.2.2) cannot take place. The same was confirmed in the Lunderstädt/Kok c.s.-case (HR 21 December 2001, *RvdW* 2002, 7) in which case the Netherlands supreme court further held that where the trustee in bankruptcy chooses to bring his "Mr Peeters q.q./Gatzen"-claim against third parties, the interest of a proper liquidation of the bankruptcy may demand that first the claim brought by the trustee in bankruptcy is decided and subsequently the claim brought against third parties by individual creditors of the debtor.

172   See Verstijlen, *supra* footnote 45, at pp. 120-134 and see also the discussion of this book of Verstijlen by Mr J.J. van Hees in *RM Themis*, 4, 2001, pp. 122-124, especially p. 123.

(1) Is the prejudiced creditor (also) independently allowed to bring a claim against the third party or is this an exclusive power belonging to the trustee in bankruptcy?
(2) In answering this first question, does it make a difference whether or not the trustee in bankruptcy intends to bring an action against the third party?
(3) Is a prejudiced creditor, following the termination of the bankruptcy, bound by possible settlements the trustee in bankruptcy made with the third party?
(4) With regards the proceeds of the claim brought by the trustee in bankruptcy against the third party, is there a sharing in the allocation of the bankruptcy costs[173]?

4.4.2   THE ROMME/BAKKER-CASE

In this case, the sole shareholder and sole director ("*Mr. J.A.M.R. Bakker* ("Bakker")") of an insurance brokerage company ("*De Brabanden Beheer B.V.*") was held personally liable on the basis of wrongful act by a creditor of the company (" *Ms. J.A.T.P.C. Romme* ("Romme")"). The company was in default in paying life annuity benefits to Romme and subsequently went into bankruptcy on 16 June 1989. These life annuity benefits resulted from an agreement Bakker, in his capacity of director of the company, had entered into with the husband of Romme on 23 May 1980. In short, Romme contended that Bakker had acted in a wrongful manner towards her because when Bakker entered into the agreement of 23 May 1980 on behalf of the company, he knew or reasonably should have known that the company would never been able to satisfy its obligations to pay the life annuity benefits.

Judgment of the Netherlands supreme court

The Netherlands supreme court reached the following conclusions:

STANDARD OF LIABILITY
(1) The Netherlands supreme court confirmed the standard used by the court of appeals, pursuant to which Bakker could be held personally liable for damages resulting from the default of the company to satisfy its obligations under the agreement of 23 May 1980, provided that Bakker, when entering into the agreement on behalf of the company, knew or reasonably should have understood that the company:
    (i)   would not, or not within a proper period of time, be able to satisfy its obligations; and

---

173   For more details on which creditors do and do not share in the allocation of bankruptcy costs, see § 3.6.

(ii) would not provide recourse for the damages resulting there from suffered by the counter party;

RULES ON ALLOCATING THE BURDEN OF PROOF

(2) The Netherlands supreme court held that situations could exist in which it is so obvious that the party having complete control over the company should be allocated with the burden of proof that, when entering into an agreement under which the company defaulted, the party having complete control knew nor should have known the company would not be able to meet its obligations or provide recourse;

(3) If in such situations the court would nevertheless allocate the burden of proof to the party looking for recourse, the court is obliged to specify which special circumstances justify this allocation; and

(4) The Netherlands supreme court further held that those situations (as meant under (2) above) may, *inter alia*, exist when it is plausible that, when the agreement was entered into, the company:

(i) had no, or insufficient, financial means at its disposal to satisfy its obligations under the agreement; and

(ii) would be dependent on another legal entity, controlled by the company, to provide it with the necessary financial means.

Summary
THE CONCEPT OF WRONGFUL ACT

Article 6:162 BW
Pursuant to article 6:162 BW a wrongful act is:

(1) a violation of a right; and

(2) an act or omission in breach of a duty imposed by law or a rule of unwritten law pertaining to proper social conduct.

THE MR PEETERS Q.Q./GATZEN-CASE

In this case, the Netherlands supreme court held that under certain circumstances the trustee in bankruptcy can bring a claim based on wrongful act against a third party involved in the prejudice of the creditors, even if the (bankrupt) debtor did not have such a claim. In practice, this "Mr Peeters q.q./Gatzen-claim" has given rise to a number of questions, the answers to which different views exist.

THE ROMME/BAKKER-CASE

In this case, the Netherlands supreme court:

(1) confirmed a standard for liability of directors based on wrongful act; and

(2) provided rules on the allocation of the burden of proof on the director instead of the party looking for recourse.

Chapter 5
PLEDGES AND MORTGAGES

Chapter 5 focuses on the contractually created security rights of pledges and mortgages, because these security rights are considered to be the strongest rights one can have in situations of insolvency in the Netherlands. After an introduction of some general aspects common to both pledges and mortgages (§ 5.1), the discussion shall include, in respect of both pledges (§ 5.2.1) and mortgages (§ 5.3.1):
(1) the different kinds of goods over which the security rights can be vested;
(2) their creation;
(3) their content; and
(4) their foreclosure procedure.

In relation to pledges, the following 3 legal concepts will be addressed:
(1) Repledge (§ 5.2.2.1);
(2) Double pledge (§ 5.2.2.2); and
(3) Reserved pledge (§ 5.2.2.3).
The discussion of pledges will be concluded by looking at some situations of concurrence of rights (§ 5.2.3).

In relation to mortgages, the foreclosure of a mortgage on immoveable goods (§ 5.3.2) and some situations of concurrence of rights (§ 5.3.3) will be briefly discussed.

5.1   General aspects of pledges and mortgages

Security rights

Security rights in the Netherlands can be categorized into[1]:
(1) personal security rights; and
(2) collateral security rights.
Collateral security rights can further be divided into:

---

[1]   See generally *"Goederenrecht"*, by Prof mr H.J. Snijders and Mr E.B. Rank-Berenschot, Kluwer 2001, Deventer, § 482, p. 385 and *"Verstrekking van zekerheden aan internationale syndicaten"*, by Prof. mr M.V. Polak and Prof. mr A.I.M. van Mierlo, NIBE no. 31 2nd edition 1998, Den Haag, § 2.3, pp. 16-28.

(i)   relative collateral security rights (including general and special privileged rights created by virtue of law, such as the general fiscal privilege of the Netherlands tax authorities[2]); and
(ii) absolute collateral security rights.

Pledges and mortgages fall within the category of absolute collateral security rights.

Rights of recourse

Pledges and mortgages are rights of recourse against a specific property of the debtor. The principles underlying the (exercise of) rights of recourse in the Netherlands may briefly be summarized as follows:

(1) Subject to the grounds of priority recognized by law, which priority only follows from mortgage, pledge and the right of privilege and other grounds provided by law, all creditors are equally entitled to take recourse for their claim against all of the property of the debtor[3].
(2) Unless otherwise provided by law, pledge and mortgage rank higher than right of privilege[4].

Scope of pledges and mortgages

Mortgages can be exclusively vested on registered goods, including:
(1) immoveable goods;
(2) registered vessels;
(3) registered aircraft; and
(4) property (or proprietary) rights, such as, for example, a building right.

In respect of all other goods, such as, for example, non-registered moveable goods and claims, pledges must be used[5].

Pledges and mortgages are limited rights. This means that they are derived from a broader right, the principal right, which is encumbered with the limited right[6].

Pledges and mortgages are also accessory rights[7]. Accessory rights are characterized by the fact that they are always linked to the claim. If the claim is transferred, an accessory right follows the claim by virtue of law. In addition, pledges

---

2   See article 21 paragraph 1 Inv.
3   See article 3:277 paragraph 1 BW read in conjunction with article 3:278 paragraph 1 BW and § 1.2.1.
4   See article 3:279 BW.
5   See article 3:227 paragraph 1 BW.
6   See article 3:227 paragraph 1 BW.
7   See article 6:142 paragraph 1 BW.

and mortgages qualify as ancillary right[8]. Ancillary rights are generally linked to another right (the principal right) to such an extent that they cannot exist independently of that other right. Ancillary rights do not necessarily have to be linked to a claim, but, similar to accessory rights, ancillary rights generally follow the right to which they are linked. As a result of these characteristics of pledges and mortgages, it is not possible under Netherlands law to create, for example, a pledge over another pledge or a mortgage over another mortgage.

General requirements for creating pledges and mortgages

Two important general requirements for validly creating pledges and mortgages under Netherlands law are:
(1) the secured obligations of a pledge or mortgage must be monetary in nature[9]; and
(2) the collateral to be pledged or mortgaged must be transferable[10].

Ad. (1)
In practice, this requirement is often satisfied for obligations that are not monetary in nature by the use of penalty clauses.

Ad. (2)
If the collateral of a pledge consists of claims, it should be noted that:
(i) claims can be made non-transferable by contract under Netherlands law [11]; and
(ii) claims may be non-transferable due to their personal nature[12].

Important features of pledges and mortgages

The most important features of pledges and mortgages can be summarized as follows:

(1) They both have *droit de suite*, meaning that – subject to applicable rules of third party protection – a pledge or mortgage continues to rest on the encumbered good where such good is transferred to a third party[13];
(2) They both are *indivisible*, meaning that partial payment of the secured obligations has no effect on a validly vested pledge or mortgage (*i.e.* a pledge or mortgage may not be partly terminated)[14];
(3) They both are subject to *the concept of object-substitution*, meaning that –

---

8   See article 3:7 BW.
9   See article 3:227 paragraph 1 BW.
10 See article 3:228 BW read in conjunction with article 3:83 paragraph 1 BW.
11 See article 3:83 paragraph 2 BW.
12 An example of a claim that is personal in nature is the corporate liability claim a trustee in bankruptcy has based on article 2:248 BW. For more information about such a corporate liability claim, see § 4.3.1.2.1.
13 See article 3:8 BW.
14 See article 3:230 BW.

by virtue of law – pledges and mortgages include a right of pledge over all claims of compensation which replace the collateral of the pledge or mortgage, including claims resulting from its depreciation (*e.g.* claims against an insurance company)[15];

(4) They both are subject to *the rule against appropriation*, meaning that any stipulation pursuant to which the pledgee or the mortgagee is given the power to appropriate the pledged or mortgaged good is considered null and void under Netherlands law[16];

(5) They both provide – in principle – for *a right of summary execution*, meaning that an additional title of enforcement is not needed[17]; and

(6) In a Netherlands bankruptcy, parties holding a valid pledge or mortgage are considered *"separatist"*, meaning that those parties may foreclose on the pledged or mortgaged collateral as if there was no bankruptcy of the debtor[18] (§ 3.6.1).

Bank-pledges and bank-mortgages

The so-called "bank-pledge" or "bank-mortgage" may be an exception to the ancillary nature of pledges and mortgages as a result of the special nature of the secured obligations involved in bank-pledges and bank-mortgages. Contrary to other pledges or mortgages, bank-pledges and bank-mortgages do not serve as security for certain claims, but for *any* present and future claim (irrespective of its nature) the pledgee/mortgagee may have or acquire against the debtor. It has been argued that bank-pledges and bank-mortgages are related to the pledgee/mortgagee to such an extent that they should be considered personal in nature and therefore the right of pledge or the right of mortgage may not follow a transfer of the collateral pursuant to a bank-pledge or bank-mortgage.

The legal basis for such an approach towards bank-pledges and bank-mortgages is found in the *Balkema*-case[19], where the Netherlands supreme court held:

> "(...) The question whether the description of the present and future claims as security for which the mortgage serves, also results, in case of assignment, in the mortgage being exclusively attached to the party in whose favor it was vested, is in principle an issue of interpretation of such description as included in the deed of mortgage. (...)"

From this it follows that, ultimately, it is an issue of interpretation of the exact wording of the deed of pledge or mortgage to decide whether or not a pledge or mortgage is an exception to the ancillary characteristic of pledges and mortgages.

---

15   See article 3:229 paragraph 1 BW.
16   See article 3:235 BW.
17   See article 3:248 BW in respect of pledges and article 3:268 BW in respect of mortgages.
18   See article 57 paragraph 1 BW.
19   HR 16 September 1988, *NJ* 1989, 10.

Termination grounds of pledges and mortgages

Being limited rights, pledges and mortgages cease to exist in the following situations:
(1) where the principal right from which the limited right is derived ceases to exist[20];
(2) where time has lapsed or the condition subsequent is met subject to which the limited right was created;
(3) where there is a waiver;
(4) in case of a renunciation, if the power to renounce has been granted, by virtue of law or upon creation of the right, to the holder of the principal right, the holder of the limited right or to both;
(5) where there is mixing of rights (*i.e.* situations in which one person has legal title to both the limited right (pledge or mortgage) and the principal right that is encumbered with the limited right);
(6) where there is foreclosure of the principal right by an arrestor, a(nother) mortgagee or a(nother) pledgee who does not have to respect the limited right derived from the principal right and, in case of a mortgage, also where there is foreclosure by an arrestor or a(nother) mortgagee who does have to respect the relevant mortgage derived from the principle right[21].
(7) where the limitation period has lapsed in respect of a legal claim of a holder of a limited right against the holder of the principal right to terminate an existing situation which is in violation of the limited right[22]; and
(8) where there is a successful invocation of third party protection by a third party acquirer of a good encumbered with a limited right[23].

Summary
GENERAL ASPECTS COMMON TO PLEDGES AND MORTGAGES

(1) Pledges and mortgages are:
    (i) absolute collateral security rights;
    (ii) rights of recourse;
    (iii) ancillary rights (and sometimes also accessory rights); and
    (iv) limited rights.
(2) Two important general requirement for creation are:
    (i) secured obligations must be monetary in nature; and
    (ii) collateral must be transferable.
(3) Important features of pledges and mortgages include:
    (i) *droit de suite*;
    (ii) indivisible;
    (iii) subject to the concept of object-substitution;
    (iv) subject to the rule against appropriation;

---

20 See article 3:81 paragraph 2 sub a-e BW.
21 See article 3:273 paragraph 1 BW.
22 See article 3:323 paragraph 1 BW.
23 See articles 3:86 BW and 3:88 BW.

(v) right of summary execution; and

(vi) *"separatist"* in a Netherlands bankruptcy.

5.2 Pledges

The discussion of pledges will be structured as follows:

(1) In § 5.2.1, the legal requirements for validly vesting a right of pledge will be set out and discussed in respect of different types of collateral;

(2) In § 5.2.2, each of the concepts of repledge, double pledge and reserved pledge will be briefly addressed; and

(3) Finally, in § 5.2.3 some situations of concurrence of pledges with other rights will be dealt with.

5.2.1 THE LEGAL REQUIREMENTS

The following 3 legal requirements for a valid transfer of a good are equally applicable to the creation of a valid pledge in the Netherlands[24] :

(1) a valid deed of establishment;

(2) a valid title or cause; and

(3) the right of the pledgor to administer and dispose of the collateral.

Ad. (1)
In respect of this requirement, special attention will be paid to how exactly a deed of establishment should be created in order to be valid and whether or not future goods can also be pledged.

Ad. (2)
In respect of this requirement, grounds for voidness and voidability shall be addressed.

Ad. (3)
In respect of this requirement, rules of third party protection will be discussed.

In the following sections, each of these 3 legal requirements shall be discussed for the following different types of collateral:

(i) Moveable, non-registered goods (§ 5.2.1.1);

(ii) Bearer or order rights (§ 5.2.1.2);

(iii) Shares (§ 5.2.1.3); and

(iv) Claims (§ 5.2.1.4).

---

24 See article 3:98 paragraph 1 BW read in conjunction with article 3:84 paragraph 1 BW.

5.2.1.1   Moveable, non-registered goods

The following two types of pledges can be created over moveable, non-registered goods:
(1)   a possessory pledge[25]; and
(2)   a non-possessory pledge[26].

Possessory pledges

A possessory pledge is created by bringing the moveable, non-registered good (such as cars, computers, *etc.*) under the control and in the power of (*i.e.* in the physical possession of):
(i)   the pledgee; or
(ii)   a third party agreed upon by both the pledgee and the pledgor jointly.
In order to create a valid possessory pledge under Netherlands law, it is essential that the pledgor is no longer in control of the moveable, non-registered good in question[27].

Non-possessory pledges

A non-possessory pledge can be created in the following two ways[28]:
(i)   by way of notarial deed; or
(ii)   by way of registered private deed.

A non-possessory pledge created by way of notarial deed has immediate effect. A non-possessory pledge created by a registered private deed only comes into effect on the day an original copy of the private deed is submitted for registration with the Registration Department of the Tax Office[29]. In the *Mr Meijs q.q./Bank of Tokyo-Mitsubishi (Holland)*-case[30] the Netherlands supreme court held in this respect that:
(a)   instead of an original copy, registration of a fax copy of the private deed suffices; and
(b)   it is sufficient for a private deed to include information from which it follows, read in conjunction with other deeds or other facts if necessary, that the deed is intended for pledging the goods mentioned therein (*i.e.* it is sufficient that the pledgee could reasonably understand from the deed that it is intended for pledging).

---

25   See article 3:236 BW.
26   See article 3:237 BW.
27   See article 3:236 paragraph 1 BW.
28   See article 3:237 paragraph 1 BW.
29   See article 3:237 paragraph 1 BW read in conjunction with article 156 Rv.
30   HR 29 June 2001, *NJ* 2001, 662.

Another difference between the two ways of creating a non-possessory pledge becomes evident where there is a default by the pledgor. In that case, the pledgee of a non-possessory pledge is entitled to demand the release of the moveable, non-registered good[31]. When the pledgor refuses to release the good[32]:

(a) the pledgee of a non-possessory pledge created by way of notarial deed, is entitled to immediately have the pledged good arrested; and

(b) the pledgee of a non-possessory pledge created by way of registered private deed, first has to obtain consent of the President of the competent district court in order to have the pledged good arrested.

A release of the pledged good results in a conversion of the non-possessory pledge into a possessory pledge. However, if the pledged good subsequently comes in the hands of the pledgor, the rules concerning non-possessory pledge apply again, thereby preventing a loss of the pledge[33]. In that case the pledgee re-acquires its initial non-possessory pledge.

Although not a constitutive element for the creation of a non-possessory pledge, the pledgor is – by virtue of law – required to declare in the deed of establishment that[34]:

(i) the pledgor is entitled to pledge the moveable, non-registered good; and

(ii) the pledged good is not encumbered with (other) limited rights, or, if already so encumbered, set out the details of such other limited rights.

Ranking

A pledge over a moveable, non-registered good provides the pledgee with a right of recourse to which – by virtue of law – priority is attached[35]. Ranking really becomes an issue in situations of double pledges and in situations of concurrence with other rights. For those situations, see § 5.2.2.2 and § 5.2.3.

The requirement for a valid deed of establishment

In the context of the legal requirement for a valid deed of establishment, it must be noted that future goods can be pledged in advance[36]. This means that a pledgor is able to make a valid deed of establishment prior to actually becoming legally entitled to the future good, during which period, the pledgor does not have the right to administer and dispose of the future good.

---

31   See article 3:237 paragraph 3 BW.
32   See article 496 paragraph 2 Rv.
33   See article 3:258 paragraph 1 BW.
34   See article 3:327 paragraph 2 BW.
35   See article 3:279 BW.
36   See article 3:98 paragraph BW read in conjunction with article 3:97 BW.

The granting of a pledge in advance over a future good qualifies as a pledge subject to a condition precedent. The condition precedent is the acquisition by the pledgor of legal title to the pledged good. The pledge becomes effective only at that moment, provided that the pledgor has not been declared bankrupt or has been granted a suspension of payment or has lost the right to administer and dispose of the pledged good in any other way.

The requirement of a valid title or cause

The legal requirement of valid title or cause concerns the legal relation that forms the basis of the pledge and justifies it. In this context the concepts of voidness and voidability are relevant. Both concepts have retroactive effect under Netherlands law[37]. The concept of voidness applies to a legal act (such as granting a pledge) where the legal act, by its content or purpose, is immoral or violates public policy law in the Netherlands[38]. Grounds that result in the applicability of the concept of voidability to a legal act, such as a pledge over a moveable, non-registered goods, include[39]:
(1)   incapacity;
(2)   mistake;
(3)   force;
(4)   abuse of circumstances;
(5)   fraud; and
(6)   *actio pauliana*[40].

The requirement of the right to administer and dispose

The general rule pursuant to article 35 Fw (§ 1.2.1.1) is that a valid pledge is not created if at the time the pledge was effected, the pledgor lacked the right to administer and dispose of the collateral. An obvious lack of the right to administer and dispose of a moveable, non-registered good exists if the legal title to it belongs to a third party. In that case, the general rule under Netherlands law is that a valid pledge cannot be created.

Notwithstanding a lack of the right to administer and dispose of the pledged good by the pledgor, a rule of third party protection deems a pledge over a moveable, non-registered good to be validly created if the pledgee acted in good faith at the time the good was brought under its control or that of a third party[41]. In addition to this rule, another third party protection rule exists by which a pledge validly

---

37   See article 3:53 paragraph 1 BW.
38   See article 3:40 paragraph 1 BW.
39   See articles 3:32 BW, 3:44 BW, 3:45 BW and 6.228 BW.
40   For more details on the *actio pauliana*, see § 4.1.
41   See article 3:238 paragraph 1 BW.

created over a moveable, non-registered good ceases to exist where the transfer of the pledged good is[41]:
(1) unauthorized;
(2) for consideration; and
(3) to a third party who at the time of acquisition of the good neither knew nor could have known of the pledge.
In cases of theft, different rules apply[42].

Methods of foreclosure

Pledges provide the holders thereof with a right of summary execution. This means that an additional title of enforcement is not needed. Under Netherlands law the following two options exist for a pledgee to foreclose on a validly pledged moveable, non-registered good:
(1) The general rule is that foreclosure takes place by way of public auction[43];
(2) The exception to the general rule is foreclosure by way of private sale[44].
However, in practice the following third way of foreclosure has been developed:
(3) By way of private sale by the trustee in bankruptcy (for the benefit of the pledgee) authorized by the supervisory judge in the bankruptcy[46].
The arrangement between the trustee in bankruptcy and the pledgee in this third way, whereby the former sells the pledged collateral for the benefit of the latter, has been qualified as a redemption of the pledge by the trustee in bankruptcy pursuant to article 58 paragraph 2 Fw (§ 3.4.2.2)[47].

Public auction

A sale by way of public auction takes place according to local customs and subject to the usual conditions. In a public auction, the pledgee also is entitled to bid.

Private sale

A private sale can take place in the following three situations[48]:
(1) At the request of the pledgee or the pledgor and, unless otherwise stipulated (*e.g.* parties can contractually agree to make the request an exclusive right of the pledgee), the President of the competent district court is entitled to determine that the pledged good can be sold in a manner other than by way of public auction;
(2) At the request of the pledgee and unless otherwise stipulated, the President of the competent district court is entitled to determine that the pledged good remains with the pledgee as purchaser thereof for an amount to be determined by the President; and

---

42   See article 3:86 paragraph 1 BW.
43   See article 3:86 paragraph 3 BW.
44   See article 3:250 paragraph 1 BW.
45   See article 3:251 paragraph 1 BW.
46   See article 176 paragraph 1 Fw read in conjunction with article 58 paragraph 2 Fw.
47   See also the Ontvanger/Mr Spruijt q.q. & ABN-case (HR 13 March 1987, *NJ* 1988, 556).
48   See article 3:251 paragraph 2 BW.

(3) The pledgee who has become entitled to foreclose can also agree with the pledgor to a manner of sale other than by way of public auction.

If the pledged good is also encumbered with another limited right and/or the pledged good is subject to an arrest, the cooperation of the holder of that limited right and/or the arrestor is also required for a sale in the situation mentioned above under (3).

General rules of foreclosure

In both a sale by way of public auction and private sale, the following general rules of foreclosure must be observed:

(1) In order to proceed with a sale, a pledgee must give at least 3 days' prior notice of the intended sale to the debtor and the pledgor, stating the place and the time of the intended sale[49]. Oftentimes, the pledgor will have contractually waived its right to receive this notice;
(2) A similar notice as mentioned above under (1) must be given to any arrestors of the pledged good and any (other) holders of limited rights with regard to the pledged good. An additional requirement for this notice is that it must also indicate, as accurately as possible, the amount for which the pledge may be redeemed. Redemption can take place up to the time of the sale, provided that the costs of foreclosure already incurred are also paid[50];
(3) Unless agreed otherwise in a contract, a pledgee must, on the day following the sale at the latest, give notice of the sale to the debtor, the pledgor, and any (other) holders of limited rights with regard to the pledged good[51];
(4) The pledgee has, in principle, the freedom to decide which of the options of foreclosure described above to use. Such may be different where:
    (i)   the claim concerned is secured by pledges on both goods of the debtor and goods of third parties[52]; or
    (ii) two or more goods of the debtor are pledged as security, whereby the pledgee proceeding with the foreclosure does not have to respect the pledge over one of the goods[53].
    When the executing pledgee commences to foreclose in both (i) and (ii) above, the third party-pledgor and the other pledgee respectively are entitled to request that the goods of the debtor are also included in the foreclosure and sold first. A subsequent refusal of such a request by the executing pledgee may be submitted for appeal to the President of the competent district court by the most interested party. In principle, no further legal remedies exist against a decision in this regard by the President of the competent district court[54];
(5) After payment of the costs of foreclosure, the pledgee is entitled to deduct the amount which is owed to the pledgee and for which the pledge was

49   See article 3:249 paragraph 1 BW.
50   See article 3:249 paragraph 2 BW.
51   See article 3:252 BW
52   See article 3:234 paragraph 1 BW.
53   See article 3:234 paragraph 2 BW.
54   See article 3:234 paragraph 3 BW.

granted from the net proceeds resulting from the sale of the pledged good[55].
The balance is paid to the pledgor; and

(6) In distributing the proceeds of the foreclosure, the pledgee must observe the
      applicable rules of the Rv concerning the ranking of debts according to their
      priority where:
      (i) other pledgees or holders of other limited rights exist, whose right to the
            pledged good have been terminated as a result of the foreclosure; or
      (ii) creditors have arrested the pledged good or the proceeds thereof.
      In this context, the duty of the pledgee to observe the applicable rules
      concerning the ranking of debts according to their priority should not be
      understood as an involvement of the pledgee in the distribution of the pro-
      ceeds to the other interested parties because the general rule is that a ranking
      arrangement takes place without the involvement of the pledgee.
      The pledgee is not entitled to pay out the amounts it owes to these other
      interested parties by way of set-off, unless[56]:
      (a) it concerns a payment to the pledgor; and
      (b) this payment is not made during bankruptcy, suspension of payment or
            liquidation of the estate of the pledgor[57].

(7) In case of a sale in execution and/or a sale pursuant to a summary execution,
      the purchaser of the moveable, non-registered good cannot make a claim on
      the basis of hidden defects[58].

5.2.1.2   Bearer or order rights

Bearer and order rights are rights incorporated in a document including a bearer-
clause stating "payable to bearer" or an order-clause stating "payable to B or to
order". For the creation of a pledge over bearer and order rights, the same rules
apply as set out in respect of the creation of a pledge over moveable, non-registered goods (§ 5.2.1.1). The only extra requirement for the creation of a possessory pledge over an order right is that an endorsement is also required[59]. An endorsement is a special notification on the back (in French: "*en dos*") of the document which embodies the order right.

The rules concerning third party protection, pledge of future goods and foreclosure are also similar to those set out above in respect of moveable, non-registered
goods.

5.2.1.3   Shares

Under Netherlands law both bearer shares and registered shares exist. Bearer
shares only exist in respect of a NV and not in respect of a BV[60]. Registered
shares exist in respect of both NVs and BVs.

---

55 See article 3:253 paragraph 1 BW.
56 See article 3:253 paragraph 2 BW.
57 Different rules apply in case the pledgor is subject to a debt reorganization of natural persons.
58 See article 7:19 BW.
59 See article 3:236 paragraph 1 BW.
60 See articles 2:82 BW and 2:190 BW.

Creating a pledge over bearer shares

For the creation of a pledge over bearer shares, the same rules apply as set out above in respect of the creation of a pledge over moveable, non-registered goods (§ 5.2.1.1).

Creating a pledge over registered shares

For the creation of a pledge over registered shares in NVs, a distinction should be made between:
(1) NVs which shares are listed on a stock exchange[61] and to which the "special rules" apply[62]; and
(2) other NVs to which the "general rules" apply[63].
Only the "general rules" apply to BVs.

The "general rules" applicable to registered shares

According to the general rules, only a notarial deed is required for the creation of a pledge[64]. Service of a copy of the notarial deed or an extract thereof on the company which shares are pledged is *not* a constitutive element for the creation of a pledge over the shares[65]. However, as long as no service on or recognition by the company has taken place, the rights attached to the pledged shares remain with the pledgor.

The pledge over the registered shares is recognized by the company when the pledge is registered in the register of shareholders of the company[66]. However, more common ways of recognition are[67]:
(1) a declaration in the notarial deed of pledge by an authorized director of the NV or BV that the NV or BV recognizes the pledge; or
(2) by way of a dated declaration on the notarial copy or extract of the deed of pledge.

The "special rules" applicable to registered shares

The special rules demand additional requirements, which will not be further discussed here.

---

61 "Stock exchange" means "any stock exchange within the meaning of article 1 sub e of the 1995 Act on the supervision of the securities trade ("*Wet toezicht effectenverkeer 1995*")". This includes both Netherlands and foreign stock exchanges.
62 See article 2:86c BW.
63 See article 2:86-2:86b BW and 2:196-2:196b BW.
64 See article 2:86 paragraph 1 BW.
65 See articles 2:86a paragraph 1 BW and 2:196a paragraph 1 BW.
66 See articles 2:86a paragraph 2 BW and 2:196a paragraph 2 BW.
67 See articles 2:86b paragraph 1 BW and 2:196b paragraph 2 BW.

The requirement of a valid title or cause

As far as grounds for voidness and voidability of a pledge over shares are concerned, see the discussion in § 5.2.1.1.

The requirement of the right to administer and dispose

Similar to pledges over moveable, non-registered goods, a rule of third party protection also exists in respect of pledges over registered shares. As long as the pledge is not properly registered in the register of shareholders of the company, a pledgee cannot invoke its pledge against the company or any third party that has relied in good faith on the information contained in the register[68].

Foreclosure

When foreclosing on pledged shares, the first and foremost rules a pledgee is required to observe are those set forth in the articles of association of the company whose shares have been pledged.

All BVs are required by law to have share transfer restrictions in their articles of association[69]. Such share transfer restrictions give the (other) shareholders of the BV, *inter alia*, a right of first refusal in respect of the pledged shares. If none of the other shareholders of the BV wishes to purchase the pledged shares, approval for the transfer of shares will be granted by the general meeting of shareholders of the BV. Subsequent to obtaining the approval, the foreclosure procedure for pledged shares is governed by the general rules on foreclosure of pledges as set forth in BW and as discussed for moveable, non-registered goods in § 5.2.1.1. In that context it should be noted that, despite being the general rule, a sale of pledged shares by way of public auction is not common in the Netherlands.

5.2.1.4   Claims

The following two types of pledges can be created in the Netherlands over claims:
(1)   a disclosed pledge[70]; and
(2)   an undisclosed pledge[71].

---

68   See articles 2:86a paragraph 3 BW and 2:196a paragraph 3 BW.
69   See article 2:195 BW. For share transfer restrictions of a NV, see article 2:87 BW.
70   See article 3:236 paragraph 2 BW read in conjunction with articles 3:98 BW and 3:94 BW.
71   See article 3:236 paragraph 1 BW.

Disclosed pledges

A disclosed pledge over claims is created by[72]:
(i)   a (notarial or private) deed of pledge; and
(ii) a notification of the pledge to the debtor of the pledged claim.
Only after the notification (which is not bound by form) has taken place, does the disclosed pledge become effective.

Undisclosed pledges

Similar to a non-possessory pledge over moveable, non-registered goods, an undisclosed pledge is also created by way of:
(i)   notarial deed; or
(ii) registered private deed[73].
Contrary to a disclosed pledge, there is no requirement of notification in order for an undisclosed pledge to become effective. As the rules for creation of an undisclosed pledge are similar to those of a non-possessory pledge, see the discussion in that regard in § 5.2.1.1.

The requirement for a valid deed of establishment

As far as undisclosed pledges are concerned, future claims can only be pledged in advance in respect of claims that are to be acquired by the pledgor from an already existing legal relationship at the time the deed of establishment is concluded (in advance)[74]. Future claims that meet this criterium are also referred to as "singular future claims", while future claims that do not meet this criterium (and thus cannot be pledged in advance) are referred to as "double future claims". In other words, future claims against yet unknown debtors cannot be pledged in advance.

A specific issue comes up when an undisclosed pledge is created over claims by way of private registered deed. This issue relates to the requirement by Netherlands law that claims must be "sufficiently identifiable"[75]. In a string of cases, including:
–   the *Stichting Spaarbank Rivierenland/Mr Gispen q.q.*-case[76];
–   the *Mr Wagemakers q.q./Rabobank Roosendaal*-case[77];

---

72   See article 3:94 paragraph1 BW.
73   See article 3:239 paragraph 1 BW.
74   See article 3:239 paragraph 1 BW.
75   See article 3:239 paragraph 1 BW.
76   HR 14 October 1994, *NJ* 1995, 447.
77   HR 20 June 1997, *NJ* 1998, 362.

– the *Mr Verhagen q.q./INB II*-case[78] ; and
– the *Zuidgeest/Furness*-case[79]

the Netherlands supreme court held that in the following situation a claim is considered to be sufficiently identifiable for the purposes of an undisclosed pledge by way of registered private deed:

> "(...) It is sufficient if such information is included in the deed (*of pledge; PJMD*) that, by using this information, it can be determined – possibly afterwards – , which claim is meant (...)"

When applied in practice, the above test encompasses a broad range of situations.

The requirement of a valid title or cause

In respect of voidness and voidability of a pledge over claims, see the discussion in this respect in § 5.2.1.1.

The requirement of the right to administer and dispose

In contrast to pledges over the goods described in § 5.2.1.1 to § 5.2.1.3, no specific rule of third party protection exists with respect to unauthorized pledges of claims.

The right to collect pledged claims

The right to collect pledged claims should not be confused with the procedure of foreclosure. The former is a separate right attached to a claim and is especially relevant prior to the commencement of a foreclosure. In respect of this right the consequences of holding a disclosed pledge or an undisclosed pledge differ substantially. In case of a disclosed pledge, the right to collect the pledged claims rests with the pledgee as of the day the disclosed pledge became effective[80]. The pledgor may collect the pledged claims only with the consent of the pledgee or the permission granted by the competent cantonal court[81]. When the right is exercised by the pledgee or by the pledgor with permission granted by the competent cantonal court, a pledge is created – by operation of law – over the collected monies[82]. However, please note that when the right to collect is exercised by the pledgor with consent of the pledgee, *no* pledge is created by operation of law over the collected monies.

In case of an undisclosed pledge, the right to collect remains with the pledgor. Only by notification of the undisclosed pledge to the debtor does the right to collect the pledged claims transfer to the pledgee[83]. Unless otherwise agreed, the

---

78   HR 19 September 1997, *NJ* 1998, 689.
79   HR 19 December 1997, *NJ* 1998, 690.
80   See article 3:246 paragraph 1 BW.
81   See article 3:246 paragraph 4 BW.
82   See article 3:246 paragraph 5 BW.
83   See article 3:246 paragraph 1 BW.

pledgee of an undisclosed pledge is entitled to notify the debtor of the pledged claims in the following two situations[84]:
(1) if the pledgor fails to perform its obligations towards the pledgee; or
(2) if the pledgee has good reason to fear that the pledgor will fail to perform its obligations.

From the *Mr Mulder q.q./CLBN*-case[85] of the Netherlands supreme court it follows that the pledgee of an undisclosed pledge remains entitled to notify the debtor of the pledged claim even after the pledgor has become bankrupt (or has been granted a suspension of payment)[86].

Foreclosure

The pledgee of a pledged claim is only entitled to foreclose on the pledged claim if the secured obligations have become due and payable[87]. Assuming that the pledgee is entitled to foreclose, a distinction can be made between:
(1) a cash payment by the debtor of the pledged claim; and
(2) a credit payment by the debtor of a pledged claim.
For a third way of foreclosure of pledged claims by the trustee in bankruptcy developed in practice, see § 5.2.1.1 under the heading "Methods of foreclosure".

Ad. (1)
In situation (1) the pledgee holds the monies on behalf of the pledgor and a pledge is created over those monies by operation of law[88]. It is, however, very important that the monies are segregated by the pledgee and remain separately identifiable from the other monies of the pledgee, since the risk exists that the pledge created over the cash paid will be lost as a result of mixing of rights[89] (*i.e.* the pledgee has legal title to both the pledge as limited right and the cash as the principal right that is encumbered with the limited right).

Ad. (2)
In situation (2) a similar risk of mixing of rights exists. This risk is addressed by using an "in-the-capacity-of account"[90] When properly set up, such an account results in a separate property. For complications that may arise in respect of the right to set-off by a pledgee of a pledged claim following a bankruptcy of the pledgor and, for a discussion of the rules that the Netherlands supreme court has set forth in this regard in the *Mr Mulder q.q./CLBN*-case, see § 4.2.1.1.5.

---

84   See article 3:239 paragraph 3 BW.
85   HR 17 February 1995, *NJ* 1996, 471.
86   For further details in respect of the Mr Mulder q.q./CLBN-case, see § 4.2.1.1.5.
87   See article 3:255 paragraph 1 BW.
88   See article 3:246 paragraph 5 BW read in conjunction with article 3:255 paragraph 1 BW.
89   See article 3:81 paragraph 1 sub e BW.
90   See article 490b paragraph 2 read in conjunction with article 445 Rv.

Pledge of a claim secured by a mortgage or a pledge

If a claim is already secured by (one or more) limited rights, for example by a mortgage over a house or a pledge over inventory, and subsequently this claim is pledged (either by way of disclosed or undisclosed pledge) does such a pledge result in an automatic transfer of the mortgage over the house or the pledge over the inventory to the pledgee?

The dominant view in the Netherlands on this question is that it should be answered in the affirmative. As a result of the pledge of the claim, the pledgee also acquires the limited rights by which the pledged claim is secured and the pledgee is entitled to exercise those limited rights in foreclosing on the pledged claim[91].

Summary
PLEDGES

The legal requirements for creating a pledge
(1) The legal requirements for creating a pledge are:
    (i)   a valid deed of establishment;
    (ii) a valid title or cause; and
    (iii) the right of the pledgor to administer and dispose of the collateral.
(2) Future goods can be pledged in advance, but in respect of future claims some limitations exist.
(3) Valid title or cause may be challenged on the basis of voidness or voidability.
(4) As a result of rules of third party protection, a pledge granted by an unauthorized pledgor can nevertheless be effective.

Different types of collateral
(1) Moveable, non-registered goods can be encumbered with the following two types of pledge:
    (i)   a possessory pledge; and
    (ii) a non-possessory pledge.
(2) Bearer or order rights.
(3) Shares can be distinguished as:
    (i)   bearer shares; and
    (ii) registered shares.
    BVs can only have registered shares while NVs can have both types of shares. Special rules apply to NVs which shares are listed on a stock exchange.

---

91 See Snijders/Rank-Berenschot, *supra* footnote 1, at § 550, p. 459 and the references made therein.

(4) Claims can be encumbered with the following two types of pledge:
     (i)   a disclosed pledge; and
     (ii) an undisclosed pledge.
     A special issue arising in respect of an undisclosed pledge created over
     claims by way of private registered deed is that the claims must be
     "sufficiently identifiable".

Foreclosure
(1) The general rule on foreclosure of a pledge is by way of public auction.
(2) An exception to the general rule is foreclosure by way of private sale.
     This exception can take place in 3 different situations. In addition, a
     fourth situation has developed in practice in which a private sale is
     conducted by the trustee in bankruptcy (for the benefit of the pledgee)
     authorized by the supervisory judge in bankruptcy.
(3) When foreclosing a pledge over shares, share transfer rules pursuant the
     articles of association of the BV or NV must first be observed.

5.2.2 REPLEDGE, DOUBLE PLEDGE AND RESERVED PLEDGE

In this part, the legal concept of repledge (§ 5.2.2.1), double pledge (§ 5.2.2.2)
and reserved pledge (§ 5.2.2.3) will be briefly addressed.

5.2.2.1 Repledge

Article 3:242 BW deals with the legal concept of repledge:

> "A pledgee is not entitled to repledge the property pledged to him, unless such right
> has been unequivocally granted to him."

In clarifying this article, the parliamentary notes[92] provide the following explanation:

> "(...) the pledgee (*repledgor; PJMD*) remains in control of the pledged asset, because
> the second pledgee (*repledgee; PJMD*) must be considered to be the holder on behalf
> of the first pledgee (*repledgor; PJMD*) (its pledgor) (...)"

> "(...) For a better understanding of the substance of the repledge clause, the under-
> signed (*the Minister of Justice; PJMD*) further states that, the clause provides the
> pledgee with the right to grant – in its own name – a new pledge over the asset which
> belongs to the pledgor. That (*new pledge; PJMD*) is higher in rank than its own
> pledge, because as a consequence of such establishment (*of the new pledge; PJMD*), a
> waiver of its rank towards the repledgee must be assumed. The repledge, as set forth in
> this explanation, does not result in a loss of ownership or of a right by the pledgor vis-
> à-vis the pledged asset. (...)"

---

92 See the parliamentary notes of Book 3 in respect of article 3:242 (3.9.24) BW, MvA II, pp.
    766-767.

Change of rank

The dominant view in the Netherlands is that a repledge results in a change of rank whereby the repledgee acquires the rank the repledgor had vis-à-vis the pledged asset and, subsequent to the repledge, the repledgor will rank immediately behind the repledgee[93]. Assuming that the repledgor had a first right of pledge over the asset, as a consequence of the repledge, the repledgee will now have a first right of pledge over the asset and the repledgor will have a second right of pledge.

Repledge in advance

The question can be asked whether or not a repledge still can become effective where:
(1) both a pledge and a subsequent repledge have been granted in advance; and
(2) the pledgee/repledgor is declared into bankruptcy prior to the moment the pledge has become effective.
It should be noted that the bankruptcy of the pledgee/repledgor does not prevent the pledge from becoming effective. As a consequence of this, it could be argued that the bankrupt estate receives a first right of pledge from the pledgor. The question whether the repledge can also become effective subsequently – leaving the bankrupt estate with a pledge that is lower in rank than that of the repledgee – is yet unsettled. In this context, a trustee in bankruptcy could challenge the repledge by arguing that the change of rank attached to the repledge violates the principle of fixation underlying the bankruptcy of the pledgee/repledgor (§ 1.2.1). Whether or not such a challenge by a trustee in bankruptcy will be successful is unclear.

5.2.2.2 Double pledge

Ranking

In situations of double pledge, the general rule under Netherlands law is: *"prior tempore, potior iure"*, meaning that the party who was first in time also acquires the first right.

Example

On day 1 A, as pledgor, grants a valid right of pledge over its car in favor of B. Subsequently on day 10, A again grants a valid right of pledge over its car, but

---

93   For a different view, see *"Herverpanding heroverwogen"*, by Mr H.A.G. Fikkers in *WPNR* 6313, 1998, pp. 301-307 and the response thereto *"De aard en het rechtskarakter van herverpanding"*, by Mr N.E.D. Faber in *WPNR* 6333, 1998, pp. 686-688. See also *"Gedachten over herverpanding"*, by Mr J.J. van Hees in *"Onzekere zekerheid"*, Insolad Jaarboek 2001, Mr J.C. van Apeldoorn c.s. (editors), Kluwer 2001, Deventer, pp 227-238.

now in favor of C. When it is assumed that no other valid pledges were vested over A's car, the ranking of the pledges will be:
(1) B with a first right of pledge; and
(2) C with a second right of pledge.

Change of rank

As an exception to the general rule set forth above, a change of rank takes place in the following situations of double pledge[94]:

(1) when – in case of two non-possessory pledges over a moveable non-registered good or over a bearer or order right – at the time of release of the pledged asset to the second pledgee (*i.e.* C in the example given above), the second pledgee neither knew nor could have known of the existence of the other pledge in favor of the first pledgee (*i.e.* party B); and

(2) when – in case of two pledges in advance over future moveable non-registered goods – the pledged asset comes into the hands of the second pledgee (*i.e.* party C) and at that time the second pledgee was acting in good faith.

Where there are two undisclosed pledges over claims, no specific provision exists under Netherlands law resulting in a similar change of rank as described above.

5.2.2.3   Reserved pledge

A reserved pledge is comparable (but not identical) to a reservation of title or ownership (§ 3.4.2.1)[95]. If an asset can be pledged, Netherlands law provides for the possibility of transferring such asset subject to a reserved pledge[96]. In that case both the legal requirements for transfer and those for creating a pledge must be observed. The following example shows that a combination of the two may be useful.

Example

A has sold and delivered a moveable, non-registered good to B. As a consequence of the sale A now has a claim for the purchase price against B. In addition to its claim for the purchase price, A also has a claim against B based on wrongful act. A could secure both its claims against B as follows:

---

94   See article 3:238 paragraph 2 BW.
95   See article 3:92 BW.
96   See article 3:81 paragraph 1 BW.

(1) a reservation of title or ownership by A could serve as security for the payment by B of the purchase price; and

(2) a reserved pledge by A could serve as security for the payment of damages by B pursuant to the claim of A based on wrongful act.

How does the reserved pledge work?

Only after the termination of the reservation of title or ownership will the reserved pledge become effective, as, only at that time will legal title to the asset transfer to party B. Nevertheless, the reserved pledge can be validly created by B before the asset is transferred and as soon as legal title to the asset is subsequently transferred to B, the reserved pledge will automatically become effective without any further formalities being required.

Summary
REPLEDGE, DOUBLE PLEDGE AND RESERVED PLEDGE

Repledge
(1) The right to repledge must be unequivocally granted by the pledgor to the pledgee/repledgor.
(2) As a consequence of the change of rank, the repledge is considered higher in rank than the (original) pledge.

Double pledge
(1) The general rule of ranking in case of two or more pledges is: "first in time, first in right".
(2) The exception to the rule is that a change of rank can take place in certain situations involving:
    (i) two non-possessory pledges over a moveable, non-registered good or over a bearer or order right; and
    (ii) two pledges in advance over future moveable, non-registered goods.

Reserved pledge
(1) The legal concept of reserved pledge is comparable (but not identical) to a reservation of title or ownership.
(2) In practice a reserved pledge may be useful in combination with a reservation of title or ownership.

5.2.3   SITUATIONS OF CONCURRENCE OF RIGHTS

In this part, the following situations of concurrence of rights will be discussed:

(1) concurrence between a non-possessory pledge and a fiscal privileged ground right (§ 5.2.3.1);
(2) concurrence between a pledge and a right of retention (§ 5.2.3.2);
(3) concurrence between a (non-possessory) pledge and a privileged right based on article 2:284 BW or article 3:285 BW or article 3:287 BW (§ 5.2.3.3); and
(4) concurrence between a pledge and a right following from an earlier precautionary arrest or arrest in execution (§ 5.2.3.4).

5.2.3.1 Concurrence between a non-possessory pledge and the fiscal privileged ground right

The scope and content of the fiscal privileged ground right

Based on the Tax Recovery Act 1990 ("Inv."), the Netherlands tax authorities have a fiscal privileged ground right[97] in respect of a number of taxes specified in the Inv.[98] The fiscal privileged ground right applies to, *inter alia*, wage tax and value added tax, but does not apply to, *inter alia*, income tax and corporate tax.

In addition, the fiscal privileged ground right only applies to moveable, non-registered goods:
(1) which are either legally owned by the tax debtor or by third parties;
(2) which are on the grounds of the tax debtor at the time of arrest by the tax authorities; and
(3) which serve as furnishing of a house or serve in the construction or use of land.

Goods that meet all 3 requirements are referred to as "ground goods". The term "ground" is of a factual nature and can generally be described as:
(i) the premises (or a part thereof) which are used by the tax debtor; and
(ii) which premises can be administered and disposed by the tax debtor independently of third parties.

"Ground goods" may be described as those goods that are destined for the more or less permanent use on the grounds in accordance with their purpose[99]. In general, ground goods include machinery and inventory, but exclude stock.

Concurrence of rights

In case of concurrence of a non-possessory pledge and the fiscal privileged ground right of the tax authorities in respect of certain ground goods, the fiscal

---

97 See article 22 Inv.
98 See article 22 paragraph 3 Inv.
99 See generally the Guideline of the Inv. (*"Leidraad Invordering 1990"*) at § 5.1.2 concerning article 22 Inv.

privileged ground right of the tax authorities has priority[100]. Outside a bank-ruptcy, the tax authorities are required to make a "ground arrest" in order to be able to invoke their fiscal privileged ground right[101]. When such ground arrest by the tax authorities is expected, a concurrence with the fiscal privileged ground right of the tax authorities may be avoided if the tax authorities are prevented from making and/or maintaining a valid ground arrest.

Ways to avoid a concurrence of rights

In practice, the following two scenarios have been used successfully to avoid a concurrence of rights with the fiscal privileged ground right of the tax authorities:

(1) The "ground lease-scenario" *("bodemverhuurconstructie")*[102]
     In this scenario, the grounds of the tax debtor are rented by the tax debtor to:
     (i)   a pledgee, as a consequence whereof the non-possessory pledge of the ground goods converts into a possessory pledge, whereby the pledgee needs to ensure that the tax debtor/pledgor does not have access to the grounds; or
     (ii) a third party, as a consequence whereof the tax debtor can no longer ad-minister and dispose of the premises independently of third parties.

(2) The "removal-scenario" *("afvoerconstructie")*[103]
     In this scenario, the ground goods of the tax debtor are removed from the ground, as a consequence whereof the goods fall outside the scope of a ground arrest because they are no longer situated on the grounds of the tax debtor.

Ground arrest

In order to be able to invoke their fiscal privileged ground right in the bankruptcy of the tax debtor, the tax authorities are not required to make a ground arrest on ground goods that are owned by the tax debtor. This is because it is assumed that the general bankruptcy arrest also serves as a ground arrest[104]. If ground goods are not owned by the bankrupt tax debtor, but by a third party, this is different and the tax authorities will have to make a ground arrest first before they can in-voke their fiscal privileged ground right. Such a ground arrest can still be made by the tax authorities during the bankruptcy of the tax debtor[105].

---

100 See article 21 paragraph 1 Inv.
101 See, for example, the Verweij-case (HR 26 May 1989, *NJ* 1990, 131).
102 A rental agreement by the trustee in bankruptcy has been sanctioned in the NMB-case (HR 12 April 1985, *NJ* 1986, 808).
103 See article 3:237 paragraph 3 BW read in conjunction with article 496 Rv.
104 See article 33 paragraph 2 Fw.
105 See the Sigmacon I-case (HR 12 May 1989, *NJ* 1990, 130).

Article 57 paragraph 3 Fw

Based on article 57 paragraph 3 Fw, the trustee in bankruptcy is obliged to look after the interests of the tax authorities vis-à-vis the pledgee having a non-possessory pledge over the ground goods of the tax debtor. This means that the pledgee (as a *separatist*) continues to be entitled to foreclose on the pledged ground goods. However, the pledgee is subsequently obliged to transfer the proceeds of the foreclosure to the trustee in bankruptcy (in an amount corresponding with the higher ranked claims of the tax authorities). This obligation to transfer the proceeds to the trustee in bankruptcy is only available if no other means exist in the bankruptcy to pay the higher ranked claims of the tax authorities[106]. If the proceeds are transferred by the pledgee to the trustee in bankruptcy, these will first be used in the allocation of the bankruptcy costs[107]. After such allocation has taken place, the remaining part of the proceeds can be used to pay the higher ranked claims of the tax authorities, following which, payment will be made to the pledgee from the remaining proceeds, if any.

5.2.3.2 Concurrence between a pledge and a right of retention

The scope and content of the right of retention

The right of retention is the right a creditor has to suspend – in the cases provided for by law – the release of an asset to a debtor until the claim of the creditor against the debtor is fully paid[108]. A bankruptcy of the debtor does not result in the loss of the right of retention by the creditor[109] (§ 3.5.2.6).

Concurrence of rights

In a concurrence between a right of retention and a more recent pledge, the right of retention is the stronger right[110]. In a concurrence between a right of retention and an earlier pledge, the retentor may also invoke its right of retention against the pledgee, provided that the claim of the retentor originates from an agreement which[111]:
(1) the debtor was entitled to enter into with respect to the pledged asset; or
(2) the retentor had no reason to doubt that the debtor was entitled to enter into.

As far as priority is concerned, the retentor has priority over the (earlier or later) pledgee in respect of the distribution of the proceeds of the retained asset in those

---

106 See the Mr Aerts q.q.-ABN AMRO-case (HR 26 June 1998, *NJ* 1998, 745).
107 See article 57 paragraph 3 Fw read in conjunction with article 182 paragraph 1 Fw.
108 See article 3:290 BW.
109 See article 60 paragraph 1 Fw.
110 See article 3:291 paragraph 1 BW.
111 See article 3:291 paragraph 2 BW.

cases in which the right of retention may be invoked against that pledgee[112]. If, in a bankruptcy, the trustee in bankruptcy demands the retained asset (which is also pledged) from the retentor in order to sell it, the pledgee is entitled to demand the release of the asset from the trustee in bankruptcy [113]. The pledgee has such right to enable him (as a *separatist*) to exercise his right of summary execution as if no bankruptcy existed. However, in that case, the trustee in bankruptcy will be obliged – on the basis of article 57 paragraph 3 Fw – to look after the interests of the retentor because the retentor is ranked higher than the pledgee in respect of the proceeds. After foreclosure of the asset, the pledgee shall therefore be required to transfer the net proceeds to the trustee in bankruptcy. After allocation of the bankruptcy costs, those proceeds shall be distributed by the trustee in bankruptcy to the retentor in payment for the claim of the retentor.

5.2.3.3   Concurrence between a (non-possessory) pledge and a privileged right based on article 3:284 Netherlands Civil Code or article 3:285 Netherlands Civil Code or article 3:287 Netherlands Civil Code

Privileged rights based on article 3:284 BW or article 3:285 BW or article 3:287 BW

The privileged rights relate to the following respective claims:
(1) A claim of costs incurred in preserving an asset (in article 3:284 BW);
(2) A claim of costs relating to labor in respect of an asset (in article 3:285 BW); and
(3) A claim of compensation for damages and insurance monies in respect of an asset (in article 3:287 BW).

Concurrence of rights

In respect of the privileged rights mentioned above, the following situations of concurrence of rights can be mentioned:

(1) In a concurrence between a privileged right based on article 3:284 BW and a non-possessory pledge, the privileged right has priority, unless the non-possessory pledge was created after the costs of preservation had been incurred[114];
(2) In a concurrence between a privileged right based on article 3:285 BW and a non-possessory pledge, the privileged right again has priority, unless[115]:

---

112   See article 3:292 BW.
113   See article 60 paragraph 2 Fw and generally *"Retentierecht en art. 57 lid 3 en 60 Fw."*, by Mr N.E.D. Faber in *NbBW*, 6, 1998, pp. 75-76.
114   See article 3:284 paragraph 3 BW.
115   See article 3:285 paragraph 2 BW.

(i) the non-possessory pledge was only created after the privileged right based on article 3:285 BW had arisen; and

(ii) the asset was brought under the control of the pledgee or a third party; and

(3) In a concurrence between a privileged right based on article 3:287 BW and a pledge (not being a converted transfer of security ownership)[116], the privileged right always has priority[117].

5.2.3.4 Concurrence between a pledge and a right following from an earlier precautionary arrest or arrest in execution

In a concurrence between a pledge and an earlier arrest in execution, the pledge can be invoked against the party that made the earlier arrest only if[118]:
(1) the pledge was created for consideration;
(2) the asset is in the hands of the pledgee; and
(3) the pledgee was acting in good faith at the time it obtained the assets in its hands.
The same applies to a situation of a concurrence between a pledge and an earlier precautionary arrest[119].

In a concurrence between a pledge and an earlier arrest (either in execution or precautionary) over shares, the party that made the earlier arrest has priority[120].

The BANQUE DE SUEZ/MR BIJKERK Q.Q.-case

As of 00.00 hours of the day a bankruptcy is adjudicated any arrests made on assets of the debtor cease to exist (§ 1.2.1). The question that presents itself in this context is whether or not a bankruptcy – in view of the situations of concurrence set forth above – results in a loss of priority for the party that made an arrest on an asset of the debtor earlier than the pledgee acquired its pledge.

In the *Banque de Suez/Mr Bijkerk q.q.*-case[121], the Netherlands supreme court held that a trustee in bankruptcy can invoke the priority of the party that made the earlier arrest vis-à-vis the pledgee. The proceeds of the sale of the asset should therefore fall in the bankrupt estate to the extent such proceeds do not exceed the

---

116 See articles 86 and 117 Ow.
117 See article 287 paragraph 2 BW.
118 See articles 453a paragraph 2 Rv and 475h paragraph 2 Rv.
119 See articles 712 Rv and 720 Rv.
120 See articles 474e Rv and 715 paragraph 1 Rv.
121 HR 13 May 1988, *NJ* 1988, 748. The essence of the Banque de Suez/Mr Bijkerk q.q.-case is now regulated in article 57 paragraph 3 Fw. For more details on article 57 paragraph 3 Fw, see § 5.2.3.1.

claim of the party that made the earlier arrest. In the distribution of those proceeds, the claim of the pledgee is subordinate to the claim of the party that made
the earlier arrest.

Summary
SITUATIONS OF CONCURRENCE OF RIGHTS

(1)   The fiscal privileged ground right of the tax authorities is a stronger
      right than a non-possessory pledge. However, a concurrence between
      the two rights may be avoided by using one of the following two
      scenarios:
      (i)   a ground lease scenario (prior to bankruptcy); or
      (ii) a removal scenario (prior to bankruptcy).

(2)   In a situation of concurrence of rights, the right of retention is a stronger
      right than a pledge. A bankruptcy of a debtor does not result in a loss of
      the right of retention, but provides the trustee in bankruptcy, pursuant to
      article 60 Fw, with a right to demand the retained asset from the retentor
      in order to sell it.

(3)   Unless the non-possessory pledge was created after the privileged rights
      based on article 3:284 BW and article 3:285 BW respectively, the
      privileged rights have priority. In respect of the privileged right based
      on article 3:285 BW, the asset must also have been brought under the
      control of the pledgee or a third party in order for the non-possessory
      pledge to have priority.

(4)   A privileged right based on article 3:287 BW has always priority over a
      pledge (not being a converted transfer of security ownership).

(5)   A pledge can be invoked against a party that made an earlier arrest only
      if:
      (i)   the pledge was created for consideration;
      (ii) the asset is in the hands of the pledgee; and
      (iii) the pledgee was acting in good faith at the time it obtained the as-
            sets in its hands.
      When there is a bankruptcy, special rules apply pursuant to the *Banque
      de Suez/Mr Bijkerk q.q.*-case.

5.3   Mortgages

The discussion of mortgages will be structured as follows:
(1) In § 5.3.1 the legal requirements for validly vesting a right of mortgage will
     be set out;
(2) In § 5.3.2 there will be a discussion of foreclosure of a mortgage over im-
     moveable goods; and
(3) In § 5.3.3 a number of situations of concurrence of mortgages with other
     rights will be dealt with.

Unless indicated otherwise, the comments made here in respect of mortgages relate to a mortgage over immoveable goods only. Mortgages over registered
moveable, goods such as vessels and aircraft and the mortgage over property (or
proprietary) rights (such as a building right) include a number of special rules
that deviate from the discussion below. These mortgages are *not* covered in this
book[122]. The same applies to the "rental clause" and the consequences of its in-
clusion in a deed of mortgage[123].

5.3.1   THE LEGAL REQUIREMENTS

Similar to pledges (§ 5.2.1), the following three requirements for a valid transfer
of a good are equally applicable to the valid creation of a mortgage in the Netherlands[124]:
(1) a valid deed of establishment;
(2) a valid title or cause; and
(3) the right of a mortgagor to administer and dispose of the collateral.
Each of these three requirements will be briefly discussed below.

5.3.1.1   A valid deed of establishment

In respect of this legal requirement a distinction can be made between:
(1) the granting of a mortgage; and
(2) the creation of a mortgage.

Granting a mortgage

In order to grant a mortgage, Netherlands law requires a notarial deed which must
meet a number of special requirements (including a detailed description of the
mortgaged property such as its type and location). This follows from:

---

122   For mortgages over aircraft, see articles 8:1310-8:1314 BW. For mortgages over inland ves-
      sels, see article 8:792-8:797 BW and for mortgages over sea vessels, see articles 8:202-8:207
      BW.
123   See article 3:264 BW.
124   See article 3:98 BW read in conjunction with article 3:84 paragraph 1 BW.

(i)   the BW[125];
(ii) the Act on the Profession of Civil Law Notary (*"Wet op het Notaris-ambt"*)[126]; and
(iii) the Land Registry Act (*"Kadasterwet"*)[127].

Creating a mortgage

In order to create a mortgage one must register it in the appropriate land register with the original copy or an extract of the notarial deed granting the mortgage[128]. If there is no entry in the register, there is no valid mortgage.

The creation in advance of a mortgage over future assets is not possible under Netherlands law[129]. However, Netherlands law does provide for the possibility of establishing a mortgage to secure the payment of future monetary obligations, provided that they are sufficiently identifiable[130]. Generally, secured future obligations are considered sufficiently identifiable if, at the time the collateral is foreclosed, the monetary obligations can be determined[131].

Ranking

Besides being a constitutive element in the creation of a mortgage, registration of a mortgage is also important for the assessment of the rank of the mortgage. The time of registration is deemed to be the time the relevant documents have been submitted for registration[132]. If two mortgages have been submitted for registration at the same time on the same day, the day on which the notarial deed was drawn up will be decisive[133]. If both notarial deeds have also been drawn up on the same day, the time on which the notarial deed was drawn up (which time must be included in the notarial deed), is decisive[134]. These general rules on ranking of mortgages also apply to mortgages established to secure the payment of future obligations.

The following can be mentioned as exceptions to the general rules on ranking of mortgages:

---

125   See, for example, article 3:260 paragraph 1 BW.
126   See, for example, article 37 of the Act on the Profession of Civil Law Notary.
127   See, for example, articles 18-24 of the Land Registry Act.
128   See article 3:89 paragraph 1 BW.
129   See article 3:98 BW read in conjunction with article 3:97 paragraph 1 BW.
130   See article 3:231 paragraph 2 BW.
131   See Snijders/Rank-Berenschot, *supra* footnote 1, § 511, pp. 417-418.
132   See article 3:19 paragraph 2 BW read in conjunction with article 3:21 paragraph 1 BW.
133   See article 3:21 paragraph 2 sub a BW.
134   See article 3:21 paragraph 2 sub b BW.

(1) a mortgage in respect of an unpaid purchase price[135];

(2) a valid change of rank agreed to between the relevant parties[136]; and

(3) a mortgage concerning overcompensation[137].

These exceptions will not be discussed further.

5.3.1.2 A valid title or cause

The legal requirement of valid title or cause concerns the legal relation that forms the basis of the mortgage and justifies it. In this context the concepts of voidness and voidability are relevant. Both concepts have retroactive effect under Netherlands law[138]. The concept of voidness applies to a legal act (such a granting a mortgage) where the legal act, by its content or purpose, is immoral or violates public policy in the Netherlands[139]. Grounds that result in the applicability of the concept of voidability to a legal act, such as a mortgage over an immoveable good, include[140]:

(1) incapacity;

(2) mistake;

(3) force;

(4) abuse of circumstances;

(5) fraud; and

(6) *actio pauliana*[141].

5.3.1.3 The right to administer and dispose of the collateral

Article 35 Fw

The general rule pursuant to article 35 paragraph 1 Fw is that a valid mortgage is not created if at the time the mortgage was effected (*i.e.* when the notarial deed granting the mortgage was submitted for registration) the mortgagor lacked the right to administer and dispose of the collateral.

For a more detailed discussion of the application of article 35 Fw, see § 1.2.1.1.

---

135   See article 3:261 BW.
136   See article 3:262 BW.
137   See article 3:177 BW.
138   See article 3:53 paragraph 1 BW.
139   See article 3:40 paragraph 1 BW.
140   See articles 3:32 BW, 3:44 BW, 3:45 BW and 6.228 BW.
141   For more details on the *actio pauliana*, see § 4.1.

Summary
MORTGAGES

The legal requirements for mortgages
(1) The legal requirements for creating a mortgage are:
   (i)   a valid deed of establishment;
   (ii) a valid title or cause; and
   (iii) the right of the mortgagor to administer and dispose of the collateral.
(2) A valid deed of establishment for a mortgage means:
   (i)   a notarial deed of mortgage; and
   (ii) registration of the notarial deed of mortgage in the proper land register.
(3) As with pledges, one should be aware of the retroactive effect of voidness and voidability for mortgages under Netherlands law.
(4) In respect of the mortgagor's right to administer and dispose of the collateral, the consequences of the principle of fixation following from article 35 Fw and the rule of third party protection pursuant to article 3:88 BW are relevant.

5.3.2   FORECLOSURE OF A MORTGAGE

A mortgagee is entitled to foreclose on the collateral if the debtor is in default with respect to any of the underlying secured obligations[142]. The right to foreclose on the mortgaged collateral is not just restricted to the mortgagee with a first mortgage over the asset; every mortgagee has this right provided that the debtor is in default against that mortgagee.

Methods of foreclosure

The two main ways of foreclosing on a mortgage in the Netherlands are:
(1) by way of public auction before a civil law notary[143]; and
(2) by way of private sale authorized by the President of the competent district court[144].
However, in practice the following third way of foreclosure has been developed:
(3) by way of private sale by the trustee in bankruptcy (for the benefit of the mortgagee) authorized by the supervisory judge in the bankruptcy[145].

---

142   See article 3:268 paragraph 1 BW.
143   See article 3:268 paragraph 1 BW.
144   See article 3:268 paragraph 2 BW.
145   See article 176 paragraph 1 Fw read in conjunction with article 58 paragraph 2 Fw.

The arrangement between the trustee in bankruptcy and the mortgagee in this third way, whereby the former sells the mortgaged collateral for the benefit of the latter, has been qualified as a redemption of the mortgage by the trustee in bankruptcy pursuant to article 58 paragraph 2 Fw (§ 3.4.2.2) [146].

Public auction

Similar to pledges, foreclosure by way of public auction is considered – at least in theory – the general rule and foreclosure by way of private sale the exception thereto. Conditions for a public auction are determined by the designated civil law notary in consultation with the mortgagee [147]. Objections against the conditions for the public auction can be submitted to the President of the competent district court by the most interested party [148]. A decision by the President of the competent district court is not subject to appeal [149]. The mortgagee or the mortgagor is entitled to request the President of the competent district court for a private sale instead of a public auction up to one week prior to the day on which the public sale in execution is scheduled to take place [150], by submitting a signed private sale and purchase agreement for authorization by the President of the competent district court [151]. If the private sale route is taken, the mortgagor, the mortgagee, an arrestor or another party having a limited right (each having a valid interest in higher proceeds), are entitled to make a higher bid than that included in the private sale and purchase agreement until the end of the hearing before the President of the competent district court.

Private sale

Foreclosure by way of private sale can be requested by either the mortgagor or the mortgagee. When requested, a signed sale and purchase agreement must be submitted to the President of the competent district court who then decides on the request, from which there is no appeal [152].

Rule against appropriation

Pursuant to the rule against appropriation, the mortgagee is not entitled to appro-

---

146   See also the Ontvanger/Mr Spruijt q.q. & ABN-case (HR 13 March 1987, *NJ* 1988, 556).
147   See article 517 paragraph 1 Rv read in conjunction with articles 519 and 546 Rv.
148   See article 518 paragraph 1 Rv read in conjunction with article 546 Rv.
149   See article 518 paragraph 2 Rv read in conjunction with article 546 Rv.
150   See article 548 paragraph 1 Rv.
151   See article 3:268 paragraph 2 BW.
152   This follows from article 3:268 paragraph 3 BW. However, in certain circumstances grounds for legal remedies against a ruling from the President of the competent district court may be based on the Rabobank/Sporting Connection-case (HR 17 June 1994, *NJ* 1995, 367).

priate the collateral and any stipulation to this effect is null and void[153]. As a consequence, the mortgagee can only acquire the collateral itself by buying the collateral either at a public auction or by a private sale authorized by the President of the competent district court.

The right to summary execution

Where the debtor is in default in respect of any of the secured obligations, the mortgagee has the right to summary execution (§ 5.1)[154]. With respect to the right of summary execution the following rules need to be observed in case of foreclosure both by way of public auction and by way of private sale authorized by the President of the competent district court:

(1) The mortgagee is required to commence foreclosure by providing notice to[155]:
    (i)   the mortgagor;
    (ii) the debtor; and
    (iii) those parties whose right or arrest follows from the public registers and whose right will expire or nullify as a consequence of the (anticipated) sale in execution.
    Another mortgagee, having a higher ranked mortgage than the mortgagee who anticipates commencing the foreclosure, is entitled to take over by announcing such intention within 14 days of receiving the notice[156];

(2) In the notice starting the foreclosure of a mortgage, a civil law notary before whom the sale in execution shall take place is designated[157]. Within 14 days of being designated, the civil law notary sets a date, time and place for the sale in execution[158], provided there are no other mortgagees who could take over the foreclosure[159]. The 14 days term starts to run as of the day the notice by the foreclosing mortgagee has been given[160]. After having set a date, time and place for the sale in execution, the civil law notary communicates this to the debtor and the other interested parties[161];

---

153   See articles 3:235 BW and 3:268 paragraph 5 BW.
154   See article 3:268 BW.
155   See article 544 paragraph 1 Rv.
156   See article 544 paragraph 3 Rv.
157   See article 544 paragraph 2 sub b Rv.
158   See article 515 paragraph 1 Rv read in conjunction with article 546 Rv.
159   See article 509 Rv.
160   See article 547 paragraph 1 Rv.
161   See article 515 paragraph 2 Rv.

(3) No sale in execution can take place prior to the lapse of 30 days after such sale has been announced by way of[162]:
   (i) posting according to local custom; and
   (ii) publication in a local daily newspaper;

(4) To the extent possible, the civil law notary is obliged to inform the debtor in writing about a sale on the day following the sale at the latest[163];

(5) The purchaser only acquires legal title to the purchased goods by registering the official report of allotment[164];

(6) As a consequence of the transfer pursuant to a sale in execution and the settlement of the purchase price[165]:
   (i) all mortgages by which the sold good was encumbered are nullified;
   (ii) registered arrests cease to exist; and
   (iii) other limited rights encumbering the asset, that cannot be invoked against the seller, cease to exist.
Similar consequences resulting in an unencumbered title take place in case of an authorized sale of a mortgaged good by the trustee in bankruptcy[166]; and

(7) In case of a sale in execution and/or a sale pursuant to a summary execution, the purchaser of the immoveable good cannot make a claim on the basis of hidden defects[167].

Summary
FORECLOSURE OF A MORTGAGE

(1) The following three ways of foreclosing on a mortgage exist:
   (i) by way of public auction before a civil law notary, pursuant to local custom and conditions set by the civil law notary;
   (ii) by way of private sale authorized by the President of the competent district court, by submitting a signed private sale and purchase agreement for authorization by the President of the competent district court; and
   (iii) by way of private sale by a trustee in bankruptcy (for the benefit of the mortgagee) authorized by the supervisory judge in bankruptcy.

---

162   See article 516 Rv read in conjunction with article 546 Rv.
163   See article 523 Rv.
164   See article 525 paragraph 1 Rv.
165   See article 3:273 paragraph 1 BW.
166   See article 188 Fw.
167   See article 7:19 BW.

(2) Registration of the official report of allotment results in a transfer of legal title to the purchaser.
(3) Foreclosure of a mortgage results in unencumbered title to the sold immoveable good.
(4) In a sale in execution and/or a sale pursuant to a summary execution, the purchaser of the immoveable good cannot make a claim on the basis of hidden defects.

5.3.3   SITUATIONS OF CONCURRENCE OF RIGHTS

In respect of mortgages the following two situations of concurrence of rights will be briefly discussed:
(1) in § 5.3.3.1 concurrence between a mortgage and a right of retention; and
(2) in § 5.3.3.2 concurrence between a mortgage and a right following from an earlier precautionary arrest or arrest in execution.

5.3.3.1   Concurrence between a mortgage and a right of retention

The scope and content of the right of retention

The right of retention is the right of a creditor to suspend – in the cases provided for by law – the release of an asset to a debtor until the claim of the creditor against the debtor is fully paid (§ 5.2.3.2). A bankruptcy of the debtor does not result in the creditor losing this right[168] (§ 3.5.2.6).

The WINTERS/KANTOOR VAN DE TOEKOMST-case

In the *Winters/Kantoor van de Toekomst*-case[169] the Netherlands supreme court gave the following guidance in respect of the execution of the right of retention on an immoveable asset:

> "(...), a creditor can only execute a right of retention on an asset if he is the holder of that asset – meaning he exercises direct or indirect factual control over such asset as determined by common opinion, the Code and the circumstances as they appear – in such manner that, (...), release is required to return the asset into the control of the debtor or the party entitled thereto. The situation in which the creditor qualifies as holder of the asset does not terminate – (...) – as long as the asset does not come into the control of the debtor or the party entitled thereto. These rules also apply to the right of retention on an immoveable asset, to the extent that, in following the general rule,

---

168   See article 60 paragraph 1 Fw.
169   HR 6 February 1998, *NJ* 1999, 303 at 5.2.

the release, as a consequence whereof the asset is returned into the control of the debtor or the party entitled thereto, will take place by vacating it.

In that regard it should be noted that the right of retention on an immoveable asset, by its nature, can not be known from the public registers and therefore can be a source of insecurity for third parties, who, in order to assess the legal status of the immoveable asset, have consulted those registers. In view thereof, such a right of retention can only be invoked against a third party, who obtained its right over the asset after the right of retention came into being, if the creditor has exercised its factual control over the asset concerned in a sufficiently clear manner, also vis-à-vis the third party. (...)"

Concurrence of rights

As it is for pledges (§ 5.2.3.2), in a situation of concurrence with a mortgage, the right of retention will also be the stronger right[170].

5.3.3.2 Concurrence between a mortgage and a right following from an earlier precautionary arrest or arrest in execution

In a situation of concurrence between a mortgage and an earlier arrest in execution, the mortgage can be invoked against the party that made the earlier arrest only if the registration of the deed of mortgage had taken place ultimately on the first day following the day of the registration of the arrest[171]:
(1) on which the office of the Service for the land register is open to the public; and
(2) the public registers are open to the public, provided that the deed of mortgage was already executed prior to the registration of the earlier arrest.

The same applies to a situation of a concurrence between a mortgage and an earlier precautionary arrest[172].

The BANQUE DE SUEZ/MR BIJKERK Q.Q.-case
In a situation of bankruptcy, the rules following from the *Banque de Suez/Mr Bijkerk q.q.*-case[173] as set forth in relation to pledges in § 5.2.3.4, also apply to mortgages.

---

170 See article 3:292 BW.
171 See article 505 paragraph 3 Rv.
172 See article 726 paragraph 1 Rv.
173 HR 13 May 1988, *NJ* 1988, 748. The essence of the Banque de Suez/Mr Bijkerk q.q.-case is now regulated in article 57 paragraph 3 Fw. For more details on article 57 paragraph 3 Fw, see § 5.2.3.1.

Summary
SITUATIONS OF CONCURRENCE OF RIGHTS

(1) In a situation of concurrence of rights, a right of retention is a stronger right than a mortgage. Bankruptcy of a debtor does not result in a loss of the right of retention, but provides the trustee in bankruptcy, pursuant to article 60 Fw, with a right to demand the retained asset from the retentor in order to sell it.

In respect of the exercise of the right of retention on an immoveable good, special rules follow from the *Winters/Kantoor van de Toekomst*-case as to exercising factual control over the retained good.

(2) In a situation of concurrence between a mortgage and an earlier arrest, the mortgage can be invoked against the party that made the earlier arrest only if the registration of the deed of mortgage had taken place ultimately on the first day following the day of the registration of the arrest:
(i)   on which the office of the Service for the land register is open to the public; and
(ii) the public registers are open to the public.
In a bankruptcy, special rules apply pursuant to the *Banque de Suez/ Mr Bijkerk q.q.*-case.

FURTHER READING

GENERAL TEXTBOOKS ON NETHERLANDS INSOLVENCY LAW

Buchem-Spapens, A.M.J. van, *"Faillissement en surséance van betaling"*, W.E.J. Tjeenk Willink 5th edition 1995, Zwolle, pp. 1-138.

Adriaansens, M.A.M., Knol, J.J. and Schee, A. van der, *"Faillissementsgids"*, Kluwer 5th edition 1998, Deventer, pp. 1-189.

Blom, R.J. *"Kernboekje Faillissement, surséance en schuldsanering 2000/2002"*, Fed 2000, Deventer, pp. 1-161.

Huizink, J.H., *"Insolventie"*, Kluwer 3rd edition 1999, Deventer, pp. 1-130.

Polak, M., and Wessels, B., (Polak-Wessels) *"Insolventierecht"*, Kluwer, Deventer:

___, Deel I, *"Faillietverklaring"*, 1999, pp. 1-310.

___, Deel II, *"Gevolgen van faillietverklaring (1)"*, 2000, pp. 1-472.

___, Deel III, *"Gevolgen van faillietverklaring (2)"* (in preparation).

___, Deel IV, *"Bestuur en beheer na faillietverklaring"*, 2002, pp. 1-328.

___, Deel V, *"Verificatie van schuldvorderingen"*, 1999, pp. 1-164.

___, Deel VI, *"Het akkoord"*, 1999, pp. 1-160.

___, Deel VII, *"Vereffening van de boedel"*, 2001, pp. 1-208.

___, Deel VIII, *"Surséance van betaling"*, 2000, pp. 1-264.

___, Deel IX, *"Schuldsaneringsregeling natuurlijke personen"*, 1999, pp. 1-287.

___, Deel X., *"Insolventierecht; overige leerstukken"* (in preparation).

Polak, N.J., and Polak, C.E., *"Faillissementrecht"*, Kluwer 8th edition 1999, Deventer, pp. 1-373.

Wessels, B., and Sint Truiden, Ph. van (editors), *"Tekst & Commentaar Faillissementswet"*, Kluwer 2nd edition 1999, Deventer, pp. 1-506.

"Praktijkboek Curatoren", Kluwer, Deventer (continuously updated loose-leaf binders).

LITERATURE ON VARIOUS INSOLVENCY LAW ISSUES

Actio pauliana/wrongful act

Hoff, G.T.J., *"Balanceren op het koord van de faillissementspauliana"*, NIBE no. 23 1995, Den Haag, pp. 1-83.

Koppen, F.P. van, *"Actio pauliana en onrechtmatige daad"*, Kluwer 1998, Deventer, pp. 1-414.

Koppen, F.P. van, *"Geen twijfel meer mogelijk: de Hoge Raad legt de Paulianabepalingen restrictief uit"*, in TvI, 6, 2000, pp. 190-196.

Timmerman, L. c.s. (editor), *"Vragen rond de faillissementspauliana"*, Insolad jaarboek 1998, Kluwer 1998, Deventer, pp. 1-92.

Verstijlen, F.M.J., *"Het onverplichtheidsvereiste bij (faillissements)pauliana"*, in TvI, 6, 1999, pp. 127-131.

Verstijlen, F.M.J., *"De onrechtmatige-daads-vordering wegens de benadeling van schuldeisers van een failliete schuldenaar: één voor allen of ieder voor zich?"*, in Ondernemingsrecht 2001-4, pp. 85-90.

Corporate liabilities and insolvency

Dongen, R.C. van, *"Identificatie in het rechtspersonenrecht: Rechtsvergelijkende beschouwingen over "Piercing the corporate veil" in het interne en internationale privaatrecht van Nederland, Duitsland, Zwitserland, New York en Texas"*, Kluwer 1995, Deventer, pp. 1 -362.

Groot, H. de, *"Bestuurdersaansprakelijkheid"*, Kluwer 2nd edition 1997, Deventer, pp. 1-308.

Heijden, C.M. van der, *"Insolventie en rechtspersoon"*, Kluwer 1996, Deventer, pp. 1-229.

Houwen, L.G.H.J., Schoonbrood-Wessels, A.P. and Schreurs, J.A.W., *"Aansprakelijkheid in concernverhoudingen"*, Kluwer 1993, Deventer, pp. 1-1197.

Lennarts, M.L., *"Concernaansprakelijkheid"*, Kluwer 1999, Deventer, pp. 1-422.

Kortmann, S.C.J.J., and Faber, N.E.D., *"Bestuurdersaansprakelijkheid en faillissement"*, in *WPNR* 6249, 1996, pp. 899-906.

Timmerman, L., *"Vereenzelviging als strijdmiddel in vennootschapsrechtelijke aansprakelijkheidsprocedures"*, in *Ondernemingsrecht* 2001-10, pp. 294-300.

Tjittes, R.P.J.L., Blom, A.B. (editors), *"Bank en aansprakelijkheid"*, Kluwer 1996, Deventer, pp. 1-230.

Vriesendorp, R.D. c.s. (editor), *"Onbehoorlijk bestuur in het insolventierecht"*, Insolad jaarboek 1997, Kluwer 1997, Deventer, pp. 1-82.

Wezeman, J.W., *"Aansprakelijkheid van bestuurders"*, Kluwer 1998, Deventer, pp. 1-516.

Criminal law and insolvencies

Borgers, M.J., and Landen, D. van der, *"Criminele Insolventie: ontneming van wederrechtelijk verkregen voordeel en faillissement"*, in *TvI*, 4, 1997, pp. 110-118.

Hilverda, C.H., *"Faillissementsfraude"*, W.E.J. Tjeenk Willink 1992, Zwolle, pp. 1-490.

Hilverda, C.H., Bartels, W.J., Dorlo, G.S.E. and Lely, J., *"Faillissementsfraude in de praktijk"*, Kluwer 1999, Deventer, pp. 1-133.

Cross-border insolvencies

Berends, A.J., *"Grensoverschrijdende insolventie"*, NIBE no. 37 1999, Den Haag, pp. 1-322.

Bos, T.M., *"Grensoverschrijdend faillissement in Europees perspectief"*, Kluwer 2000, Deventer, pp. 1-445.

Galen, R.J. van, and Apeldoorn, J.C. van, *"Grensoverschrijdende aspecten van insolventieprocedures buiten verdrag"* in *"Mededelingen van de Nederlandse Vereniging voor Internationaal Recht, number 117: grensoverschrijdende insolventieprocedures"*, Kluwer 1998, Deventer, pp. 1-153.

Debt reorganization of natural persons

Polak, M., and Wessels, B., (Polak-Wessels) *"Insolventierecht"*, Kluwer 1999, Deventer, Deel IX, *"Schuldsaneringsregeling natuurlijke personen"*, pp. 1-287.

Verschoof, R.J., *"Schuldsaneringsregeling voor natuurlijke personen"*, NIBE no. 36 1998, Den Haag, pp. 1-206.

Employees and insolvency

Jacobs, A.T.J.M. c.s., *"Werknemersrechten in faillissement (Een rechtsvergelijkende beschouwing)"*, Boom Juridische Uitgevers 2000, Den Haag, pp. 1-81.

Loesberg, E., *"Internationale aspecten van ontslag van werknemers tijdens insolventie van de werkgever"*, in *ArbeidsRecht*, 12, 1998, pp. 17-20.

Luttmer-Kat, A.M. c.s. (editor), *"Werknemers en insolventie van de werkgever: is de balans in evenwicht?"*, Insolad jaarboek 1999, Kluwer 2000, Deventer, pp. 1-100.

Polak, M.V., *"De curator, de werknemer, zijn internationale dienstbetrekking en haar beëindiging"*, in *"De curator, een octopus"*, Kortmann, S.C.J.J. c.s. (editors), W.E.J. Tjeenk Willink 1996, Deventer, pp. 313-328.

Restart

Couwenberg, O., *"Resolving Financial Distress in the Netherlands, a case study approach"*, 1997, pp. 1-270.

Eeghen, L.J. van, "*Verkenning van belangen bij doorstart en faillissement*", in *TVVS*, 4, 1996, pp. 93-98.

Eeghen, L.J. van, "*Benadeling van crediteuren en voorbereide doostart faillissementen*", in *NJB*, 36, 1997, pp. 1665-1669.

Hesper, R.H.G., "*Faillissement en doorstart in het licht van de Europese steunbepalingen*", in *TvI*, 3, 1996, pp. 57-60.

Joosten, E.P.M., "*Overdracht van ondernemingen uit faillissement*", W.E.J. Tjeenk Willink 1998, Deventer, pp.1-276.

Kaar, R.H. van het, and Knegt, R., "*Doorstart na faillisement: de positie van werknemers*", in *NJB*, 39, 1996, pp. 1622-1627.

Oosterhout, H.B., "*De doorstart van een insolvente onderneming*", Kluwer 1998, Deventer, pp. 1-164.

Ophof, H.P.J. c.s., "*Jubileumnummer "Doorstart", Veertig jaar TVVS*", in *TVVS*, 7, 1997, pp. 199-214.

Security rights and insolvency

Polak, M.V., and Mierlo, A.I.M. van "*Verstrekking van zekerheden aan internationale syndicaten*", NIBE no. 31 1998, Den Haag, pp. 1-153.

Suspension of payment

Leuftink, A.L., "*Surséance van betaling*", Kluwer, 1995, Deventer, pp. 1-369.

Polak, M., and Wessels, B., (Polak-Wessels) "*Insolventierecht*", Kluwer 2000, Deventer, Deel VIII,, , "*Surséance van betaling*", pp. 1-264.

Tax and insolvency

Houte, C.P.M. van, "*Belastingschulden in faillissement*", in *WFR*, 6430, 2001, pp. 504-515.

Kortmann, S.C.J.J. c.s. (editor), "*Faillissement en fiscus*", Insolad jaarboek 2000, Kluwer 2001, Deventer, pp. 1-137.

Tekstra, A.J., "*Fiscale aspecten van insolventies*", Koninklijke Vermande 2nd edition 1999, Den Haag, pp. 1-358.

Veeger, J.L., "*Fiscale concernaansprakelijkheid en insolventie*", in *TvI*, 6, 1999, pp. 125-127.

Trustee in bankruptcy

Verstijlen, F.M.J., "*De Faillissementscurator: een rechtsvergelijkend onderzoek naar de taak, bevoegdheden en persoonlijke aansprakelijkheid van de faillissementscurator*", W.E.J. Tjeenk Willink 1998, Deventer, pp. 1-449.

Winding up in a bankruptcy

Boekraad, G.A.J., "*Afwikkeling van de faillissementsboedel*", W.E.J. Tjeenk Willink 1997, Deventer, pp. 1-323.

Galen, R.J. van, "*Drie typen schulden bij faillissement (I)*", in *WPNR* 6225, 1996, pp. 393-397.

Galen, R.J. van, "*Drie typen schulden bij faillissement (II, slot)*", in *WPNR* 6226, 1996, pp. 413-417.

Galen, R.J. van, "*De rangorde onder boedelschulden in faillissement (I)*", in *WPNR* 6266, 1997, pp. 255-258.

Galen, R.J. van, "*De rangorde onder boedelschulden in faillissement (II, slot)*", in *WPNR* 6267, 1997, pp. 275-279.

Polak, M., and Wessels, B., (Polak-Wessels) "*Insolventierecht*", Kluwer 2001, Deventer, Deel VII, "*Vereffening van de boedel*", pp. 1-208.

BIBLIOGRAPHY

Articles

Dijk, M.C.M. van, "*Stelplicht en bewijslast in zaken van bestuurdersaansprakelijkheid*" in *NbBW*, 2, 2001, pp. 14-19.

Draaisma, M.J., "*E-mailblokkade*", in *TvI*, 4, 1997, pp. 101-102

Faber, N.E.D., "*Monopolist, afkoelingsperiode en faillissement*", in *NbBW*, 11, 1998, pp. 124-128.

Galen, R.J. van, and Apeldoorn, J.C. van, "*Grensoverschrijdende aspecten van insolventieprocedures buiten verdrag*" in "*Mededelingen van de Nederlandse Vereniging voor Internationaal Recht, number 117: grensoverschrijdende insolventieprocedures*", Kluwer 1998, Deventer, pp. 1-153.

Faber, N.E.D., "*Retentierecht en art. 57 lid 3 en 60 Fw.*", in *NbBW*, 6, 1998, pp. 75-76.

Faber, N.E.D., "*De aard en het rechtskarakter van herverpanding*", in *WPNR* 6333, 1998, pp. 686-688.

Fikkers, H.A.G., "*Herverpanding heroverwogen*", in *WPNR* 6313, 1998, pp. 301-307.

Hees, A. van, "*Voorwaarden voor het instellen van de pauliana*", in "*Vragen rond de faillissementspauliana*", Insolad jaarboek 1998, Timmerman, L. (editor), Kluwer 1998, Deventer, pp. 1-11.

Hees, J.J. van, "*Levering van registergoederen en aandelen tijdens faillissement: curator en notaris in een lastig parket*", in "*De curator, een octopus*", Kortmann, S.C.J.J. c.s. (editors), W.E.J. Tjeenk Willink 1996, Deventer, pp. 123-138.

Hees, J.J. van, "*Bespreking van het boek "De Faillissementscurator" van Mr F.M.J Verstijlen*", in *RM Themis*, 4, 2001, pp. 122-124.

Hees, J.J. van, "*Gedachten over herverpanding*", in "*Onzekere zekerheid*", Insolad Jaarboek 2001, Apeldoorn, J.C. van c.s. (editors), Kluwer 2001, Deventer, pp. 227-238.

Huizink, J.B., "*Nogmaals artikel 47 Fw*", in *WPNR* 6429, 2001, pp. 33-34.

Jol, J.T., "*Aspecten van verrekening tijdens faillissement en surséance van betaling*", in "*De curator, een octopus*", Kortmann, S.C.J.J c.s. (editors), W.E.J. Tjeenk Willink 1996, Deventer, pp. 201-218

Jong, E.A. de, "*Het spookbeeld van de décharge herrezen*", in *Ondernemingsrecht* 2001-8, pp. 232-235.

Kortmann, S.C.J.J., "*De afkoelingsperiode van de Art. 63a Fw; ondoordachte wetgeving*", in "*Financieringen en aansprakelijkheid*", Kortmann, S.C.J.J. (editor), W.E.J. Tjeenk Willink 1994, Zwolle, pp. 149-161

Kortmann, S.C.J.J., "*Haastige Spoed ... Opmerkingen naar aanleiding van het voorstel tot wijziging van de Faillissementswet*", in *TvI*, 1, 2000, pp. 26-34.

Kortmann, S.C.J.J. and Faber, N.E.D., "*De faillissementscurator: vertegenwoordiger of niet?*", in "*De curator, een octopus*", Kortmann, S.C.J.J c.s. (editors), W.E.J. Tjeenk Willink 1996, Deventer, pp. 139-172.

Kortmann, S.C.J.J. and Veder, P.M., "*De Europese Insolventieverordening*", in *WPNR* 6421, 2000, pp. 764-774.

Kroft, W.P.J., "*De curator en de medezeggenschap van werknemers*", in "*De curator, een octopus*", Kortmann, S.C.J.J c.s. (editors), W.E.J. Tjeenk Willink 1996, Deventer, pp. 49-62.

Oven, J.C. van, "*Bestuurdersaansprakelijkheid ingevolge de Tweede Misbruikwet*", in "*Onbehoorlijk bestuur in het insolventierecht*", Insolad jaarboek 1997, Vriesendorp, R.D. (editor), Kluwer 1997, Deventer, pp. 1-14.

Pabbruwe, H.J., *"De achtergestelde geldlening nog eens ontrafeld"*, in *WPNR* 6338, 1998, pp. 766-771.

Polak, M.V., *"De curator, de werknemer, zijn internationale dienstbetrekking en haar beëindiging"*, in *"De curator, een octopus"*, Kortmann, S.C.J.J c.s. (editors), W.E.J. Tjeenk Willink 1996, Deventer, pp. 313-328.

Ranitz, S.H. de, *"Crediteurenbelang versus "andere belangen""*, in *"De curator, een octopus"*, Kortmann, S.C.J.J c.s. (editors), W.E.J. Tjeenk Willink 1996, Deventer, pp. 187-199.

Timmerman, L., *"Bewijslastverdeling bij doorbraak van aansprakelijkheid"*, *TVVS*, 9, 1993, p. 234.

Vriesendorp, R.D., *"Doorstarten en onbehoorlijk bestuur"*, in *"Onbehoorlijk bestuur in het insolventierecht"*, Insolad jaarboek 1997, Vriesendorp, R.D. (editor), Kluwer 1997, Deventer, pp. 65-82.

Vriesendorp, R.D., *"Wetgever: de hoogste tijd voor een insolventiewet"*, in *TvI*, 3, 1997, pp. 63-68.

Wessels, B., *"Enkele insolventievragen bij de positie van de achtergestelde crediteur"*, in *TvI*, 1, 1995, pp. 7-12.

Wessels, B., *"Over art. 212A-212F Faillissementswet (nieuw)"*, in *NbBW*, 4, 1999, pp. 38-42.

Winter, J.W., *"Curator, jaarrekening en voortzetting van het bedrijf"* in *"De curator, een octopus"*, Kortmann, S.C.J.J c.s. (editors), W.E.J. Tjeenk Willink 1996, Deventer, pp. 37-48.

Books

Beckman, H., *"De jaarrekening-vrijstelling voor afhankelijke groepsmaatschappijen: Een analyse van artikel 2:403 BW en zijn voorgangers"*, Kluwer 1995, Deventer, pp. 1-812.

Boekraad, G.A.J., *"Afwikkeling van de faillissementsboedel"*, W.E.J. Tjeenk Willink 1997, Deventer, pp. 1-323.

Dongen, R.C. van, *"Identificatie in het rechtspersonenrecht: Rechtsvergelijkende beschouwingen over "Piercing the corporate veil" in het interne en internationale privaatrecht van Nederland, Duitsland, Zwitserland, New York en Texas"*, Kluwer 1995, Deventer, pp. 1 -362.

Feltz, G.W. van der, *"Geschiedenis van de Wet op het Faillissement en de Surséance van Betaling"*, part 2-I, 1896, Kortmann, S.C.J.J. and Faber, N.E.D. (editors) W.E.J. Tjeenk Willink 1994, Zwolle, pp. 1-560.

Feltz, G.W. van der, *"Geschiedenis van de Wet op het Faillissement en de Surséance van Betaling"*, part 2-II, 1897, Kortmann, S.C.J.J and Faber, N.E.D. (editors), W.E.J. Tjeenk Willink 1994, Zwolle, pp. 1-498.

Feltz, G.W. van der, *"Geschiedenis van de Wet op het Faillissement en de Surséance van Betaling"*, part 2-III, 1896, Kortmann, S.C.J.J and Faber, N.E.D. (editors), W.E.J. Tjeenk Willink 1995, Zwolle, pp. 1-809.

Hees, A. van, *"De achtergestelde vordering, in het bijzonder de achtergestelde lening"*, Kluwer 1989, Deventer, pp. 1- 170.

Hees, J.J. van, *"Leasing"*, W.E.J. Tjeenk Willink 1997, Deventer, pp. 1- 227.

Houwen, L.G.H.J., Schoonbrood-Wessels, A.P. and Schreurs, J.A.W. *"Aansprakelijkheid in concernverhoudingen"*, Kluwer 1993, Deventer, pp. 1-1197.

Leuftink, A.L., *"Surséance van betaling"*, Kluwer 1995, Deventer, pp. 1-369

Polak, M.V. and Mierlo, A.I.M. van, *"Verstrekking van zekerheden aan internationale syndicaten"*, NIBE no. 31 2nd edition 1998, Den Haag, pp. 1-153.

Snijders, H.J., and Rank-Berenschot, E.B., *"Goederenrecht"*, Kluwer 3rd edition 2001, Deventer, 1-616.

Verstijlen, F.M.J., *"De Faillissementscurator: een rechtsvergelijkend onderzoek naar de taak, bevoegdheden en persoonlijke aansprakelijkheid van de faillissementscurator"*, W.E.J. Tjeenk Willink 1998, Deventer, pp. 1-449.

Wessels, B. and Sint Truiden, Ph. van (editors), "*Tekst & Commentaar Faillissementswet*", Kluwer 2nd edition 1999, Deventer, pp. 1-506.
Wezeman, J.W., "*Aansprakelijkheid van bestuurders*", Kluwer 1998, Deventer, pp. 1-516.

Miscellaneous

"*Directives in bankruptcies and suspensions of payment*", in "*Vademecum Advocatuur: Wet & Regelgeving*", 2001, pp. 485-511.

TABLE OF CASES

Netherlands supreme court

Courts of appeals

District courts

TRANSLATED TERMS

English into Dutch

Abuse of circumstances, *misbruik van omstandigheden*

Abuse of right, *misbruik van bevoegdheid*

Accessory rights, *nevenrechten*

Administrator in suspension of payment, *bewindvoerder*

Agencies, *agentuurovereenkomsten*

Aggrieved party, *benadeelde* or *gelaedeerde*

Agreement of engagement, *opdracht*

Agreements with mutual performances, *wederkerige overeenkomsten*

Allocation of the bankruptcy costs, *omslag van de faillissementskosten*

Allow, *toewijzen*

Ancillary rights, *afhankelijke rechten*

Announcement, *aanzegging* or *bekendmaking*

Announcement by way of posting, *aanplakking*

Apparent mismanagement, *kennelijk onbehoorlijk bestuur*

Appeal, *hoger beroep*

Appropriation, *toeëigening*

Arrest, *beslag*

Arrest in execution, *executoriaal beslag*

Arrestor, *beslaglegger*

Assignments, *cessies*

Assignment by way of security, *cessie tot zekerheid*

Attorney of record, *procureur*

Automatic general arrest, *algemeen beslag van rechtswege*

Auction, *veiling*

Backservice obligation, *affinanciering van de backservice*

Bailiff's notification, *exploot*

Bankruptcy, *faillissement*

Bankruptcy account, *faillissementsrekening*

Bankruptcy chambers, *faillissementskamers*

Bankruptcy costs general in nature, *algemene faillissementskosten*

Bankruptcy costs specific in nature, *bijzondere faillissementskosten*

Bankrupt estate, *faillissementsboedel*

Bare legal title, *bloot eigendom*

Bearer or order rights, *rechten aan toonder of order*

Bearer shares, *aandelen aan toonder*

Board of directors, *bestuur*

Building right, *opstalrecht*

Cantonal court, *kantonrechter*

Capacity, *handelingsbekwaamheid*

Cash payment, *chartale betaling*

Central Bank of the Netherlands, *De Nederlandsche Bank* or *DNB*

Central counter party, *centrale wederpartij*

Change of rank, *rangwisseling*

Claim for compensation of value, *waardevergoedingsvordering*

Claims, *vorderingen*

Claims not subject to verification, *niet voor verificatie vatbare vorderingen*

Clearing house, *verrekeningsinstituut*

Collateral, *goederen bezwaard met een zekerheidsrecht*

Collateral security rights, *goederenrechtelijke zekerheden*

Collected monies, *geïnde*

Collective bargaining agreement, *collectieve arbeidsovereenkomst*

Common opinion, *verkeersopvatting*

Compensation for damages and insurance monies in respect of an asset, *schadevergoeding en verzekeringspenningen*

Composition (proposal), *akkoord(-voorstel)*

Concurrence of rights, *samenloop van rechten*

Condition precedent, *opschortende voorwaarde*

Condition subsequent, *ontbindende voorwaarde*

Consequences of a proprietary nature, *zakelijke werking*

Conspire, *samenspannen*

Consultation, *overleg*

Corporate tax, *vennootschapsbelasting*

Costs incurred in preserving an asset, *kosten tot behoud van een goed*

Costs relating to labor in respect of an asset, *kosten wegens bearbeiding*
Court of appeals, *Gerechtshof*
Court order, *beschikking*
Credit claims, *girale tegoeden*
Credit payments, *girale betalingen*
Creditors with factual preference, *dwangcrediteuren*
Current-account, *rekening courant*

Debtor, *schuldenaar*
Debt reorganization of natural persons, *schuldsanering natuurlijke personen*
Declaration of law, *verklaring voor recht*
Deed of establishment, *vestigingshandeling*
Default, *verzuim*
Default attributable to, *toerekenbare tekortkoming* or *wanprestantie*
Deficit in the bankruptcy, *tekort in het faillissement*
Dilute, *verwateren*
Discharge, *décharge*
Disclosed pledge, *openbaar pandrecht*
Discontinuation, *opheffing*
Dissolution, *ontbinding*
District court, *Arrondissementsrechtbank*
Double future claims, *dubbel toekomstige vorderingen*
Double pledge, *dubbele verpanding*
Due and payable, *opeisbaar*
Duty to investigate, *onderzoeksplicht*

Emergency Arrangement, *Noodregeling*
Employment agreements, *arbeidsovereenkomsten*
End-of-term arrangements, *afvloeiingsregelingen*
Endorsement, *endossement*
Enforceable, *afdwingbaar*
Estate claim, *boedelschuld*
Estate creditors, *boedelcrediteuren*
Eviction, *ontruiming*
Execution, *tenuitvoerlegging*
Ex officio, ambtshalve
Extra-judicial invalidation, *buitengerechtelijke vernietiging*
Extra-judicial statement, *buitengerechtelijke verklaring*

Factual acts, *feitelijke handelingen*
Force, *bedreiging*
For consideration, *anders dan om niet*
Foreclosure, *uitwinning*
Formation of goods, *zaaksvorming*

Final plan of distribution, *slotuitdelingslijst*
Final and not open to appeal, *in kracht van gewijsde gaan* or *verbindend worden*
Final suspension of payment, *definitieve surséance van betaling*
First necessities of life, *eerste levensbehoeften*
Fiscal privilege, *fiscaal voorrecht*
Fiscal privileged ground right, *fiscaal bodemrecht*
Fraud, *bedrog*
Further appeal to the Netherlands supreme court, *in cassatie gaan*
Future goods, *toekomstige goederen*

General bankruptcy arrest, *algemeen faillissementsbeslag*
Generally accepted principles, *in het verkeer geldende opvattingen*
General partnership, *vennootschap onder firma*
Goods traded on the commodity market and delivered at a fixed time or within a pre-set period, *termijnzaken*
Gross negligence, *grove nalatigheid*
Ground, *bodem*
Ground arrest, *bodembeslag*
Ground for annulment, *vernietigingsgrond*
Ground goods, *bodemzaken*
Ground lease-scenario, *bodemverhuurconstructie*
Group relations, *concernverhoudingen*
Guarantors pursuant to a surety, *borgen*

Hidden defects, *verborgen gebreken*
Hire-purchase agreements, *huurkoop overeenkomsten*

Identification, *vereenzelviging*
Immaterial default, *onbelangrijk verzuim*
Immoral, *in strijd met de goede zeden*
Immoveable goods, *onroerende zaken*
Improper discontinuation, *oneigenlijke opheffing*
Improper subordination, *onzuivere achterstelling*
In advance, *bij voorbaat*
Incapacity, *handelingsonbekwaamheid*
Income tax, *inkomstenbelasting*
Incidental circumstances, *bijkomende omstandigheden*
In good faith, *te goeder trouw*
Insolvency stay, *afkoelingsperiode*
Intention, *oogmerk*

In-the-capacity-of account, *kwaliteitsrekening*
In the control of, *in de macht van*
Introduced in the system, *ingevoerd in het systeem*
Inviolable, *onaantastbaar*
Invoke, *inroepen*

Judiciary, *rechtelijke macht*
Judicial interference, *gerechtelijke tussenkomst*

Knowledge, *wetenschap*

Lawsuits, *gerechtelijke procedures*
Lease agreement, *pachtovereenkomst*
Legal act, *rechtshandeling*
Legal entity, *rechtspersoon*
Legal obligation, *rechtsplicht*
Limitation periods, *verjaringstermijnen*
Limited partnership, *commanditaire vennootschap*
Limited rights, *beperkte rechten*
Liquidation, *vereffening*
Liquidation of an estate, *vereffening van een nalatenschap*
Liquidator, *vereffenaar*
Lists of pledged goods, *pandlijsten*
Long-term agreement, *duurovereenkomst*
Loss of a benefit, *verlies van een voordeel*

Mandate, *lastgeving*
Manifest error, *onmiskenbare vergissing*
Means of recourse, *verhaalsmogelijkheden*
Mismanagement, *wanbeleid* or *onbehoorlijk bestuur*
Mistake, *dwaling*
Mixing of property or goods, *vermenging*
Monetary claims, *geldvorderingen*
Monetary obligations, *geldschulden*
Mortgage, *hypotheek*
Moveable goods, *roerende zaken*
Mutual debtorship, *wederzijds schuldenaarschap*

National Gazette of the Netherlands, *Nederlandse Staatscourant*
Negative estate, *negatieve boedel*
Netherlands supreme court, *Hoge raad der Nederlanden*
Non-disclosed pledge, *stil pandrecht*
Non-possessory pledge, *vuistloos pandrecht* or *bezitloos pandrecht*
Non-preferential creditors, *concurrente crediteuren*

Notarial deed, *authentieke akte verleden ten overstaan van een notaris*
Not due and payable, *niet opeisbaar*
Notice, *aanzegging*
Nullification, *vernietiging*

Object-substitution, *zaaksvervanging*
Obligation to provide further security rights, *verplichting tot nadere zekerheidsstelling*
Obligation to restore the original situation, *verplichting tot ongedaanmaking*
Obligatory legal acts, *verplichte rechtshandelingen*
Official report of allotment, *proces-verbaal van toewijzing*
Omission to act, *nalaten*
On balance, *per saldo*
Ordinary creditors, *concurrente crediteuren*
Overcompensation, *overbedeling*

Payments by transfer into accounts, *giraal betalingsverkeer*
Parliamentary notes, *parlementaire geschiedenis*
Permit to terminate an employment agreement, *ontslagvergunning*
Piercing of the corporate veil, *directe doorbraak van aansprakelijkheid*
Plan of distribution, *uitdelingslijst*
Pledge, *pandrecht*
Policy determinators, *beleidsbepalers*
Possessory pledge, *vuistpand*
Precautionary arrest, *conservatoir beslag*
Preferential creditors, *bevoorrechte crediteuren*
Prejudice, *benadeling*
Prima facie evidence, *aannemelijk maken*
Principal bank, *huisbank*
Principle of reasonableness and fairness, *beginsel van redelijkheid en billijkheid*
Priority rights, *voorrangsrechten*
Privileged rights, *voorrechten*
Private deed, *onderhandse akte*
Private sale, *onderhandse verkoop*
Proceeds, *opbrengst*
Proper discontinuation, *eigenlijke opheffing*
Proper subordination, *zuivere achterstelling*
Property, *zaak*
Property (or proprietary) right, *zakelijk recht*
Protection from eviction, *ontruimingsbescherming*
Prove, *bewijzen*
Provisional suspension of payment, *voorlopige surséance van betaling*

Proxies, *volmachten*
Public auction, *openbare verkoop*
Purchase in installments, *koop op afbetaling*
Purpose and purport, *doel en strekking*

Ranking arrangement, *rangregeling*
Ratification, *homologatie*
Redemption, *inlossing*
Reference proceeding, *renvooi procedure*
Registration Department of the Tax Office,
    Inspectie der Registratie en Successie
Registered claim, *vordering op naam*
Registered good, *registergoed*
Registered shares, *aandelen op naam*
Register of bankruptcies,
    faillissementsregister
Relative effect of an annulment, *relatieve
    nietigheid*
Release, *afgifte*
Removal-scenario, *afvoerconstructie*
Render account for ones acts, *rekening en
    verantwoording afleggen*
Rental agreements, *huurovereenkomsten*
Rental clause, *huurbeding*
Renunciation, *opzegging*
Renunciation of a claim against the estate,
    boedelafstand
Repledge, *herverpanding*
Request for a dismissal, *ontslag van instantie*
Reservation of title or ownership,
    eigendomsvoorbehoud
Reserved pledge, *voorbehouden pandrecht*
Restart, *doorstart*
Retroactive effect, *terugwerkende kracht*
Revocation, *intrekking*
Right of preference, *voorrecht*
Right of priority, *voorrangsrecht*
Right of recourse, *verhaalsrecht*
Right of retention, *retentierecht*
Right of summary execution, *recht van
    parate executie*
Right of usufruct, *recht van vruchtgebruik*
Right to administer and dispose,
    beschikkingsbevoegdheid
Right to advise, *adviesrecht*
Right to consent, *instemmingsrecht*
Right to recollect, *recht van reclame*
Right to remain silent, *zwijgrecht*
Right to request a review, *verzet*
Rule of third party protection, *regel van
    derdenbescherming*
Rule of unwritten law pertaining to proper
    social conduct, *hetgeen volgens
    ongeschreven recht in het
    maatschappelijke verkeer betaamt*

Satisfaction, *voldoening*
Secured obligations, *gezekerde vorderingen*
Security rights, *zekerheidsrechten*
Security ownership, *zekerheidseigendom*
Separate property, *afgescheiden vermogen*
Seriously to blame, *ernstig verwijt zijn te
    maken*
Serve as furnishing, *dienen tot stoffering*
Service for the landregister, *Dienst voor het
    kadaster*
Set-off, *verrekening*
Set-off notification, *verrekeningsverklaring*
Settlement, *schikking*
Settlement agent, *afwikkelende instantie*
Several and jointly liable co-debtors,
    hoofdelijk medeschuldenaren
Share transfer restrictions,
    blokkeringsregeling
Singular future claims, *enkelvoudig
    toekomstige vorderingen*
Social security board, *bedrijfsvereniging* or
    *uitvoeringsinstantie sociale
    verzekeringen*
Subordination, *achterstelling*
Subordinated creditors, *achtergestelde
    crediteuren*
Substitute damages, *vervangende
    schadevergoeding*
Substitution, *indeplaatsstelling*
Sufficiently identifiable, *voldoende
    bepaalbaar*
Supervisory judge, *rechter-commissaris*
Supervisory board, *raad van commissarissen*
Supplementary damages, *aanvullende
    schadevergoeding*
Surety, *borgtochtovereenkomst*
Suspensory effect, *schorsende werking*

Tax authorities, *belastingdienst*
Tax debtor, *belastingschuldige*
Terms of forfeiture, *vervaltermijnen*
Third party stipulation, *derdenbeding*
Title of enforcement, *executoriale titel*
To service, *betekenen*
Trade union, *werknemersvakbond*
Transferable, *overdraagbaar*
Transfer of title or ownership,
    eigendomsoverdracht
Transfer pursuant to particular title,
    overdracht onder bijzondere titel
Transfer of a business, *overgang van
    onderneming*
Transfer order, *overboekingsopdracht*
Trustee in bankruptcy, *curator*

Undue payment, *onverschuldigde betaling*
Unencumbered title, *zuivering*

Valid title or cause, *geldige titel*
Value added tax, *omzetbelasting*
Voidness, *nietigheid*
Voidability, *vernietigbaarheid*
Voluntary legal acts, *onverplichte
    rechtshandelingen*

Wages, *loon*
Wages Guarantee Arrangement,
    Loongarantieregeling
Wages tax, *loonbelasting*
Waiver, *afstand*
Wilfull misconduct, *grove schuld*
Workout, *buitengerechtelijke sanering*
Works Council, *ondernemingsraad*
Wrongful act, *onrechtmatige daad*

Dutch into English

Aandelen aan toonder, *bearer shares*
Aandelen op naam. *registered shares*
Aannemelijk maken, *prima facie evidence*
Aanplakking, *announcement by way of
    posting*
Aanzegging, *notice*
Accoord(voorstel), *composition(proposal)*
Achtergestelde credituren, *subordinated
    creditors*
Achterstelling, *subordination*
Advierecht, *right to advise*
Afdwingbaar, *enforceable*
Affinanciering van de backservice,
    backservice obligation
Afgescheiden vermogen, *separate property*
Afgifte, *release*
Afhankelijke rechten, *ancillary rights*
Afkoelingsperiode, *insolvency stay*
Afstand, *waiver*
Afvloeiingsregelingen, *end-of-term arrange-
    ments*
Afvoerconstructie, *removal-scenario*
Afwikkelende instantie, *settlement agent*
Agentuurovereenkomsten, *agencies*
Algemeen beslag van rechtswege, *automatic
    general arrest*
Algemeen faillissementsbeslag, *general
    bankruptcy arrest*
Algemene faillissementskosten, *bankruptcy
    costs general in nature*
Ambtshalve, *ex officio*
Anders dan om niet, *for consideration*
Arbeidsovereenkomsten, *employment
    agreements*
Arrondissementsrechtbank, *district court*

Bedrijfsvereniging, *social security board*
Bedreiging, *force*
Bedrog, *fraud*

Beginsel van redelijkheid en billijkheid,
    principle of reasonableness and fairness
Bekendmaking, *announcement*
Belastingdienst, *tax authorities*
Belastingplichtige, *tax debtor*
Beleidsbepalers, *policy determinators*
Benadeelde, *aggrieved party*
Benadeling, *prejudice*
Beperkte rechten, *limited rights*
Beschikking, *court order*
Beschikkingsbevoegdheid, *right to adminis-
    ter and dispose*
Beslag, *arrest*
Beslaglegger, *arrestor*
Bestuur, *board of directors*
Betekenen, *to service*
Bevoorrechte crediteuren, *preferential
    creditors*
Bewijzen, *prove*
Bewindvoerder, *administrator in suspension
    of payment*
Bezitloos pandrecht, *non-possessory pledge*
Bijkomende omstandigheden, *incidental
    circumstances*
Bij voorbaat, *in advance*
Bijzondere faillissementskosten, *bankruptcy
    costs specific in nature*
Blokkeringsregeling, *share transfer restric-
    tions*
Bloot eigendom, *bare legal title*
Bodem, *ground*
Bodembeslag, *ground arrest*
Bodemverhuurconstructie, *ground lease-
    scenario*
Bodemzaken, *ground goods*
Boedelafstand, *renunciation of a claim
    against the estate*
Boedelcrediteuren, *estate creditors*
Boedelschuld, *estate claim*
Borgen, *guarantors pursuant to a surety*
Borgtochtovereenkomst, *surety*

Buitengerechtelijke verklaring, *extra-judicial statement*
Buitengerechtelijke sanering, *workout*
Buitengerechtelijke vernietiging, *extra-judicial invalidation*

Cassatie, *further appeal to the Netherlands supreme court*
Centrale wederpartij, *central counter party*
Cessies, *assignments*
Cessie tot zekerheid, *assignment by way of security*
Chartale betaling, *cash payment*
Collectieve arbeidsovereenkomst, *collective bargaining agreement*
Commanditaire vennootschap, *limited partnership*
Concernverhoudingen, *group relations*
Concurrente crediteuren, *non-preferential or ordinary creditors*
Conservatoir beslag, *precautionairy arrest*
Curator, *trustee in bankruptcy*

Décharge, *discharge*
Definitieve surséance van betaling, *final suspension of payment*
De Nederlandsche Bank (DNB), *Central Bank of the Netherlands*
Derdenbeding, *third party stipulation*
Dienen tot stoffering, *serve as furnishing*
Dienst voor het kadaster, *Service for the landregister*
Directe doorbraak van aansprakelijkheid, *piercing the corporate veil*
Doel en strekking, *purpose and purport*
Doorstart, *restart*
Dubbele verpanding, *double pledge*
Dubbel toekomstige vorderingen, *double future claims*
Duurovereenkomst, *long-term agreement*
Dwaling, *mistake*
Dwangcrediteuren, *creditors with factual preference*

Eerste levensbehoeften, *first necessities of life*
Eigendomsoverdracht, *transfer of title*
Eigendomsvoorbehoud, *reservation of title or ownership*
Eigenlijke opheffing, *proper discontinuation*
Endossement, *endorsement*
Enkelvoudig toekomstige vorderingen, *singular future claims*
Ernstig verwijt maken, *seriously to blame*
Executoriaal beslag, *arrest in execution*

Exercutoriale titel, *title of enforcement*
Exploot, *bailiff's notification*

Faillissement, *bankruptcy*
Faillissementsboedel, *bankrupt estate*
Faillissementskamers, *bankruptcy chambers*
Faillissementsregister, *register of bankruptcies*
Faillissementsrekening, *bankruptcy account*
Feitelijke handelingen, *factual acts*
Fiscaal bodemrecht, *fiscal privileged ground right*
Fiscaal voorrecht, *fiscal privilege*

Geïnde, *collected monies*
Gelaedeerde, *aggrieved party*
Geldige titel, *valid title or cause*
Geldschulden, *monetary obligations*
Geldvorderingen, *monetary claims*
Gerechtelijke procedures, *lawsuites*
Gerechtelijke tussenkomst, *judicial interference*
Gerechtshof, *Court of appeals*
Gezekerde vorderingen, *secured obligations*
Giraal betalingsverkeer, *payments by transfer in accounts*
Girale betalingen, *credit payments*
Girale tegoeden, *credit claims*
Goederen bezwaard met een zekerheidsrecht, *collateral*
Goederenrechtelijke zekerheden, *collateral security rights*
Grove nalatigheid, *gross negligence*
Grove schuld, *wilfull misconduct*

Handelingsbekwaamheid, *capacity*
Handelingsonbekwaamheid, *incapacity*
Hetgeen volgens ongeschreven recht in het maatschappelijke verkeer betaamt, *rule of unwritten law pertaining to proper social conduct*
Herverpanding, *repledge*
Hoge Raad der Nederlanden, *Netherlands supreme court*
Hoger beroep, *appeal*
Homologatie, *ratification*
Hoofdelijk medeschuldenaren, *several and jointly liable co-debtors*
Huisbank, *principal bank*
Huurbeding, *rental clause*
Huurkoop overeenkomsten, *hire-purchase agreements*
Huurovereenkomsten, *rental agreements*
Hypotheek, *mortgage*

In de macht van, *in the control of*
Indeplaatsstelling, *substitution*
Ingevoerd in het systeem, *introduced in the system*
In het verkeer geldende opvattingen, *generally accepted principles*
Inkomstenbelasting, *income tax*
In kracht van gewijsde gaan, *final and not open to appeal*
Inlossing, *redemption*
Inroepen, *invoke*
Inspectie der Registratie en Successie, *Registration Department of the Tax Office*
Instemmingsrecht, *right to consent*
In strijd met de goede zeden, *immoral*
Intrekking, *revocation*

Kantonrechter, *cantonal court*
Kennelijk onbehoorlijk bestuur, *apparent mismanagement*
Koop op afbetaling, *purchase in installments*
Kosten tot behoud van een goed, *costs incurred in preserving an asset*
Kosten wegens bearbeiding, *costs relating to labor in respect of an asset*
Kwaliteitsrekening, *in-the-capacity-of account*

Lastgeving, *mandate*
Loon, *wages*
Loonbelasting, *wages tax*
Loongarantieregeling, *Wages Guarantee Arrangement*

Misbruik van bevoegdheid, *abuse of right*
Misbruik van omstandigheden, *abuse of circumstances*

Nalaten, *omission to act*
Nederlandse Staatscourant, *National Gazette of the Netherlands*
Negatieve boedel, *negative estate*
Nevenrechten, *accessory rights*
Nietigheid, *voidness*
Niet opeisbaar, *not due and payable*
Niet voor verificatie vatbare vorderingen, *claims not subject to verification*
Noodregeling, *Emergency Arrangement*
Notariële akte, *notarial deed*

Omslag van de faillissementskosten, *allocation of the bankruptcy costs*
Omzetbelasting, *value added tax*
Onaantastbaar, *inviolable*

Onbehoorlijk bestuur, *mismanangement*
Onbelangrijk verzuim, *immaterial default*
Onderhandse akte, *private deed*
Onderhandse verkoop, *private sale*
Ondernemingsraad, *Works Council*
Onderzoeksplicht, *duty to investigate*
Oneigenlijke opheffing, *improper discontinuation*
Onmiskenbare vergissing, *manifest error*
Onrechtmatige daad, *wrongful act*
Onroerende zaken, *immoveable goods*
Ontbindende voorwaarde, *condition subsequent*
Ontbinding, *dissolution*
Ontruiming, *eviction*
Ontruimingsbescherming, *protection from eviction*
Ontslag van instantie, *request for dismissal*
Ontslagvergunning, *permit to terminate an employment agreement*
Onverplichte rechtshandelingen, *voluntary legal acts*
Onverschuldige betaling, *undue payment*
Onzuivere achterstelling, *improper subordination*
Oogmerk, *intention*
Opbrengst, *proceeds*
Opdracht, *agreement of engagement*
Opeisbaar, *due and payable*
Openbaar pandrecht, *disclosed pledge*
Openbare verkoop, *public auction*
Opheffing, *discontinuation*
Opschortende voorwaarde, *condition precedent*
Opstalrecht, *building right*
Opzegging, *renunciation*
Overbedeling, *overcompensation*
Overboekingsopdracht, *transfer order*
Overdraagbaar, *transferable*
Overdracht onder bijzondere titel, *transfer pursuant to particular title*
Overgang van onderneming, *transfer of a business*
Overleg, *consultation*

Pachtovereenkomsten, *lease agreements*
Pandlijsten, *lists of pledged goods*
Pandrecht, *pledge*
Parlementaire geschiedenis, *parliamentary notes*
Per saldo, *on balance*
Proces-verbaal van toewijzing, *official report of allotment*
Procureur, *attorney of record*

Raad van commissarissen, *supervisory board*
Rangregeling, *ranking arrangement*
Rangwisseling, *change of rank*
Ratificatie, *ratification*
Rechtelijke macht, *judiciary*
Rechten aan order of toonder, *bearer or order rights*
Rechter-commissaris, *supervisory judge*
Rechtshandeling, *legal act*
Rechtspersoon, *legal entity*
Rechtsplicht, *legal obligation*
Recht van parate executie, *right of summary proceedings*
Recht van reclame, *right to recollect*
Recht van vruchtgebruik, *right of usufruct*
Regel van derdenbescherming, *rule of third party protection*
Registergoed, *registered good*
Rekening courant, *current-account*
Rekening en verantwoording afleggen, *render account for ones acts*
Relatieve nietigheid, *relative effect of an annulment*
Renvooi procedure, *reference proceeding*
Retentierecht, *right of retention*
Roerende zaken, *moveable goods*

Samenloop van rechten, *concurrence of rights*
Samenspannen, *conspire*
Schadevergoeding en verzekeringspenningen, *compensation for damages and insurance monies in respect of an asset*
Schikking, *settlement*
Schorsende werking, *suspensory effect*
Schuldenaar, *debtor*
Schuldsanering natuurlijke personen, *debt reorganization of natural persons*
Slotuitdelingslijst, *final plan of distribution*
Stil pandrecht, *non-disclosed pledge*

Te goeder trouw, *in good faith*
Tekort in het faillissement, *deficit in the bankruptcy*
Tenuitvoerlegging, *execution*
Termijnzaken, *goods traded on the commodity market and delivered at a fixed time or within a pre-set period*
Terugwerkende kracht, *retroactive effect*
Toeëigening, *appropriation*
Toekomstige goederen, *future goods*
Toerekenbare tekortkoming, *default attributable to*
Toewijzen, *allow*

Uitdelingslijst, *plan of distribution*
Uitvoeringsinstantie sociale verzekeringen, *social security board*
Uitwinning, *foreclosure*

Veiling, *auction*
Vennootschap onder firma, *general partnerschip*
Vennootschapsbelasting, *corporate tax*
Verbindend worden, *final and not open to appeal*
Verborgen gebreken, *hidden defects*
Vereenzelviging, *identification*
Vereffenaar, *liquidator*
Vereffening, *liquidation*
Vereffening van een nalatenschap, *liquidation of an estate*
Verhaalsmogelijkheden, *means of recourse*
Verhaalsrecht, *right of recourse*
Verjaringstermijnen, *limitation periods*
Verkeersopvatting, *common opinion*
Verklaring voor recht, *declaration of law*
Verlies van een voordeel, *loss of a benefit*
Vermenging, *mixing of goods*
Vernietigbaarheid, *voidability*
Vernietiging, *nullification*
Vernietigingsgrond, *ground for annulment*
Verplichte rechtshandelingen, *obligatory legal acts*
Verplichting tot nadere zekerheidsstelling, *obligation to provide further security rights*
Verplichting tot ongedaanmaking, *obligation to restore the original situation*
Verrekening, *set-off*
Verrekkeningsinstituut, *clearing house*
Verrekeningsverklaring, *set-off notification*
Vervaltermijnen, *terms of forfeiture*
Verwateren, *dilute*
Verzet, *right to request a review*
Verzuim, *default*
Vestingshandeling, *deed of establishment*
Voldoende bepaalbaar, *sufficiently identifiable*
Voldoening, *satisfaction*
Volmachten, *proxies*
Voorbehouden pandrecht, *reserved pledge*
Voorlopige surséance van betaling, *provisional suspension of payment*
Voorrangsrechten, *priority rights*
Voorrechten, *privileged rights* of *rights of preference*
Vorderingen, *claims*
Vordering op naam, *registered claim*

Vuistloos pandrecht, *non-possessory pledge*
Vuistpand, *possessory pledge*

Waardevergoedingvordering, *claim for compensation of value*
Wanbeleid, *mismanagement*
Wanprestatie, *default attributable to*
Wederkerige overeenkomsten, *agreements with mutual performances*
Wederzijds schuldenaarschap, *mutual debtorship*
Werknemersvakbond, *trade union*
Wetenschap, *knowledge*

Zaak, *property*
Zaaksvervanging, *object substitution*
Zaaksvorming, *formation of goods*
Zakelijke werking, *consequences of a proprietary nature*
Zakelijk recht, *property (or proprietary) right*
Zekerheidseigendom, *security ownership*
Zekerheidsrechten, *security rights*
Zuivere achterstelling, *proper subordination*
Zuivering, *unencumbered title*
Zwijgrecht, *right to remain silent*

Annex
ENGLISH VERSION OF EU INSOLVENCY REGULATION

**Council regulation (EC) No 1346/2000
of 29 May 2000
on insolvency proceedings**
(Official Journal L 160, 30/06/2000, p. 0001-0013; only European Community's legislation printed in the *Official Journal of the European Communities* is deemed to be authentic)

THE COUNCIL OF THE EUROPEAN UNION,

Having regard to the Treaty establishing the European Community, and in particular Articles 61(c) and 67(1) thereof,
Having regard to the initiative of the Federal Republic of Germany and the Republic of Finland,
Having regard to the opinion of the European Parliament(1),
Having regard to the opinion of the Economic and Social Committee(2),

Whereas:

(1)   The European Union has set out the aim of establishing an area of freedom, security and justice.

(2)   The proper functioning of the internal market requires that cross-border insolvency proceedings should operate efficiently and effectively and this Regulation needs to be adopted in order to achieve this objective which comes within the scope of judicial cooperation in civil matters within the meaning of Article 65 of the Treaty.

(3)   The activities of undertakings have more and more cross-border effects and are therefore increasingly being regulated by Community law. While the insolvency of such undertakings also affects the proper functioning of the internal market, there is a need for a Community act requiring coordination of the measures to be taken regarding an insolvent debtor's assets.

(4)   It is necessary for the proper functioning of the internal market to avoid incentives for the parties to transfer assets or judicial proceedings from one Member State to another, seeking to obtain a more favourable legal position (forum shopping).

(5)   These objectives cannot be achieved to a sufficient degree at national level and action at Community level is therefore justified.

(6)   In accordance with the principle of proportionality this Regulation should be confined to provisions governing jurisdiction for opening insolvency proceedings and judgments which are delivered directly on the basis of the insolvency proceedings and are closely connected with such proceedings. In addition, this Regulation should contain provisions regarding the recognition of those judgments and the applicable law which also satisfy that principle.

(7)   Insolvency proceedings relating to the winding-up of insolvent companies or other legal persons, judicial arrangements, compositions and analogous proceedings are ex-

cluded from the scope of the 1968 Brussels Convention on Jurisdiction and the Enforcement of Judgments in Civil and Commercial Matters(3), as amended by the Conventions on Accession to this Convention(4).

(8)   In order to achieve the aim of improving the efficiency and effectiveness of insolvency proceedings having cross-border effects, it is necessary, and appropriate, that the provisions on jurisdiction, recognition and applicable law in this area should be contained in a Community law measure which is binding and directly applicable in Member States.

(9)   This Regulation should apply to insolvency proceedings, whether the debtor is a natural person or a legal person, a trader or an individual. The insolvency proceedings to which this Regulation applies are listed in the Annexes. Insolvency proceedings concerning insurance undertakings, credit institutions, investment undertakings holding funds or securities for third parties and collective investment undertakings should be excluded from the scope of this Regulation. Such undertakings should not be covered by this Regulation since they are subject to special arrangements and, to some extent, the national supervisory authorities have extremely wide-ranging powers of intervention.

(10)   Insolvency proceedings do not necessarily involve the intervention of a judicial authority; the expression "court" in this Regulation should be given a broad meaning and include a person or body empowered by national law to open insolvency proceedings. In order for this Regulation to apply, proceedings (comprising acts and formalities set down in law) should not only have to comply with the provisions of this Regulation, but they should also be officially recognised and legally effective in the Member State in which the insolvency proceedings are opened and should be collective insolvency proceedings which entail the partial or total divestment of the debtor and the appointment of a liquidator.

(11)   This Regulation acknowledges the fact that as a result of widely differing substantive laws it is not practical to introduce insolvency proceedings with universal scope in the entire Community. The application without exception of the law of the State of opening of proceedings would, against this background, frequently lead to difficulties. This applies, for example, to the widely differing laws on security interests to be found in the Community. Furthermore, the preferential rights enjoyed by some creditors in the insolvency proceedings are, in some cases, completely different. This Regulation should take account of this in two different ways. On the one hand, provision should be made for special rules on applicable law in the case of particularly significant rights and legal relationships (e.g. rights in rem and contracts of employment). On the other hand, national proceedings covering only assets situated in the State of opening should also be allowed alongside main insolvency proceedings with universal scope.

(12)   This Regulation enables the main insolvency proceedings to be opened in the Member State where the debtor has the centre of his main interests. These proceedings have universal scope and aim at encompassing all the debtor's assets. To protect the diversity of interests, this Regulation permits secondary proceedings to be opened to run in parallel with the main proceedings. Secondary proceedings may be opened in the Member State where the debtor has an establishment. The effects of secondary proceedings are limited to the assets located in that State. Mandatory rules of coordination with the main proceedings satisfy the need for unity in the Community.

(13)   The "centre of main interests" should correspond to the place where the debtor conducts the administration of his interests on a regular basis and is therefore ascertainable by third parties.

(14)   This Regulation applies only to proceedings where the centre of the debtor's main interests is located in the Community.

(15)   The rules of jurisdiction set out in this Regulation establish only international jurisdiction, that is to say, they designate the Member State the courts of which may open insolvency proceedings. Territorial jurisdiction within that Member State must be established by the national law of the Member State concerned.

(16)   The court having jurisdiction to open the main insolvency proceedings should be enabled to order provisional and protective measures from the time of the request to open proceedings. Preservation measures both prior to and after the commencement of the insolvency proceedings are very important to guarantee the effectiveness of the insolvency proceedings. In that connection this Regulation should afford different possibilities. On the one hand, the court competent for the main insolvency proceedings should be able also to order provisional protective measures covering assets situated in the territory of other Member States. On the other hand, a liquidator temporarily appointed prior to the opening of the main insolvency proceedings should be able, in the Member States in which an establishment belonging to the debtor is to be found, to apply for the preservation measures which are possible under the law of those States.

(17)   Prior to the opening of the main insolvency proceedings, the right to request the opening of insolvency proceedings in the Member State where the debtor has an establishment should be limited to local creditors and creditors of the local establishment or to cases where main proceedings cannot be opened under the law of the Member State where the debtor has the centre of his main interest. The reason for this restriction is that cases where territorial insolvency proceedings are requested before the main insolvency proceedings are intended to be limited to what is absolutely necessary. If the main insolvency proceedings are opened, the territorial proceedings become secondary.

(18)   Following the opening of the main insolvency proceedings, the right to request the opening of insolvency proceedings in a Member State where the debtor has an establishment is not restricted by this Regulation. The liquidator in the main proceedings or any other person empowered under the national law of that Member State may request the opening of secondary insolvency proceedings.

(19)   Secondary insolvency proceedings may serve different purposes, besides the protection of local interests. Cases may arise where the estate of the debtor is too complex to administer as a unit or where differences in the legal systems concerned are so great that difficulties may arise from the extension of effects deriving from the law of the State of the opening to the other States where the assets are located. For this reason the liquidator in the main proceedings may request the opening of secondary proceedings when the efficient administration of the estate so requires.

(20)   Main insolvency proceedings and secondary proceedings can, however, contribute to the effective realisation of the total assets only if all the concurrent proceedings pending are coordinated. The main condition here is that the various liquidators must cooperate closely, in particular by exchanging a sufficient amount of information. In order to ensure the dominant role of the main insolvency proceedings, the liquidator in such proceedings should be given several possibilities for intervening in secondary insolvency proceedings which are pending at the same time. For example, he should be able to propose a restructuring plan or composition or apply for realisation of the assets in the secondary insolvency proceedings to be suspended.

(21)   Every creditor, who has his habitual residence, domicile or registered office in the
         Community, should have the right to lodge his claims in each of the insolvency pro-
         ceedings pending in the Community relating to the debtor's assets. This should also
         apply to tax authorities and social insurance institutions. However, in order to ensure
         equal treatment of creditors, the distribution of proceeds must be coordinated. Every
         creditor should be able to keep what he has received in the course of insolvency pro-
         ceedings but should be entitled only to participate in the distribution of total assets in
         other proceedings if creditors with the same standing have obtained the same propor-
         tion of their claims.

(22)   This Regulation should provide for immediate recognition of judgments concerning
         the opening, conduct and closure of insolvency proceedings which come within its
         scope and of judgments handed down in direct connection with such insolvency pro-
         ceedings. Automatic recognition should therefore mean that the effects attributed to
         the proceedings by the law of the State in which the proceedings were opened extend
         to all other Member States. Recognition of judgments delivered by the courts of the
         Member States should be based on the principle of mutual trust. To that end, grounds
         for non-recognition should be reduced to the minimum necessary. This is also the ba-
         sis on which any dispute should be resolved where the courts of two Member States
         both claim competence to open the main insolvency proceedings. The decision of the
         first court to open proceedings should be recognised in the other Member States
         without those Member States having the power to scrutinise the court's decision.

(23)   This Regulation should set out, for the matters covered by it, uniform rules on con-
         flict of laws which replace, within their scope of application, national rules of private
         international law. Unless otherwise stated, the law of the Member State of the open-
         ing of the proceedings should be applicable (lex concursus). This rule on conflict of
         laws should be valid both for the main proceedings and for local proceedings; the lex
         concursus determines all the effects of the insolvency proceedings, both procedural
         and substantive, on the persons and legal relations concerned. It governs all the con-
         ditions for the opening, conduct and closure of the insolvency proceedings.

(24)   Automatic recognition of insolvency proceedings to which the law of the opening
         State normally applies may interfere with the rules under which transactions are car-
         ried out in other Member States. To protect legitimate expectations and the certainty
         of transactions in Member States other than that in which proceedings are opened,
         provisions should be made for a number of exceptions to the general rule.

(25)   There is a particular need for a special reference diverging from the law of the open-
         ing State in the case of rights in rem, since these are of considerable importance for
         the granting of credit. The basis, validity and extent of such a right in rem should
         therefore normally be determined according to the lex situs and not be affected by the
         opening of insolvency proceedings. The proprietor of the right in rem should there-
         fore be able to continue to assert his right to segregation or separate settlement of the
         collateral security. Where assets are subject to rights in rem under the lex situs in one
         Member State but the main proceedings are being carried out in another Member
         State, the liquidator in the main proceedings should be able to request the opening of
         secondary proceedings in the jurisdiction where the rights in rem arise if the debtor
         has an establishment there. If a secondary proceeding is not opened, the surplus on
         sale of the asset covered by rights in rem must be paid to the liquidator in the main
         proceedings.

(26)   If a set-off is not permitted under the law of the opening State, a creditor should nev-
         ertheless be entitled to the set-off if it is possible under the law applicable to the

claim of the insolvent debtor. In this way, set-off will acquire a kind of guarantee function based on legal provisions on which the creditor concerned can rely at the time when the claim arises.

(27)   There is also a need for special protection in the case of payment systems and financial markets. This applies for example to the position-closing agreements and netting agreements to be found in such systems as well as to the sale of securities and to the guarantees provided for such transactions as governed in particular by Directive 98/26/EC of the European Parliament and of the Council of 19 May 1998 on settlement finality in payment and securities settlement systems(5). For such transactions, the only law which is material should thus be that applicable to the system or market concerned. This provision is intended to prevent the possibility of mechanisms for the payment and settlement of transactions provided for in the payment and set-off systems or on the regulated financial markets of the Member States being altered in the case of insolvency of a business partner. Directive 98/26/EC contains special provisions which should take precedence over the general rules in this Regulation.

(28)   In order to protect employees and jobs, the effects of insolvency proceedings on the continuation or termination of employment and on the rights and obligations of all parties to such employment must be determined by the law applicable to the agreement in accordance with the general rules on conflict of law. Any other insolvency-law questions, such as whether the employees' claims are protected by preferential rights and what status such preferential rights may have, should be determined by the law of the opening State.

(29)   For business considerations, the main content of the decision opening the proceedings should be published in the other Member States at the request of the liquidator. If there is an establishment in the Member State concerned, there may be a requirement that publication is compulsory. In neither case, however, should publication be a prior condition for recognition of the foreign proceedings.

(30)   It may be the case that some of the persons concerned are not in fact aware that proceedings have been opened and act in good faith in a way that conflicts with the new situation. In order to protect such persons who make a payment to the debtor because they are unaware that foreign proceedings have been opened when they should in fact have made the payment to the foreign liquidator, it should be provided that such a payment is to have a debt-discharging effect.

(31)   This Regulation should include Annexes relating to the organisation of insolvency proceedings. As these Annexes relate exclusively to the legislation of Member States, there are specific and substantiated reasons for the Council to reserve the right to amend these Annexes in order to take account of any amendments to the domestic law of the Member States.

(32)   The United Kingdom and Ireland, in accordance with Article 3 of the Protocol on the position of the United Kingdom and Ireland annexed to the Treaty on European Union and the Treaty establishing the European Community, have given notice of their wish to take part in the adoption and application of this Regulation.

(33)   Denmark, in accordance with Articles 1 and 2 of the Protocol on the position of Denmark annexed to the Treaty on European Union and the Treaty establishing the European Community, is not participating in the adoption of this Regulation, and is therefore not bound by it nor subject to its application,

HAS ADOPTED THIS REGULATION:

CHAPTER I
GENERAL PROVISIONS
Article 1
Scope

1. This Regulation shall apply to collective insolvency proceedings which entail the partial or total divestment of a debtor and the appointment of a liquidator.

2. This Regulation shall not apply to insolvency proceedings concerning insurance undertakings, credit institutions, investment undertakings which provide services involving the holding of funds or securities for third parties, or to collective investment undertakings.

Article 2
Definitions

For the purposes of this Regulation:

(a) "insolvency proceedings" shall mean the collective proceedings referred to in Article 1(1). These proceedings are listed in Annex A;

(b) "liquidator" shall mean any person or body whose function is to administer or liquidate assets of which the debtor has been divested or to supervise the administration of his affairs. Those persons and bodies are listed in Annex C;

(c) "winding-up proceedings" shall mean insolvency proceedings within the meaning of point (a) involving realising the assets of the debtor, including where the proceedings have been closed by a composition or other measure terminating the insolvency, or closed by reason of the insufficiency of the assets. Those proceedings are listed in Annex B;

(d) "court" shall mean the judicial body or any other competent body of a Member State empowered to open insolvency proceedings or to take decisions in the course of such proceedings;

(e) "judgment" in relation to the opening of insolvency proceedings or the appointment of a liquidator shall include the decision of any court empowered to open such proceedings or to appoint a liquidator;

(f) "the time of the opening of proceedings" shall mean the time at which the judgment opening proceedings becomes effective, whether it is a final judgment or not;

(g) "the Member State in which assets are situated" shall mean, in the case of:
    –   tangible property, the Member State within the territory of which the property is situated,
    –   property and rights ownership of or entitlement to which must be entered in a public register, the Member State under the authority of which the register is kept,
    –   claims, the Member State within the territory of which the third party required to meet them has the centre of his main interests, as determined in Article 3(1);

(h) "establishment" shall mean any place of operations where the debtor carries out a non-transitory economic activity with human means and goods.

Article 3
International jurisdiction

1. The courts of the Member State within the territory of which the centre of a debtor's main interests is situated shall have jurisdiction to open insolvency proceedings. In the case of a company or legal person, the place of the registered office shall be presumed to be the centre of its main interests in the absence of proof to the contrary.

2. Where the centre of a debtor's main interests is situated within the territory of a Member State, the courts of another Member State shall have jurisdiction to open insolvency proceedings against that debtor only if he possesses an establishment within the territory of that other Member State. The effects of those proceedings shall be restricted to the assets of the debtor situated in the territory of the latter Member State.

3. Where insolvency proceedings have been opened under paragraph 1, any proceedings opened subsequently under paragraph 2 shall be secondary proceedings. These latter proceedings must be winding-up proceedings.

4. Territorial insolvency proceedings referred to in paragraph 2 may be opened prior to the opening of main insolvency proceedings in accordance with paragraph 1 only:

    (a) where insolvency proceedings under paragraph 1 cannot be opened because of the conditions laid down by the law of the Member State within the territory of which the centre of the debtor's main interests is situated; or

    (b) where the opening of territorial insolvency proceedings is requested by a creditor who has his domicile, habitual residence or registered office in the Member State within the territory of which the establishment is situated, or whose claim arises from the operation of that establishment.

Article 4

Law applicable

1. Save as otherwise provided in this Regulation, the law applicable to insolvency proceedings and their effects shall be that of the Member State within the territory of which such proceedings are opened, hereafter referred to as the "State of the opening of proceedings".

2. The law of the State of the opening of proceedings shall determine the conditions for the opening of those proceedings, their conduct and their closure. It shall determine in particular:

    (a) against which debtors insolvency proceedings may be brought on account of their capacity;

    (b) the assets which form part of the estate and the treatment of assets acquired by or devolving on the debtor after the opening of the insolvency proceedings;

    (c) the respective powers of the debtor and the liquidator;

    (d) the conditions under which set-offs may be invoked;

    (e) the effects of insolvency proceedings on current contracts to which the debtor is party;

    (f) the effects of the insolvency proceedings on proceedings brought by individual creditors, with the exception of lawsuits pending;

    (g) the claims which are to be lodged against the debtor's estate and the treatment of claims arising after the opening of insolvency proceedings;

    (h) the rules governing the lodging, verification and admission of claims;

    (i) the rules governing the distribution of proceeds from the realisation of assets, the ranking of claims and the rights of creditors who have obtained partial satisfaction after the opening of insolvency proceedings by virtue of a right in rem or through a set-off;

    (j) the conditions for and the effects of closure of insolvency proceedings, in particular by composition;

    (k) creditors' rights after the closure of insolvency proceedings;

    (l) who is to bear the costs and expenses incurred in the insolvency proceedings;

    (m) the rules relating to the voidness, voidability or unenforceability of legal acts detrimental to all the creditors.

Article 5
Third parties' rights in rem
1. The opening of insolvency proceedings shall not affect the rights in rem of creditors or third parties in respect of tangible or intangible, moveable or immoveable assets - both specific assets and collections of indefinite assets as a whole which change from time to time - belonging to the debtor which are situated within the territory of another Member State at the time of the opening of proceedings.
2. The rights referred to in paragraph 1 shall in particular mean:
    (a) the right to dispose of assets or have them disposed of and to obtain satisfaction from the proceeds of or income from those assets, in particular by virtue of a lien or a mortgage;
    (b) the exclusive right to have a claim met, in particular a right guaranteed by a lien in respect of the claim or by assignment of the claim by way of a guarantee;
    (c) the right to demand the assets from, and/or to require restitution by, anyone having possession or use of them contrary to the wishes of the party so entitled;
    (d) a right in rem to the beneficial use of assets.
3. The right, recorded in a public register and enforceable against third parties, under which a right in rem within the meaning of paragraph 1 may be obtained, shall be considered a right in rem.
4. Paragraph 1 shall not preclude actions for voidness, voidability or unenforceability as referred to in Article 4(2)(m).

Article 6
Set-off
1. The opening of insolvency proceedings shall not affect the right of creditors to demand the set-off of their claims against the claims of the debtor, where such a set-off is permitted by the law applicable to the insolvent debtor's claim.
2. Paragraph 1 shall not preclude actions for voidness, voidability or unenforceability as referred to in Article 4(2)(m).

Article 7
Reservation of title
1. The opening of insolvency proceedings against the purchaser of an asset shall not affect the seller's rights based on a reservation of title where at the time of the opening of proceedings the asset is situated within the territory of a Member State other than the State of opening of proceedings.
2. The opening of insolvency proceedings against the seller of an asset, after delivery of the asset, shall not constitute grounds for rescinding or terminating the sale and shall not prevent the purchaser from acquiring title where at the time of the opening of proceedings the asset sold is situated within the territory of a Member State other than the State of the opening of proceedings.
3. Paragraphs 1 and 2 shall not preclude actions for voidness, voidability or unenforceability as referred to in Article 4(2)(m).

Article 8
Contracts relating to immoveable property
The effects of insolvency proceedings on a contract conferring the right to acquire or make use of immoveable property shall be governed solely by the law of the Member State within the territory of which the immoveable property is situated.

Article 9
Payment systems and financial markets
1. Without prejudice to Article 5, the effects of insolvency proceedings on the rights and obligations of the parties to a payment or settlement system or to a financial market shall be governed solely by the law of the Member State applicable to that system or market.
2. Paragraph 1 shall not preclude any action for voidness, voidability or unenforceability which may be taken to set aside payments or transactions under the law applicable to the relevant payment system or financial market.

Article 10
Contracts of employment
The effects of insolvency proceedings on employment contracts and relationships shall be governed solely by the law of the Member State applicable to the contract of employment.

Article 11
Effects on rights subject to registration
The effects of insolvency proceedings on the rights of the debtor in immoveable property, a ship or an aircraft subject to registration in a public register shall be determined by the law of the Member State under the authority of which the register is kept.

Article 12
Community patents and trade marks
For the purposes of this Regulation, a Community patent, a Community trade mark or any other similar right established by Community law may be included only in the proceedings referred to in Article 3(1).

Article 13
Detrimental acts
Article 4(2)(m) shall not apply where the person who benefited from an act detrimental to all the creditors provides proof that:
–   the said act is subject to the law of a Member State other than that of the State of the opening of proceedings, and
–   that law does not allow any means of challenging that act in the relevant case.

Article 14
Protection of third-party purchasers
Where, by an act concluded after the opening of insolvency proceedings, the debtor disposes, for consideration, of:
–   an immoveable asset, or
–   a ship or an aircraft subject to registration in a public register, or
–   securities whose existence presupposes registration in a register laid down by law,
the validity of that act shall be governed by the law of the State within the territory of which the immoveable asset is situated or under the authority of which the register is kept.

Article 15
Effects of insolvency proceedings on lawsuits pending
The effects of insolvency proceedings on a lawsuit pending concerning an asset or a right of which the debtor has been divested shall be governed solely by the law of the Member State in which that lawsuit is pending.

CHAPTER II
RECOGNITION OF INSOLVENCY PROCEEDINGS

Article 16
Principle
1.   Any judgment opening insolvency proceedings handed down by a court of a Member State which has jurisdiction pursuant to Article 3 shall be recognised in all the other Member States from the time that it becomes effective in the State of the opening of proceedings.
      This rule shall also apply where, on account of his capacity, insolvency proceedings cannot be brought against the debtor in other Member States.
2.   Recognition of the proceedings referred to in Article 3(1) shall not preclude the opening of the proceedings referred to in Article 3(2) by a court in another Member State. The latter proceedings shall be secondary insolvency proceedings within the meaning of Chapter III.

Article 17
Effects of recognition
1.   The judgment opening the proceedings referred to in Article 3(1) shall, with no further formalities, produce the same effects in any other Member State as under this law of the State of the opening of proceedings, unless this Regulation provides otherwise and as long as no proceedings referred to in Article 3(2) are opened in that other Member State.
2.   The effects of the proceedings referred to in Article 3(2) may not be challenged in other Member States. Any restriction of the creditors' rights, in particular a stay or discharge, shall produce effects vis-à-vis assets situated within the territory of another Member State only in the case of those creditors who have given their consent.

Article 18
Powers of the liquidator
1.   The liquidator appointed by a court which has jurisdiction pursuant to Article 3(1) may exercise all the powers conferred on him by the law of the State of the opening of proceedings in another Member State, as long as no other insolvency proceedings have been opened there nor any preservation measure to the contrary has been taken there further to a request for the opening of insolvency proceedings in that State. He may in particular remove the debtor's assets from the territory of the Member State in which they are situated, subject to Articles 5 and 7.
2.   The liquidator appointed by a court which has jurisdiction pursuant to Article 3(2) may in any other Member State claim through the courts or out of court that moveable property was removed from the territory of the State of the opening of proceedings to the territory of that other Member State after the opening of the insolvency proceedings. He may also bring any action to set aside which is in the interests of the creditors.
3.   In exercising his powers, the liquidator shall comply with the law of the Member State within the territory of which he intends to take action, in particular with regard to procedures for the realisation of assets. Those powers may not include coercive measures or the right to rule on legal proceedings or disputes.

Article 19
Proof of the liquidator's appointment
The liquidator's appointment shall be evidenced by a certified copy of the original decision appointing him or by any other certificate issued by the court which has jurisdiction.

A translation into the official language or one of the official languages of the Member State within the territory of which he intends to act may be required. No legalisation or other similar formality shall be required.

Article 20
Return and imputation
1. A creditor who, after the opening of the proceedings referred to in Article 3(1) obtains by any means, in particular through enforcement, total or partial satisfaction of his claim on the assets belonging to the debtor situated within the territory of another Member State, shall return what he has obtained to the liquidator, subject to Articles 5 and 7.
2. In order to ensure equal treatment of creditors a creditor who has, in the course of insolvency proceedings, obtained a dividend on his claim shall share in distributions made in other proceedings only where creditors of the same ranking or category have, in those other proceedings, obtained an equivalent dividend.

Article 21
Publication
1. The liquidator may request that notice of the judgment opening insolvency proceedings and, where appropriate, the decision appointing him, be published in any other Member State in accordance with the publication procedures provided for in that State. Such publication shall also specify the liquidator appointed and whether the jurisdiction rule applied is that pursuant to Article 3(1) or Article 3(2).
2. However, any Member State within the territory of which the debtor has an establishment may require mandatory publication. In such cases, the liquidator or any authority empowered to that effect in the Member State where the proceedings referred to in Article 3(1) are opened shall take all necessary measures to ensure such publication.

Article 22
Registration in a public register
1. The liquidator may request that the judgment opening the proceedings referred to in Article 3(1) be registered in the land register, the trade register and any other public register kept in the other Member States.
2. However, any Member State may require mandatory registration. In such cases, the liquidator or any authority empowered to that effect in the Member State where the proceedings referred to in Article 3(1) have been opened shall take all necessary measures to ensure such registration.

Article 23
Costs
The costs of the publication and registration provided for in Articles 21 and 22 shall be regarded as costs and expenses incurred in the proceedings.

Article 24

Honouring of an obligation to a debtor

1.   Where an obligation has been honoured in a Member State for the benefit of a debtor who is subject to insolvency proceedings opened in another Member State, when it should have been honoured for the benefit of the liquidator in those proceedings, the person honouring the obligation shall be deemed to have discharged it if he was unaware of the opening of proceedings.

2.   Where such an obligation is honoured before the publication provided for in Article 21 has been effected, the person honouring the obligation shall be presumed, in the absence of proof to the contrary, to have been unaware of the opening of insolvency proceedings; where the obligation is honoured after such publication has been effected, the person honouring the obligation shall be presumed, in the absence of proof to the contrary, to have been aware of the opening of proceedings.

Article 25

Recognition and enforceability of other judgments

1.   Judgments handed down by a court whose judgment concerning the opening of proceedings is recognised in accordance with Article 16 and which concern the course and closure of insolvency proceedings, and compositions approved by that court shall also be recognised with no further formalities. Such judgments shall be enforced in accordance with Articles 31 to 51, with the exception of Article 34(2), of the Brussels Convention on Jurisdiction and the Enforcement of Judgments in Civil and Commercial Matters, as amended by the Conventions of Accession to this Convention.

The first subparagraph shall also apply to judgments deriving directly from the insolvency proceedings and which are closely linked with them, even if they were handed down by another court.

The first subparagraph shall also apply to judgments relating to preservation measures taken after the request for the opening of insolvency proceedings.

2.   The recognition and enforcement of judgments other than those referred to in paragraph 1 shall be governed by the Convention referred to in paragraph 1, provided that that Convention is applicable.

3.   The Member States shall not be obliged to recognise or enforce a judgment referred to in paragraph 1 which might result in a limitation of personal freedom or postal secrecy.

Article 26 (6)

Public policy

Any Member State may refuse to recognise insolvency proceedings opened in another Member State or to enforce a judgment handed down in the context of such proceedings where the effects of such recognition or enforcement would be manifestly contrary to that State's public policy, in particular its fundamental principles or the constitutional rights and liberties of the individual.

CHAPTER III
SECONDARY INSOLVENCY PROCEEDINGS

Article 27
Opening of proceedings
The opening of the proceedings referred to in Article 3(1) by a court of a Member State and which is recognised in another Member State (main proceedings) shall permit the opening in that other Member State, a court of which has jurisdiction pursuant to Article 3(2), of secondary insolvency proceedings without the debtor's insolvency being examined in that other State. These latter proceedings must be among the proceedings listed in Annex B. Their effects shall be restricted to the assets of the debtor situated within the territory of that other Member State.

Article 28
Applicable law
Save as otherwise provided in this Regulation, the law applicable to secondary proceedings shall be that of the Member State within the territory of which the secondary proceedings are opened.

Article 29
Right to request the opening of proceedings
The opening of secondary proceedings may be requested by:
(a)   the liquidator in the main proceedings;
(b)   any other person or authority empowered to request the opening of insolvency proceedings under the law of the Member State within the territory of which the opening of secondary proceedings is requested.

Article 30
Advance payment of costs and expenses
Where the law of the Member State in which the opening of secondary proceedings is requested requires that the debtor's assets be sufficient to cover in whole or in part the costs and expenses of the proceedings, the court may, when it receives such a request, require the applicant to make an advance payment of costs or to provide appropriate security.

Article 31
Duty to cooperate and communicate information
1.   Subject to the rules restricting the communication of information, the liquidator in the main proceedings and the liquidators in the secondary proceedings shall be duty bound to communicate information to each other. They shall immediately communicate any information which may be relevant to the other proceedings, in particular the progress made in lodging and verifying claims and all measures aimed at terminating the proceedings.
2.   Subject to the rules applicable to each of the proceedings, the liquidator in the main proceedings and the liquidators in the secondary proceedings shall be duty bound to cooperate with each other.
3.   The liquidator in the secondary proceedings shall give the liquidator in the main proceedings an early opportunity of submitting proposals on the liquidation or use of the assets in the secondary proceedings.

Article 32
Exercise of creditors' rights
1.   Any creditor may lodge his claim in the main proceedings and in any secondary proceedings.
2.   The liquidators in the main and any secondary proceedings shall lodge in other proceedings claims which have already been lodged in the proceedings for which they were appointed, provided that the interests of creditors in the latter proceedings are served thereby, subject to the right of creditors to oppose that or to withdraw the lodgement of their claims where the law applicable so provides.
3.   The liquidator in the main or secondary proceedings shall be empowered to participate in other proceedings on the same basis as a creditor, in particular by attending creditors' meetings.

Article 33
Stay of liquidation
1.   The court, which opened the secondary proceedings, shall stay the process of liquidation in whole or in part on receipt of a request from the liquidator in the main proceedings, provided that in that event it may require the liquidator in the main proceedings to take any suitable measure to guarantee the interests of the creditors in the secondary proceedings and of individual classes of creditors. Such a request from the liquidator may be rejected only if it is manifestly of no interest to the creditors in the main proceedings. Such a stay of the process of liquidation may be ordered for up to three months. It may be continued or renewed for similar periods.
2.   The court referred to in paragraph 1 shall terminate the stay of the process of liquidation:
      –   at the request of the liquidator in the main proceedings,
      –   of its own motion, at the request of a creditor or at the request of the liquidator in the secondary proceedings if that measure no longer appears justified, in particular, by the interests of creditors in the main proceedings or in the secondary proceedings.

Article 34
Measures ending secondary insolvency proceedings
1.   Where the law applicable to secondary proceedings allows for such proceedings to be closed without liquidation by a rescue plan, a composition or a comparable measure, the liquidator in the main proceedings shall be empowered to propose such a measure himself.
      Closure of the secondary proceedings by a measure referred to in the first subparagraph shall not become final without the consent of the liquidator in the main proceedings; failing his agreement, however, it may become final if the financial interests of the creditors in the main proceedings are not affected by the measure proposed.
2.   Any restriction of creditors' rights arising from a measure referred to in paragraph 1 which is proposed in secondary proceedings, such as a stay of payment or discharge of debt, may not have effect in respect of the debtor's assets not covered by those proceedings without the consent of all the creditors having an interest.
3.   During a stay of the process of liquidation ordered pursuant to Article 33, only the liquidator in the main proceedings or the debtor, with the former's consent, may propose measures laid down in paragraph 1 of this Article in the secondary proceedings; no other proposal for such a measure shall be put to the vote or approved.

Article 35
Assets remaining in the secondary proceedings
If by the liquidation of assets in the secondary proceedings it is possible to meet all claims allowed under those proceedings, the liquidator appointed in those proceedings shall immediately transfer any assets remaining to the liquidator in the main proceedings.

Article 36
Subsequent opening of the main proceedings
Where the proceedings referred to in Article 3(1) are opened following the opening of the proceedings referred to in Article 3(2) in another Member State, Articles 31 to 35 shall apply to those opened first, in so far as the progress of those proceedings so permits.

Article 37 (7)
Conversion of earlier proceedings
The liquidator in the main proceedings may request that proceedings listed in Annex A previously opened in another Member State be converted into winding-up proceedings if this proves to be in the interests of the creditors in the main proceedings.
The court with jurisdiction under Article 3(2) shall order conversion into one of the proceedings listed in Annex B.

Article 38
Preservation measures
Where the court of a Member State which has jurisdiction pursuant to Article 3(1) appoints a temporary administrator in order to ensure the preservation of the debtor's assets, that temporary administrator shall be empowered to request any measures to secure and preserve any of the debtor's assets situated in another Member State, provided for under the law of that State, for the period between the request for the opening of insolvency proceedings and the judgment opening the proceedings.

CHAPTER IV
PROVISION OF INFORMATION FOR CREDITORS AND LODGEMENT OF THEIR CLAIMS

Article 39
Right to lodge claims
Any creditor who has his habitual residence, domicile or registered office in a Member State other than the State of the opening of proceedings, including the tax authorities and social security authorities of Member States, shall have the right to lodge claims in the insolvency proceedings in writing.

Article 40
Duty to inform creditors
1. As soon as insolvency proceedings are opened in a Member State, the court of that State having jurisdiction or the liquidator appointed by it shall immediately inform known creditors who have their habitual residences, domiciles or registered offices in the other Member States.
2. That information, provided by an individual notice, shall in particular include time

limits, the penalties laid down in regard to those time limits, the body or authority empowered to accept the lodgement of claims and the other measures laid down. Such notice shall also indicate whether creditors whose claims are preferential or secured in rem need lodge their claims.

Article 41

Content of the lodgement of a claim

A creditor shall send copies of supporting documents, if any, and shall indicate the nature of the claim, the date on which it arose and its amount, as well as whether he alleges preference, security in rem or a reservation of title in respect of the claim and what assets are covered by the guarantee he is invoking.

Article 42

Languages

1.   The information provided for in Article 40 shall be provided in the official language or one of the official languages of the State of the opening of proceedings. For that purpose a form shall be used bearing the heading "Invitation to lodge a claim. Time limits to be observed" in all the official languages of the institutions of the European Union.

2.   Any creditor who has his habitual residence, domicile or registered office in a Member State other than the State of the opening of proceedings may lodge his claim in the official language or one of the official languages of that other State. In that event, however, the lodgement of his claim shall bear the heading "Lodgement of claim" in the official language or one of the official languages of the State of the opening of proceedings. In addition, he may be required to provide a translation into the official language or one of the official languages of the State of the opening of proceedings.

CHAPTER V
TRANSITIONAL AND FINAL PROVISIONS

Article 43

Applicability in time

The provisions of this Regulation shall apply only to insolvency proceedings opened after its entry into force. Acts done by a debtor before the entry into force of this Regulation shall continue to be governed by the law which was applicable to them at the time they were done.

Article 44

Relationship to Conventions

1.   After its entry into force, this Regulation replaces, in respect of the matters referred to therein, in the relations between Member States, the Conventions concluded between two or more Member States, in particular:

(a)   the Convention between Belgium and France on Jurisdiction and the Validity and Enforcement of Judgments, Arbitration Awards and Authentic Instruments, signed at Paris on 8 July 1899;

(b)   the Convention between Belgium and Austria on Bankruptcy, Winding-up, Arrangements, Compositions and Suspension of Payments (with Additional Protocol of 13 June 1973), signed at Brussels on 16 July 1969;

(c)   the Convention between Belgium and the Netherlands on Territorial Jurisdiction, Bankruptcy and the Validity and Enforcement of Judgments, Arbitration Awards and Authentic Instruments, signed at Brussels on 28 March 1925;

(d)   the Treaty between Germany and Austria on Bankruptcy, Winding-up, Arrangements and Compositions, signed at Vienna on 25 May 1979;

(e)   the Convention between France and Austria on Jurisdiction, Recognition and Enforcement of Judgments on Bankruptcy, signed at Vienna on 27 February 1979;

(f)   the Convention between France and Italy on the Enforcement of Judgments in Civil and Commercial Matters, signed at Rome on 3 June 1930;

(g)   the Convention between Italy and Austria on Bankruptcy, Winding-up, Arrangements and Compositions, signed at Rome on 12 July 1977;

(h)   the Convention between the Kingdom of the Netherlands and the Federal Republic of Germany on the Mutual Recognition and Enforcement of Judgments and other Enforceable Instruments in Civil and Commercial Matters, signed at The Hague on 30 August 1962;

(i)   the Convention between the United Kingdom and the Kingdom of Belgium providing for the Reciprocal Enforcement of Judgments in Civil and Commercial Matters, with Protocol, signed at Brussels on 2 May 1934;

(j)   the Convention between Denmark, Finland, Norway, Sweden and Iceland on Bankruptcy, signed at Copenhagen on 7 November 1933;

(k)   the European Convention on Certain International Aspects of Bankruptcy, signed at Istanbul on 5 June 1990.

2.   The Conventions referred to in paragraph 1 shall continue to have effect with regard to proceedings opened before the entry into force of this Regulation.

3.   This Regulation shall not apply:

(a)   in any Member State, to the extent that it is irreconcilable with the obligations arising in relation to bankruptcy from a convention concluded by that State with one or more third countries before the entry into force of this Regulation;

(b)   in the United Kingdom of Great Britain and Northern Ireland, to the extent that is irreconcilable with the obligations arising in relation to bankruptcy and the winding-up of insolvent companies from any arrangements with the Commonwealth existing at the time this Regulation enters into force.

Article 45
Amendment of the Annexes
The Council, acting by qualified majority on the initiative of one of its members or on a proposal from the Commission, may amend the Annexes.

Article 46
Reports
No later than 1 June 2012, and every five years thereafter, the Commission shall present to the European Parliament, the Council and the Economic and Social Committee a report on the application of this Regulation. The report shall be accompanied if need be by a proposal for adaptation of this Regulation.

Article 47
Entry into force
This Regulation shall enter into force on 31 May 2002.

This Regulation shall be binding in its entirety and directly applicable in the Member States in accordance with the Treaty establishing the European Community.
Done at Brussels, 29 May 2000.

For the Council
The President
A. Costa

(1)   Opinion delivered on 2 March 2000 (not yet published in the Official Journal).
(2)   Opinion delivered on 26 January 2000 (not yet published in the Official Journal).
(3)   OJ L 299, 31.12.1972, p. 32.
(4)   OJ L 204, 2.8.1975, p. 28; OJ L 304, 30.10.1978, p. 1; OJ L 388, 31.12.1982, p. 1; OJ L 285, 3.10.1989, p. 1; OJ C 15, 15.1.1997, p. 1.
(5)   OJ L 166, 11.6.1998, p. 45.
(6)   Note the Declaration by Portugal concerning the application of Articles 26 and 37 (OJ C 183, 30.6.2000, p. 1).
(7)   Note the Declaration by Portugal concerning the application of Articles 26 and 37 (OJ C 183, 30.6.2000, p. 1).

ANNEX A
Insolvency proceedings referred to in Article 2(a)

BELGIË-/BELGIQUE
- Het faillissement//La faillite
- Het gerechtelijk akkoord//Le concordat judiciaire
- De collectieve schuldenregeling//Le règlement collectif de dettes
DEUTSCHLAND
- Das Konkursverfahren
- Das gerichtliche Vergleichsverfahren
- Das Gesamtvollstreckungsverfahren
- Das Insolvenzverfahren
ΕΛΛΑΔΑ
– Η πτώχευση
– Η ειδική εκκαθάριση
– Η προσωρινή διαχείριση εταιρείας. Η διοίκηση και η διαχείριση των πιστωτών
– Η υπαγωγή επιχείρησης υπό επίτροπο με σκοπό τη σύναψη συμβιβασμού με τους πιστωτές
ESPAÑA
- Concurso de acreedores
- Quiebra
- Suspensión de pagos
FRANCE
- Liquidation judiciaire
- Redressement judiciaire avec nomination d'un administrateur
IRELAND
- Compulsory winding up by the court
- Bankruptcy

- The administration in bankruptcy of the estate of persons dying insolvent
- Winding-up in bankruptcy of partnerships
- Creditors' voluntary winding up (with confirmation of a Court)
- Arrangements under the control of the court which involve the vesting of all or part of the property of the debtor in the Official Assignee for realisation and distribution
- Company examinership

ITALIA
- Fallimento
- Concordato preventivo
- Liquidazione coatta amministrativa
- Amministrazione straordinaria
- Amministrazione controllata

LUXEMBOURG
- Faillite
- Gestion contrôlée
- Concordat préventif de faillite (par abandon d'actif)
- Régime spécial de liquidation du notariat

NEDERLAND
- Het faillissement
- De surséance van betaling
- De schuldsaneringsregeling natuurlijke personen

ÖSTERREICH
- Das Konkursverfahren
- Das Ausgleichsverfahren

PORTUGAL
- O processo de falência
- Os processos especiais de recuperação de empresa, ou seja:
- A concordata
- A reconstituição empresarial
- A reestruturação financeira
- A gestão controlada

SUOMI-/FINLAND
- Konkurssi//konkurs
- Yrityssaneeraus//företagssanering

SVERIGE
- Konkurs
- Företagsrekonstruktion

UNITED KINGDOM
- Winding up by or subject to the supervision of the court
- Creditors' voluntary winding up (with confirmation by the court)
- Administration
- Voluntary arrangements under insolvency legislation
- Bankruptcy or sequestration

ANNEX B
Winding up proceedings referred to in Article 2(c)

BELGIË-/BELGIQUE
- Het faillissement//La faillite
DEUTSCHLAND
- Das Konkursverfahren
- Das Gesamtvollstreckungsverfahren
- Das Insolvenzverfahren
ΕΛΛΑΔΑ
– Η πτώχευση
– Η ειδική εκκαθάριση
ESPAÑA
- Concurso de acreedores
- Quiebra
- Suspensión de pagos basada en la insolvencia definitiva
FRANCE
- Liquidation judiciaire
IRELAND
- Compulsory winding up
- Bankruptcy
- The administration in bankruptcy of the estate of persons dying insolvent
- Winding-up in bankruptcy of partnerships
- Creditors' voluntary winding up (with confirmation of a court)
- Arrangements under the control of the court which involve the vesting of all or part of the property of the debtor in the Official Assignee for realisation and distribution
ITALIA
- Fallimento
- Liquidazione coatta amministrativa
LUXEMBOURG
- Faillite
- Régime spécial de liquidation du notariat
NEDERLAND
- Het faillissement
- De schuldsaneringsregeling natuurlijke personen
ÖSTERREICH
- Das Konkursverfahren
PORTUGAL
- O processo de falência
SUOMI-/FINLAND
- Konkurssi//konkurs
SVERIGE
- Konkurs
UNITED KINGDOM
- Winding up by or subject to the supervision of the court
- Creditors' voluntary winding up (with confirmation by the court)
- Bankruptcy or sequestration

ANNEX C
Liquidators referred to in Article 2(b)

BELGIË-/BELGIQUE
- De curator//Le curateur
- De commissaris inzake opschorting//Le commissaire au sursis
- De schuldbemiddelaar//Le médiateur de dettes

DEUTSCHLAND
- Konkursverwalter
- Vergleichsverwalter
- Sachwalter (nach der Vergleichsordnung)
- Verwalter
- Insolvenzverwalter
- Sachwalter (nach der Insolvenzordnung)
- Treuhänder
- Vorläufiger Insolvenzverwalter

ΕΛΛΑΔΑ
- Ο σύνδικος
- Ο προσωρινός διαχειριστής. Η διοικούσα επιτροπή των πιστωτών
- Ο ειδικός εκκαθαριστής
- Ο επίτροπος

ESPAÑA
- Depositario-administrador
- Interventor o Interventores
- Síndicos
- Comisario

FRANCE
- Représentant des créanciers
- Mandataire liquidateur
- Administrateur judiciaire
- Commissaire à l'exécution de plan

IRELAND
- Liquidator
- Official Assignee
- Trustee in bankruptcy
- Provisional Liquidator
- Examiner

ITALIA
- Curatore
- Commissario

LUXEMBOURG
- Le curateur
- Le commissaire
- Le liquidateur
- Le conseil de gérance de la section d'assainissement du notariat

NEDERLAND
- De curator in het faillissement
- De bewindvoerder in de surséance van betaling
- De bewindvoerder in de schuldsaneringsregeling natuurlijke personen

ÖSTERREICH
- Masseverwalter
- Ausgleichsverwalter
- Sachwalter
- Treuhänder
- Besondere Verwalter
- Vorläufiger Verwalter
- Konkursgericht
PORTUGAL
- Gestor judicial
- Liquidatário judicial
- Comissão de credores
SUOMI-/FINLAND
- Pesänhoitaja//boförvaltare
- Selvittäjä//utredare
SVERIGE
- Förvaltare
- God man
- Rekonstruktör
UNITED KINGDOM
- Liquidator
- Supervisor of a voluntary arrangement
- Administrator
- Official Receiver
- Trustee
- Judicial factor

INDEX